The Fullness of Life

Martin Dybicz

Make the time

En Route Books and Media, LLC
5705 Rhodes Avenue
St. Louis, MO 63109

Cover credit: TJ Burdick

Library of Congress Control Number: 2019933989

Copyright © 2019 Martin Dybicz

All rights reserved.

ISBN-10: 1-950108-02-3

ISBN-13: 978-1-950108-02-2

To Marygin, who has colored my world with love in so many ways.

Table of Contents

Introduction 1

Part 1: What Is Reality and How Do We Know It? 5

Chapter I: What Is Reality? 7

    What Are Two Different Philosophies of Reality? 7

    Which Philosophy Is Right? 9

    What about When There Are Many Different Perceptions or Opinions about Something? 10

    What about When Something Is Not Known for Sure? 11

    What Makes a Thing Real? 12

    Are Spiritual Things Subjective or Objective? 13

    In What Key Ways Are Relationships Objective? 14

Chapter II: Why Start with Philosophy? 19

    Can We Avoid Philosophy? 19

    What is the Philosophical Environment in Which We Live? 20

    Is Catholic Faith Judgmental of Subjectivists? 22

    What Is the Real Meaning of Love? 23

    What Is the Real Meaning of Tolerance? 25

Chapter III: How Do We Know Reality? What Is Truth?...........................27

    What Is Truth? 27

    What Is One of the Two Most Basic Ways to Know Reality/Get Truth? 29

    What Is the Other Most Basic Way to Know Reality/Get Truth? 29

    What Is the Right Relationship between Faith and Reason? 31

    What Does *Not* Put Us in Touch with Reality? 35

    What Should We Now Realize about Being Catholic? 36

Part 2: How Do We Know God? 41

Chapter I: Does Everyone Seek God? 43

    What Do We Want More Than Anything Else? 43

    What Is New about the Human Search for Transcendence? 45

    What about Those Who Have Given Up on God or Religion? 45

Chapter II: How Do We Know God by Using Only Reason? 49

    What Are the Five Proofs? 49

    The First Proof: From Effect to Cause 50

    The Second Proof: From Change 52

    The Third Proof: From Predictability 53

    The Fourth Proof: From Necessity.. 55

    The Fifth Proof: From Degrees 56

    What Do We Know from the Five Proofs? 57

    Does Evil Disprove the Existence of God? 59

Chapter III: How Do We Know God from His Revelation? 63

Why Is God's Revelation Not Obvious to Everyone? 63

What Else Are Revelation and Faith Besides Knowledge? 64

What Is Natural Revelation? 66

What Is Supernatural Revelation? 70

Who Should Interpret Revelation? 72

Where Do Revelation and Faith Meet? 75

Why Doesn't God Reveal Himself Directly? Why Is He behind a Curtain/Veil? 77

Summary: What Is the Fullness of Revelation and Faith? 77

Part 3: How Should We Read Sacred Scripture? 83

Chapter I: What Are Important Basics about Sacred Scripture? 85

Why Is Sacred Scripture Important? 85

What Are the Parts of the Bible? 86

How Did the Bible Come to Be? 88

How Does Biblical Notation Work? 91

Chapter II: What Language and Meanings Are in Sacred Scripture? . 95

Using Scripture with This Book 95

What Are the Four Senses of Scripture? 96

What Is a Key to Reading Sacred Scripture? 97

Why Is Some of Scripture's Language Figurative? 98

How Do We Know When Scripture Is Literal or Figurative? 98

Is Scripture's Figurative Language Objectively True or Subjectively True? 100

Chapter III: What Does God Reveal through Genesis 1-3? 103

Is Genesis 1-3 Literal or Figurative? 103

What Is the Doctrine of Original Sin? 106

What about Evolution? 109

Examples of How True Faith and True Science Support Each Other 110

How Does Original Sin Help Us Understand Revelation? 111

Part 4: What Does God Reveal through the Old Testament? . 115

Chapter I: What Does God Reveal through Genesis 4-11? 117

Chapter II: What Does God Reveal to and through the Patriarchs? . 121

What Is Essential Background for the Patriarchs? 121

How Does Abraham Respond to God? 123

What Does God Reveal to and through Abraham? 125

What Does God Reveal to and through the Other Patriarchs?..126

What Are the Names of the People Descended from Abraham? 127

What Are the Languages of the People Descended from Abraham? 128

Chapter III: What Does God Reveal to and through Moses? 131

What Is Essential Background for Moses? 131

How Does Moses Respond to God? 132

What Does God Reveal to and through Moses? 134

What Is New about the Chosen People's Faith Response to God because of His Revelation through Moses? 135

Chapter IV: What Is the History of the Chosen People? 141

Chapter V: What Does God Reveal through the History of the Chosen People? 147

    How Does the "Vineyard Song" Summarize the History of the Chosen People? 147

    How Did the Covenant Make the Chosen People Different from All Other Ancient Peoples? 149

    How Does the Old Testament Express That God Will Reveal Himself <u>beyond</u> the Old Testament? 151

Chapter VI: What Are Other Key Passages in the Old Testament? ... 153

    What Are Other Key Passages about the Patriarchs? 153

    What Are Other Key Passages about Important Women? 153

    What Are Other Key Passages about David? 154

    What Are Other Key Passages about the Prophets? 154

    What Are Other Key Passages of Wisdom Literature? 155

    What Are Other Key Passages about the Different Ways God Revealed Himself? 155

Part 5: What Does God Reveal through the New Testament? **157**

Chapter I: What Is Essential Background for the New Testament? . 159

    What Are the Books of the New Testament? 159

    What Is the Relationship between the Old Testament and the New Testament? 160

    What Will Be the Focus of Our New Testament Study? 161

    Can We Be Sure That Jesus Existed? 161

    How Trustworthy Is the New Testament for Knowing the Real Jesus? 162

Chapter II: How Did the Gospels Come to Be?..........................167

    How Were the Gospels Written?..167

    Why Are There Four Gospels? 168

Chapter III: What Do the Synoptic Gospels Reveal about Jesus? 173

    What Are Important Points about Jesus' Birth?......................173

    Did Jesus Sin? 176

    What Does Jesus Teach in the Synoptics?................................176

    When the Jews Hear Jesus Preach the Kingdom, What Do They Think He Means? 176

    What Does Jesus Not Mean about the Kingdom?.....................177

    What Does Jesus Do in the Synoptics? 178

    Does Jesus Fulfill the Old Testament Revelations about the Messiah? 178

Chapter IV: What Does the Gospel of John Reveal about Jesus?...........183

    What Is Important about the Prologue of John's Gospel? 183

    Does Jesus Claim to Be God in John's Gospel? 184

    What Does Jesus Teach in John's Gospel?................................184

    What Does Jesus Do in John's Gospel?......................................185

Chapter V: What Is Revealed about Jesus in All Four Gospels?.............187

    Who Is John the Baptist? 187

    To What Else Do All Four Gospels Witness?.............................. 188

    What Are Important Points about the Passion of Jesus? 189

    What Is the Most Important Point about the Death of Jesus?.. 191

    What Are Important Points about the Resurrection of Jesus? .192

The Fullness of Life

What Is the Most Important Point about the Resurrection of Jesus? 193

Chapter VI: Does Reason Support Faith in the Resurrection? 197

How Can We Use Reason to Know the Resurrection Is Real? .. 197

What Are the Five Possibilities about the Resurrection? 199

What Are the Reasons against the *Recovery* Theory? 200

What Are the Reasons against the Hallucination Theory? 202

What Are the Reasons against the Conspiracy Theory? 203

What Are the Reasons against the Myth Theory? 204

What Is Reasonable to Conclude? 204

Chapter VII: What Is the New Covenant? 207

How Did Jesus' Physical Presence on Earth End? 207

What Will Happen When Jesus Returns? 208

What Is God's Plan for the Time between the First Coming of Christ and the Second Coming of Christ? 210

What Is the Gospel? 210

What Is the New Covenant? 211

How Does the Parable of the Vineyard Tenants Summarize the New Covenant? 211

What Are Some Key Examples of How the New Testament Fulfills the Old Testament? 212

Chapter VIII: What Are Other Key Passages in the New Testament? 215

What Are Other Key Passages from the Gospels on Jesus' Teachings? 215

What Are Other Key Passages from the Gospels on Jesus' Parables?..216

What Are Other Key Passages from the Gospels on Events in Jesus' Life? 216

What Are Other Key Passages from the Gospels on Jesus' Miracles?..217

What Are Other Key Passages from the Acts of the Apostles? .. 217

What Are Other Key Passages from the Epistles/Letters? 218

What Are Other Key Passages from the Book of Revelation? ...219

Part 6: What Is the Fullness of Revelation? 221

Chapter I: What Is the Fullness of Who Jesus Is? 223

    How Does Jesus' Claim to Be God Fit in History? 223

    What Are the Three Possibilities about Who Jesus Is? 224

    What Does Jesus' Divinity Mean <u>about Him</u>?............................ 225

    What Does Jesus' Divinity Mean <u>for Us</u>? 227

Chapter II: What Is the Fullness of Who God Is? 229

    What Is the Most Important Doctrine of the Catholic Faith? .. 229

    What Is Important to Understand about the Nicene Creed? ... 230

    How Do We Know God Is the Trinity? 232

    How Does Knowing That God is the Trinity Help Us Understand Why We Exist? 234

Chapter III: What Is the Fullness of Following Jesus Christ? 237

    Why Does the Church Exist? 237

    Who Belongs to the Church? 238

What Is the Relationship of the Catholic Church to All Non-Catholic Religions? 240

Why Be Catholic? 243

Chapter IV: What Is the Role of the Magisterium in the Church? 247

What Makes the Catholicism Different from Every Other Religion? 247

What Is the Power of the Magisterium? 248

What Is Infallibility? 249

Does the Magisterium Teach Anything Besides Doctrine and Discipline? 251

Must a Good Catholic Always Agree with the Magisterium? 252

Chapter V: What Is the Role of St. Mary in Salvation History? 257

Why Is St. Mary the "Blessed Virgin"? 257

Why Is St. Mary the "Blessed Mother"? 258

How Has God Revealed Himself through St. Mary? 259

Why Should We Pray to St. Mary? 261

Part 7: What Is Living Fully? 265

Chapter I: What Is Human Nature? 267

How Do We Know What Human Nature Is? 267

What Does Reason Teach Us about Human Nature? 268

What Does Faith Teach Us about Human Nature? 270

Who Am I? 272

What Is Real Self-Esteem? 273

Chapter II: What Is the Purpose of Life? 277

What Has God Revealed Is the Purpose of Life? 277

What Is the Best Formula for Happiness? 278

What Goal of Life Should We Want? 279

If God Wants Us to Be Happy, Why Is There Suffering? 281

Chapter III: What Do Feelings Have to Do with Happiness? 287

Is It Wrong to Feel Good? 287

What Should We Do with Our Feelings? 289

Are Feelings Ever Sinful? 290

What Are Good Words to Live by? 291

How Do We Find Happiness in Relationships? 291

Chapter IV: What Is the Role of Sexuality in Happiness? 295

What Is Sexuality? 296

Are Males and Females Equal? 297

Is There Evidence from <u>Reason</u> That Males and Females Are Different? 297

What Do We Know from <u>Faith</u> about the Difference between Males and females? 300

How Are Males and Females Complementary? 301

What Is the Purpose of Sex? 303

Why Isn't Feeling Good the Purpose of Sex? 304

Part 8: What Is the Fullness of Responding to Revelation? ..309

Chapter I: Why End with This Part? 311

Chapter II: What Is the Fullness of Responding to God in Morality? 313

What Is Morality? 313

Should Everyone Be Moral? 314

What Is Conscience?..316

What Is Social Justice?...317

What Is the Essence of Revealed Morality?.............................318

Why Is Love a Commandment?..318

What Are the Ten Commandments?..320

What Is the Connection between the Great Commandments and the Ten Commandments?..321

What Is the Difference between Mortal Sin and Venial Sin?...322

Chapter III: What Is the Fullness of Responding to God in Worship?..325

What Is Worship?..325

Why Does the Catholic Church Worship?...............................326

What Is the Essence of Catholic Worship?..............................327

What Are the Sacraments?...327

What Is Necessary for the Sacraments to Be Effective?..........329

How Does the Church Use Time to Worship God?................330

Chapter IV: What Makes the Eucharist Especially Important?..............335

What Is the Holy Eucharist?..335

How Is the Liturgy of the Eucharist a Meal and a Sacrifice?...336

How Should Catholics Participate in Non-Catholic Worship?.338

How Should Non-Catholics Participate at Mass?....................338

How Is Communion Received Worthily?................................339

Chapter V: What Else Is Important to Know about the Sacraments?....343

What Is Important to Know about Baptism?..........................343

What Is Important to Know about Confirmation?.................344

- What Is Important to Know about Confession? 345
- What Is Important to Know about Anointing of the Sick? 346
- What Is Important to Know about Holy Orders? 346
- What Is Necessary for a Sacramental Marriage? 347

Chapter VI: What Is the Fullness of Responding to God in Prayer? 349
- What Is Prayer? 349
- What Does Jesus Teach Us about Prayer? 350
- What Are Ways to Pray? 351
- What Advice Have Holy Men and Women Given? 352
- What Are Discernment and Spiritual Direction? 357

Chapter VII: What Is the Fullness of Sharing the Faith? 361
- Why Share the Faith? 361
- What Are Basic Forms of Sharing the Faith? 363
- What Are Key Methods of Sharing the Faith with Non-Catholics? 364
- What Are Key Methods of Sharing the Faith in the Family? 365

Chapter VIII: What Is Living Fully? 369

INTRODUCTION

Do you want your life to be the most it can be? Do you want the greatest and best life you can have? Do you want the fullness of life? Of course, you do. We all do.

This book is for anyone who wants the fullness of life. It explains what the fullness of life is and how to have it.

"I came that they might have life, and have it to the full" is Jesus Christ's statement of His purpose (John 10:10). "They" is every human being. "They" is us! Jesus wants each one of us to have the fullness of life, life in abundance, life overflowing. And He proclaims and promises that He is "the way and the truth and the life" (John 14:6).

This book shows that Jesus Christ is the only One Who can provide the fullness of life.

This book is for those who want to know Jesus Christ better and are open to following Him. It is for those who know little or nothing about Jesus. It also is for those who learned something about Jesus but then lost interest in Him. And it is for those who are already actively interested in Jesus and seek to review or deepen their relationship with Him.

This book, furthermore, shows that living fully is found in being Catholic. It is meant to give an overview of the Catholic Faith that conveys the profundity of the Catholic Faith while also being readable. It is not written for theologians and scholars. In the interest of being as brief as possible, it is more concerned with showing the interconnectedness of the different parts of the Catholic Faith than it is with showing the depth of each part of the Faith. Greater depth can be found in the many footnotes and sources cited.

Our English word *catholic* comes from two ancient Greek words *kat' holon*. *Kat'* is a contraction of the preposition *kata*, which means "according to." *Holon* means "whole." So *catholic* literally means "according to the whole," and so "complete" or "full." This book aims to show the complete Faith and the completeness of the Faith. It aims for the whole truth about the fullness of life, about Jesus Christ, and about the Catholic Faith. It aims to avoid reductionism.

This book intends to be faithful to the *Catechism of the Catholic Church* as the sure norm for teaching the Church's Faith and Catholic doctrine (*Fidei Depositum*, 3), while making those necessary adaptations called for by the *Catechism* (*CCC*, 24). No part of this book contradicts the *Catechism*. Doctrines from the Catechism are not quoted, but footnotes show when doctrines are being paraphrased and summarized. By identifying and emphasizing doctrine, this book attempts to follow the wise advice: "In essential things, unity; in non-essential things, liberty; in all things, charity."[1] Assenting to doctrine is what should unify Catholics.

The structure of this book has been adapted from "Core I" and "Core II" of the United States Conference of Catholic Bishops' *Doctrinal Elements of a Curriculum Framework for the Development of Catechetical Materials for Young People of High School Age* (2008). It covers everything in that *Curriculum Framework* while going beyond it so that this book is an overview of the entire Catholic Faith, unlike Cores I and II which are more limited in scope. This book is suitable for those who are of any age beyond high school as well as for those of high school age.

The titles of parts and chapters and the chapter subtitles are in the form of questions. Catechisms have traditionally used a question-and-answer format. More than that, knowledge essentially comes from asking good questions and finding good answers, as we learned from Socrates about 400 BC.[2] Indeed, to be human is to ask questions—human beings are the "question-asking animal."

You will find many slashes in the text whenever there is a term that every reader might not know or just to help with understanding. After the

---

1 According to Douglas Beaumont, this wise advice came from a very unwise person, Marco Antonio de Dominis: https://douglasbeaumont.com/2013/06/18/the-origin-of-in-essentials-unity/

2 Socrates (c. 470-399 BC) is rightfully known as the Father of Philosophy. Most of what we know about him comes from writings by his prize pupil, Plato (c. 428-348 BC). Socrates' method was to engage others in sustained dialogues/conversations, which did not, however, result in a systematic, comprehensive philosophy. Systematic philosophy was left to Plato and Plato's prize pupil, Aristotle. This book is a structured Socratic dialogue—a dialogue that DOES result in a systematic, comprehensive catechesis/instruction of Catholic Faith.

The Fullness of Life

slash is a synonym or two so that the meaning of the first term is more obvious.

At the end of every chapter, there is an exercise for PERSONAL FAITH RESPONSE and a glossary for review or future reference.

May we all find the fullness of life.

PART 1

WHAT IS REALITY AND HOW DO WE KNOW IT?

Chapter I: WHAT IS REALITY?

Chapter II: WHY START WITH PHILOSOPHY?

Chapter III: HOW DO WE KNOW REALITY? WHAT IS TRUTH?

PART 1: WHAT IS REALITY AND HOW DO WE KNOW IT?

Chapter I
WHAT IS REALITY?

SOURCES

- The philosophy of St. Thomas Aquinas,[3] including the writings not only of St. Thomas himself, but also of Jacques Maritain, Stefan Swiezawski, Josef Pieper, Ralph McInerny, James Schall, SJ, Reginald F. O'Neill, SJ, and Bernard Wuellner, SJ.

- Pope John Paul II, *Fides et Ratio*, 1998.

WHAT ARE TWO DIFFERENT PHILOSOPHIES OF REALITY?

We must begin our study of Jesus Christ and the Catholic Faith with philosophy, as will be made clearer by the end of Part 1. Philosophy is a set of ideas or a way of thinking about the most basic things. It is subdivided into Metaphysics (the study of being and its nature/essence), Epistemology (the study of knowing), Ethics/Morality (the study of what makes action good or bad), Aesthetics (the study of beauty), and Logic (the study of reasoning). This chapter is on Metaphysics. Chapter III is on Epistemology.

Now there are two DIFFERENT ways we human beings can experience or see the SAME thing. (1) We can each experience or see the same thing

---

[3] For the importance of St. Thomas Aquinas, see *Fides et Ratio*, 43-45, 57-58, 78, 85.

in our own way, e.g.[4], you experience chocolate ice cream as a good taste, and I experience chocolate ice cream as a bad taste, and this is called subjectivity. (2) We can experience or see the same thing as it really is, e.g., we see that a scoop of ice cream is not a scoop of mashed potatoes, and this is called objectivity.

Everyone **agrees** that two different people can experience the same thing in different ways, have different perceptions, have different tastes or preferences, e.g., everyone agrees that different people like different ice cream flavors. Everyone agrees that human beings can be subjective.

What people **disagree** about is whether, or about what, human beings can be objective. And this disagreement is, at root, a disagreement *about things* (Metaphysics) and *about our ability to know things* (Epistemology). The question at issue in this chapter is: Are things themselves whatever we think, feel, believe they are, which would mean that things themselves are subjective; OR are things themselves what they are regardless of what we feel, think, believe about them, which would mean that things themselves are objective?

From this disagreement, two different philosophies of reality result:

1) Subjectivism, which says that a thing is whatever someone thinks or feels it is.

2) Objectivism, which says that a thing is what it is regardless of what someone thinks or feels it is.

A person who has the philosophy of Subjectivism is an Subjectivist, and a person who has the philosophy of Objectivism is a Objectivist.[5]

---

4 *E.g.* will be used a lot in this book and means "for example." (It abbreviates the Latin *exempli gratia*, commonly translated as "for the sake of example.")

5 The terms *Objectivism/Objectivist* and *Subjectivism/Subjectivist* have been used in different ways by different philosophers. For example, Ayn Rand called her philosophy "Objectivism." The Objectivism being presented in this book is Thomism, the philosophy of St. Thomas Aquinas—NOT the philosophy of Ayn Rand or any other philosopher. Other good, Thomistic names for *Objectivism* and *Subjectivism*, as they are meant in this book, are *Realism* and *Relativism*.

WHICH PHILOSOPHY IS RIGHT?

It cannot be true that a thing is subjective and is not subjective at the same time and in the same way, just as it cannot be true that the door of a room is open and is not open at the same time in the same way, just as it cannot be true that X is Y and is not Y at the same time and in the same way, just as two contradictions/disagreements cannot both be true at the same time and in the same way. Subjectivism and Objectivism (two contradictory philosophies!) cannot both be right. We must choose one or the other.

So we must answer the subtitle. In order to begin doing so, let's use our previous example. Whether we like chocolate ice cream over vanilla ice cream or vanilla over chocolate, chocolate is still chocolate (and NOT vanilla), vanilla is still vanilla (and NOT chocolate), and ice cream is still ice cream (and NOT mashed potatoes). This means that when we are subjective about flavors, we are **subjective about the objective realities** (1) that a particular flavor is what the flavor is and (2) that the thing that has a particular flavor is the thing that it is.

Let's also use a classic picture to help us answer the subtitle. What do you FIRST see in the picture to the left? A young lady or an old lady? Answer before you read the next sentence. Regardless of what you saw first, what is in the picture is both a young lady and an old lady.[6]

When some people see the young lady first and other people see the old lady first, they rightly and unavoidably are being subjective. But the reason that some see the young lady first, that others see the old lady first, and that eventually both ladies can be seen is because both the young lady and the old lady **are objectively there**.

---

6 If you see only the young lady, the young lady's right ear is the old lady's right eye, the young lady's right eye lash is the old lady's left eye lash, the young lady's right jaw is the bottom of the right side of the old lady's nose, and the young lady's necklace is the right side of the old lady's mouth.

If you only see the old lady, reverse the process: the old lady's right eye is the young lady's right ear, etc.

No one sees the Statue of Liberty in this picture. And that is because the Statue of Liberty is not objectively in the picture. In the case of this picture, everyone is being subjective about the objective reality of the picture.

Both the ice cream example and the young lady-old lady example show that whenever we are subjective—whether about particular things or about reality as a whole—***we are always subjective about objective realities***. To be subjective about a thing does NOT make that thing itself subjective. When we are subjective about a thing, that thing still is objective. It still is what it is no matter how subjective we are about it.

The philosophy that is right is Objectivism, and the philosophy that is mistaken is Subjectivism. As Pope St. John Paul the Great affirmed,

> Intelligence is not confined to observable data alone. It can with genuine certitude attain to [objective] reality itself as knowable . . . A radically phenomenalist or relativist philosophy [which is Subjectivism] would be ill-adapted to help in the deeper exploration of the riches found in the Word of God. . . . The inspired authors [of the Bible] intended to formulate true statements, capable, that is, of expressing objective reality. [Our thinking is in need of] transcending empirical data in order to attain something absolute, ultimate, and foundational [that is, objective reality] in its search for truth."[7]

In order to find the fullness of life, we must be Objectivist. Jesus was an Objectivist. Being Objectivist is essential/necessary/required to be Catholic. Let's look at some challenges to that.

WHAT ABOUT WHEN THERE ARE MANY DIFFERENT PERCEPTIONS OR OPINIONS ABOUT SOMETHING?

Another way to define a Subjectivist is as one who thinks that no perception/opinion is better than any other perception/opinion.

Let's use an example to help us answer our new subtitle: your wallet. If you were to ask different people to guess how much cash is in your wallet, you would get different perceptions or opinions. Would each perception or opinion about the amount of cash in your wallet be right? Of

---

[7] *Fides et Ratio*, 82-83.

course not.

The actual amount of cash in the wallet is NOT subjective—the amount of cash in the wallet does NOT change depending on whatever the perception is. The amount of cash in your wallet is objective—the amount of cash in your wallet IS WHAT IT IS independently of whatever the perception is. Each different perception of the amount of cash is closer to or farther from the objective reality of the actual amount. Each perception or opinion about the amount of cash is in a range from worst to best. Each perception/opinion is NOT equally good.

What is true about the many different perceptions/opinions of the amount of cash in the wallet is true when there are many different perceptions/opinions about ANYTHING. It does NOT matter how many perceptions or opinions there are about something—whether there are 2 or 7,000,000,000. Each perception or opinion about a thing is EITHER closer to OR farther from the objective reality of that thing. One perception/opinion is more accurate or less accurate than another perception/opinion.

So whenever different people have different perceptions or opinions about something, about anything, the next question should be: Who has the best or most accurate perception or opinion? The often-heard statement "Different people have different perceptions or opinions" actually describes what? NOT what is OUTSIDE people's minds—NOT reality. "Different people have different perceptions or opinions" only describes what is INSIDE people's minds. The question is: Whose mind is more in touch with reality?

WHAT ABOUT WHEN SOMETHING IS NOT KNOWN FOR SURE?

Sticking with the wallet example, if you never told the others the actual amount of cash, and so they **never knew** the actual amount of cash in the wallet, then what? Each perception or opinion or belief about the amount of cash would STILL be in a range from worst to best. Each perception or opinion about the amount of cash would NOT be equally true.

Take any other example. Before the beginning of the Major League Baseball season, every different perception of or opinion about the next World Series winner is STILL in a range from worst to best; each perception of or opinion about the next winner is NOT equally true. Before Columbus sailed west of Spain in 1492, every different perception or opinion about what lay to the west of Spain was STILL in a range from worst to best; each perception or opinion about what lay to the west was NOT equally true. Before a trial begins, the different perceptions or opinions about whether the accused is innocent or guilty is either true or false—the accused is either innocent or guilty of the charge; each perception or opinion is NOT equally true—the accused CANNOT be both innocent and guilty of the charge.

If we **never know** the actual truth about ANYTHING, then what? Each perception or opinion about that thing is STILL in a range from worst to best (or in the case of only true or false, then either true or false). Each perception/opinion about that thing CANNOT be equally true. When something is unknown/uncertain/unproved/mysterious, it still is what it is and NOT whatever we feel it is. While different opinions or beliefs may be equally unsure, they can NEVER be equally true. Do not make the mistake many people make (usually unintentionally) of equating "could be true" with "is true" or mistaking "could be real" with "is real."

WHAT MAKES A THING REAL?

From now on, we will use the word *real* to mean *objectively real*; and we will use the word *reality* to mean *objective reality*.

The first characteristic something must have in order for it to be real is **existence**, which means that it is, it exists, it has being independently of human thoughts, feelings, wants, e.g., Tokyo IS the capital of Japan whether or not someone thinks about it or cares about it. Existence makes a thing to NOT be a fiction, fantasy, myth, figment of one's imagination, illusion, or delusion. The word for all the things that exist is **reality**.

The second characteristic something must have in order for it to be real is that it has an essence, identity, nature,[8] which makes it what it is and therefore what makes it different from other things.[9] A chair is dif-

---

8 The word *nature* has two different meanings: (1) essence, e.g., "human nature," and (2) the part of reality that is not man-made, not artificial, not synthetic, e.g., "natural ingredients."

9 An imaginary/fictitious/mythical thing also has an objective essence (e.g., Batman is not Wonder Woman). It even has an objective existence; but its existence is in the human mind (and expressions of the human mind, e.g., movies),

ferent from a table, a desk, a couch, and even a stool because they have different essences. The essence of something is expressed in its definition. All these years whenever you have learned something's definition, you have learned its essence.[10] E.g., the essence of a chair is (and here is its definition): legs, a seat, a back, designed for one person at a time.

So what makes a thing real/have reality is (1) having existence and (2) having essence.

ARE SPIRITUAL THINGS SUBJECTIVE OR OBJECTIVE?

Because no real thing is subjective (although we can be subjective about things), and because there are real spiritual things, therefore no real spiritual thing is subjective. In other words, all real spiritual things are objectively real.

And because every real thing has existence and an essence, therefore every real spiritual thing has existence and an essence.[11]

Since God must have an objective existence in order to be real, which of the following is true? (A) God exists for those who believe in Him but not for those who do not believe in Him or (B) God either exists or does not exist regardless of whether someone believes in God or not. A later chapter will show that (B) is true and (A) is false.

Since God must have an objective essence in order to be real, which of the following is true? (A) God is who God is—my belief about God might be mistaken even though I am very sincere about my belief, or (B) God is whoever/whatever someone believes God is—my belief about God might be very different from yours and neither of us is mistaken. A later chapter will show that (A) is true and (B) is false.

---

not in reality.

10 Essence is subdivided into: (1) That about a thing which is unchanging about it if it is going to stay itself, which is called its *substance* and (2) that about a thing which can change while the thing still stays itself, which is called an *accident* (which in this case means something incidental, NOT unintended), e.g., the color of a chair is an accident of it because you can change a chair's color, and the chair stays a chair.

11 Essence includes both substance and accident. However, God is the one being not only which has an unchanging substance, but also about which there is nothing accidental/changing. Which is one more reason why only God is God/the Supreme Being and nothing else is God.

Yes, different people have different perceptions/opinions/beliefs of God. But each perception/opinion/belief of God is NOT equally true. Different perceptions/opinions/beliefs of God are closer to or further from the reality of God. "Different people have different beliefs about God" describes NOT what is OUTSIDE people's minds, BUT only what is INSIDE people's minds. Again, when different minds hold different beliefs about God, the question is: Whose mind is in touch with the reality of God?

Remember that this chapter is about metaphysics—NOT about ethics/morality. Absolutely nothing has been concluded about whether personal disbelief in God is moral or immoral. Absolutely nothing has been concluded about public policy, e.g., tolerance of difference beliefs. Issues like these are treated in later chapters, beginning in the next one.

Remember, also that there is a difference between subjectivity and Subjectivism. Being subjective (NOT Subjectivist!) in Catholic Faith can be in harmony with God's Will. E.g., when you prefer to sit while praying and I prefer to kneel, we are both being subjective. That subjectivity is proper for Catholic Faith as long as we are praying to the one true God. The many spiritualities and religious orders in the Church's history attest to the Catholic ability to be properly subjective.

Congratulations on now knowing more philosophy than most college graduates, including graduates from the most selective colleges. Congratulations, too, if you had already known more philosophy than we have just covered—hopefully this review was helpful.

IN WHAT KEY WAYS ARE PERSONAL RELATIONSHIPS OBJECTIVE?

One goal of this book is to help with personal relationships.

We do have and we have had many relationships in our lives, e.g., family, friendships, acquaintances, co-workers, neighbors, classmates, teammates, etc., etc.

In each relationship, you are NOT a subjective reality—you are NOT whoever the other person thinks/feels/believes you are. You are an objective reality—you are who you are and some people understand you and other people do not understand you. Different perceptions/opinions of you are closer to or farther from the reality of you.

The Fullness of Life

Likewise, your perceptions/opinions of others are closer to or farther from the reality of them. In each of your relationships, the other person is NOT a subjective reality—they are NOT whoever you think/feel/believe they are. The other person is an objective reality. They are who they are. You understand some of them and you do not understand some of them. Or some you understand better than others. Different perceptions/opinions of them are closer to or farther from the reality of them.

Relationships are objective in these important ways. They involve people who are who they are, whether or not each person is being honest with the other. The relationship itself is what it is—good or bad—whether or not those in the relationship admit it.

In order to have an objectively good relationship with anyone, whether a close relationship or at least a relationship that does not harm us, we need to know who they really are, strengths and weaknesses. In order to have an objectively good relationship with God, we need to know who He really is. In order to participate constructively in relationships with others and with God, we need to know who we really are, strengths and weaknesses.

A wise man is one who savors things as they really are.

—St. Bernard of Clairvaux

PERSONAL FAITH RESPONSE

Check any statements below that describe you.

In order to LIVE FULLY:

1. _____I will face reality and NOT deny or escape reality in favor of "my reality."

2. _____I will be objective about myself and be honest with myself about my own strengths and weaknesses.

3. _____I will be objective about others and be accurate about others' strengths and weaknesses.

4. _____I will help others to face reality as constructively as I can.

5. _____I want other people to understand me.

6. _____I want to understand other people.

7. _____I want to know who God really is.

VOCABULARY (ESSENCES!)

Philosophy: A set of ideas/a way of thinking about the most basic things.

Subjectivity: Experiencing/seeing a thing in one's own way.

Objectivity: Experiencing/seeing a thing as it really is.

Subjectivism: The philosophy that humans can ONLY be subjective, and NOT objective, about things, and so a thing is whatever someone thinks/feels it is.

Objectivism: The philosophy that humans can be BOTH objective AND subjective about things, and so a thing is what it is regardless of what someone thinks/feels it is.

Existence: Existing/having being independently of human thoughts/feelings/wants.

Reality: All the things that exist.

Essence: The identity/nature of a thing that makes it what it is and NOT something else.

PART 1: WHAT IS REALITY AND HOW DO WE KNOW IT?

Chapter II

WHY START WITH PHILOSOPHY?

SOURCES

- Joseph Cardinal Ratzinger, *Truth and Tolerance* (Ignatius Press, 2004).

- Joseph Cardinal Ratzinger, Homily at the Mass for the Election of the Roman Pontiff, 2005.

- Pope Benedict XVI, "The Regensburg Lecture," 2006.

CAN WE AVOID PHILOSOPHY?

Is it now becoming clear why it is so important to start with Philosophy? Everyone is a metaphysician—everyone has a view of reality. "The human being by nature is a philosopher."[12] Human beings cannot not philosophize just as they cannot not breathe in order to live. The question is not whether we will philosophize or not, the question is whether we will philosophize well or poorly. The metaphysical reality is that everyone is a metaphysician!

One's philosophy affects one's faith. Our assumptions about reality,

---

12 Pope John Paul II, *Fides et Ratio*, 64, 1998.

truth, and meaning affect what we end up believing. False philosophy leads to false belief. True Faith can only be based on true philosophy. The reality is that everyone is a Subjectivist or an Objectivist about everything, including about God, whether they realize it or not. The issue of whether things are objective or subjective will never go away—it will be at the root of all our thinking and all that we do the rest of our lives. If we reflect enough, we will see that we have always had this issue in the back of our minds, and we have acted accordingly—usually in a random, eclectic way since the great majority of people are not taught how to think systematically in good philosophy.

And it is clear that this book is claiming to be about real things. God is real!

In this book, we are doing what good seminary education has traditionally done. "I wish to repeat clearly that the study of philosophy is fundamental and indispensable to the structure of theological studies and to the formation of candidates for the priesthood. It is not by chance that the curriculum of theological studies is preceded by a time of special study of philosophy."13 We will only study enough philosophy in order to think clearly and have true Faith.

WHAT IS THE PHILOSOPHICAL ENVIRONMENT IN WHICH WE LIVE?

In our society today, many people believe that anything involving belief and values, such as religion and sexuality, is completely subjective (e.g., "I believe God exists and you believe God doesn't exist, but we're both right in our own way"). We live in a society that has become increasingly Subjectivist.

Yet from the time of Socrates (the Father of Philosophy), which was about 400 BC, until about 1920 AD in Europe and until the 1960s in America,14 religion and morality were considered EITHER objectively

---

13 *Fides et Ratio*, 62.
14 This true about society in general. Intellectuals/those for whom thinking is their primary occupation especially began attacking the philosophical consensus begun by Socrates during the Protestant Reformation and the Enlightenment.

true OR objectively false, but NOT subjective.15

So we are living at a critical time in human history, which is all the more why we need to start with Philosophy.

Here are some examples of the Subjectivism with which we live:

- We are often told to follow our dream/heart/passion.

- It is legal for a woman to decide for herself when human life begins, and so abortion has been legal in the United States since 1973.

- Same-sex "marriage" was legalized in 2015 to be just as good as marriage of a man and a woman. One of the Supreme Court Justices who ruled in favor of same-sex marriage had previously (and mistakenly) written, "At the heart of liberty is the right to define one's own concept of existence, of meaning, of the universe, and of the mystery of human life." You can't get more Subjectivist than that.

- People are increasingly encouraged to identify as whatever gender they want, including a "gender" beyond masculine and feminine.

- People are often made to feel guilty when disagreeing with someone else's non-traditional beliefs or actions.

- There are many people (you?) who would be surprised to hear, as you did in the last chapter, that God is an objective reality—that God is not whoever/whatever someone believes God is.

For the sake of argument, if Subjectivism is right, then the above examples are examples of progress and growth. But if Objectivism is right, which it is, then the above examples are examples of regress and decay, of confusion and dehumanization.

Pope Benedict XVI said that Subjectivism[16] has become so dominant in our times that it is now a dictatorship. Another sign that Subjectivism has become dominant is that we have gone from being philosophically and

---

15 The ancient Romans were the first people to have a word for reality itself, and our word *reality* comes from their word *realitis*.

16 He actually said the "dictatorship of Relativism," which amounts to the same thing.

theologically oriented to being psychologically and sociologically[17] oriented. We have gone from being a society in the habit of asking, "True or false?" and "Right or wrong?" to being a society asking, "What does he feel?" and "What do they believe?" It is not that psychology and sociology are bad. It is that psychology and sociology need to be supplemented with theology and philosophy, e.g., "Is he or are they in touch with reality?"

Therefore, we, and all human beings, have the same choice, which takes place every minute of every day: To be an Objectivist and face reality OR to be a Subjectivist and escape reality, including the reality about religion and sexuality.

God help you! You live in a society where there are only more ways to escape reality—more bad ideas, more false gods, more delusions, more things to which you can become addicted, more ways for your life to crash and burn. (Don't confuse escaping reality with real recreation, which is healthy, temporary, and prepares you to face reality better.)

In order to face reality, we need the help and support of others. We, in turn, should try to help others face reality. The goal of this book is to show you that the best way to face reality is to be a follower and a friend of Jesus Christ in the Catholic Church He founded, which is also the best way to help others.

As you read this book, keep in mind that it is about the essence/nature/substance of the Catholic Faith. It is NOT about what Catholics, as individuals or as a group, believe or do, which would make it a book on psychology or sociology. The thoughts, feelings, and actions of Catholics can be out of touch with reality, including out of touch with the reality of what the Catholic Faith IS.

IS CATHOLIC FAITH JUDGMENTAL OF SUBJECTIVISTS?

Are Subjectivists automatically guilty of sin and going to Hell? No. Are Subjectivists less than human and without the same human rights as Objectivists? No. The right way to be Catholic is to never judge the soul (since only God can do that) or human dignity (since no one, no matter how much he might try to de-humanize another or even himself can take

---

[17] Psychology is the study of a person's motivations and personality. Sociology is the study of how groups act and believe.

The Fullness of Life

away God-given human dignity).[18]

However, Catholic Faith does judge the philosophy of Subjectivism to be mistaken.[19]

It is not humanly possible to never judge/evaluate/assess anything about anyone. This is not just sociologically true, it is philosophically true—it is true about the reality (metaphysics!) of human nature. Everyone judges something about others. If it is not their soul, then it is their politics, music, health-related habits (e.g., cigarette smoking), competence, whether their choices are worth imitating or not, something. The only way human beings could not judge would be for humans to rely exclusively on instinct and automatic response to stimulus, which is impossible.

The question is not whether TO judge; the question is WHAT to judge. Let's use as an example the common experience of being in a Math class. In Math class, we judge whether others have right or wrong answers without judging their souls or human dignity. We know that someone can get the wrong answer to a Math problem and still be a good person who is loved by God and has human rights! We should judge outside Math class what we judge inside Math class. Outside Math class, we should always judge whether thinking and behavior (of myself as well as others) is right or wrong without judging souls or human dignity.

WHAT IS THE REAL MEANING OF LOVE?

The question of love arises because our Subjectivist culture—and Subjectivist elements within the Church—have taught us that it is unloving to judge. Here is what St. Pius X (pope, 1903-1914) wrote in *Our Apostolic Mandate* (1906):

> But Catholic doctrine tells us that the primary duty of love does not lie in . . . the theoretical or practical indifference towards the errors and vices in which we see our brethren plunged, but in the zeal for their intellectual and moral improvement as well as for their material well-being. . . . Further, while Jesus was kind to sinners and to those who

---

[18] *Catechism of the Catholic Church (CCC)*, 1700-1715.
[19] But didn't Jesus say to never judge (in Matthew 7:1)? We will cover interpreting Scripture in later chapters. In the meantime, here are only a few examples of how Jesus Himself judges: John 2:13-16; Matthew 10:33, 23:27-28, 25:41.

went astray, He did not respect their false ideas, however sincere they might have appeared. He loved them all, but He instructed them in order to convert them and save them.

So our motivation for judging thoughts and behaviors is *love*. It is crucial to get love right. Essentially, love is NOT a feeling/emotion (although love involves it); love IS an act of the will/a choice/a commitment that wants what is good for others[20] ("zeal for their intellectual and moral improvement as well as for their material well-being," as St. Pius X put it) and that does NOT simply want to give others what they want. Likewise, hate is NOT essentially a feeling/emotion (although hate involves it); hate IS an act of the will/a choice/a commitment that wants what is bad for others. E.g., because Christ told us to love everyone, even our enemies, therefore is it a sin to have negative feelings toward those who have treated us badly? No. It is a sin to be committed to what is bad for those who have treated us badly.

St. Augustine brilliantly summarized Christ's message of love as: "Hate the sin, but love the sinner."[21] In doing so, we need to avoid two false extreme. One is to so hate sin that we hate sinners. The other is to so love sinners that we love/excuse/deny sins.

Usually St. Augustine's instruction means: Disapproving of the mistaken thought or action of someone while respecting the dignity of the person with the mistaken thought or action as a fellow human being and a fellow child of God.[22] A common mistake in our Subjectivist society is to think that because we should respect/love everyone we should therefore approve of everyone's non-traditional thoughts and behaviors. However, criticizing someone's false beliefs or immoral actions is NOT being hateful but is being loving when we honestly want them to know the truth and do the right thing, which is wanting what is good for them. E.g., it is loving to judge negatively someone's drug addiction. Since there are unloving ways of expressing our judgments, we should express our judgments as constructively as possible.

Be forewarned! Constructively criticizing others can be very difficult and unappreciated when they are overly sensitive or stubborn. All too often, the temptation is to play the if-you-criticize-me-you-don't-love-me

---

20 *CCC*, 1766, 1822-1829.
21 Letter 211, paragraph 11 (423 AD); *CCC*, 1928-1948, 2464-2499.
22 *CCC*, 1846-1876.

card. Let us not be manipulated by this tactic. Let us not use it ourselves.

We can apply St. Augustine's instruction to ourselves (even though he did not make this application). We can hate our sins while loving ourselves. We can avoid the one extreme of so hating our sins that we hate ourselves. We can avoid the other extreme of so loving ourselves that we love/excuse/deny our own sins.

WHAT IS THE REAL MEANING OF TOLERANCE?

A related issue in our Subjectivist society is tolerance. *To tolerate* is from the Latin which means NOT "to accept" and NOT "to celebrate," BUT "to put up with." So real tolerance is tolerating/putting up with (1) things that are subjectively bad which we do not need to like or (2) things that are objectively bad.[23]

Real tolerance is NOT thinking that someone's beliefs and behaviors (especially if they're non-traditional) are just as good as anyone else's beliefs and behaviors. Real tolerance is NOT agreeing that no beliefs and behaviors (especially if they're non-traditional) are ever mistaken. Real tolerance is NOT accepting and celebrating others' beliefs and behaviors (especially if they're non-traditional) as good for them. Real tolerance IS supporting others' right to have mistaken beliefs and behaviors as long as their mistaken beliefs and behaviors do not harm anyone, including themselves.

Just as we should not be offended when someone claims his belief/opinion is true and our belief/opinion is false, others should be offended when we claim our belief/opinion is true and theirs is false. Objectivists are often accused of being bigots by Subjectivists; but if Subjectivism is right, then there is nothing but bias! The only escape from bias is having objectivity. All people should seek the objective truth about God, religion, morality, sexuality, and the meaning of life.

---

23 *CCC*, 1730-1748.

PERSONAL FAITH RESPONSE

Check any statements below that describe you.

In order to LIVE FULLY:

1. ____I will neither mindlessly cling to the past nor mindlessly cling to the present—I will intelligently choose the right philosophy.

2. ____I will free my mind from Subjectivism because I cannot find good reasons to disagree with the previous chapter.

3. ____I will judge the thoughts and behaviors of myself and others without judging anyone's soul or dignity.

4. ____I will hate sins but love sinners—I will hate my sins but love myself, and I will hate others' sins but love others.

5. ____I will tolerate mistaken ideas and behaviors as long as no one is hurt.

> *In our doing and acting everything depends on this, that we comprehend objects clearly and treat them according to their nature.*
>
> —Goethe

VOCABULARY

Judging: Evaluating whether thinking and behavior are right or wrong without judging souls or human dignity.

Love: An act of the will/a choice/a commitment that wants what is good for others.

Tolerance: Supporting others' right to have mistaken beliefs and behaviors as long as their beliefs and behaviors do not harm anyone.

PART 1: WHAT IS REALITY AND HOW DO WE KNOW IT?

Chapter III

HOW DO WE KNOW REALITY? WHAT IS TRUTH?

SOURCES

- The philosophy of St. Thomas Aquinas, including the writings not only of St. Thomas himself, but also of Jacques Maritain, Stefan Swiezawski, Josef Pieper, Ralph McInerny, James Schall, SJ, Reginald F. O'Neill, SJ, and Bernard Wuellner, SJ.

- Pope John Paul II, *Fides et Ratio*, 1998.

- Joseph Cardinal Ratzinger, *Truth and Tolerance* (Ignatius Press, 2004).

WHAT IS TRUTH?

After answering countless True-or-False questions year after year in school, it is easy to answer the subtitle, right? So try it now. Take a moment and define the word *truth*. If you were telling someone what truth is, what would you tell them?

It is easy to have started using very early in our lives hugely important words—e.g., *love, justice, reality, happiness*, etc.—and then continue to use them without ever having straightened out what they really mean.

Let's make sure we are not doing that with *truth*.

In order to know the essence of truth, let's start with the door of the room in which you are currently sitting. Is the statement *The door of the room is open* true or false? The answer depends on whether the statement matches/fits/agrees with/corresponds to the reality of the door.

Truth is the match/fit/agreement/correspondence of a thought (or its spoken or written expression) to reality. A thought (or its expression) is false when it does NOT correspond to/fit/match reality. Truth is knowing reality as reality actually is. Knowledge is having the truth about reality.

Truth is INSIDE the mind. Reality is OUTSIDE the mind. Truth is always objective. It can never be subjective, which is not to deny that different people can be subjective in terms of their perceptions, responses, tastes, and preferences.

When someone disagrees with the truth, he is mistaken. It is important to know the difference between a mistake and a lie. What mistakes and lies have in common is that there is something false about both of them. Someone tells a lie when he wants others to think something is true that he knows is really false, e.g., "The dog ate my homework." Someone makes a mistake when he sincerely believes something is true that is really false, e.g., "The answer to the Math problem is 30" when it really is 300. All lies are falsehoods, but not all falsehoods are lies.

It is also important to know that there is a difference between an "epistemological wrong" and a "moral wrong." Remember that Epistemology is the study of knowing. We all make epistemological mistakes—we misunderstand something, we get our facts wrong, etc. We all also make moral mistakes—we choose to do something that is morally wrong, we commit a sin, etc. It is NOT automatically a sin to have a false idea, including a false idea about God. It is a sin to be willfully ignorant and willfully stubborn about not admitting the truth.

There are two basic ways of knowing reality and thus getting truth.

The Fullness of Life

WHAT IS ONE OF THE TWO MOST BASIC WAYS TO KNOW REALITY/GET TRUTH?

One way to know the answer to a Math problem is to figure it out yourself. Likewise, one of the two most basic ways human beings know reality is by figuring out reality, which has traditionally gone by the name of Reason. Reason uses (1) evidence/data, which is something concrete/specific/particular—an example from Criminology is finger prints or DNA and an example from History is a ruin, artifact, or document and (2) logic, which is putting together evidence/ data in a way that makes sense—an example from Criminology is "Therefore, the butler did it" and an example from History is "Therefore, the first city was Jericho."24

When humans use Reason correc-tly, they get objective truth that corresponds to/fits/matches/agrees with reality. Math, Science, History, and all academic subjects—including Philosophy—other than Theology are forms/examples of Reason.25 On the other hand, the history of Math, Science, and the other forms of Reason is full of mistakes being made. When the word *Reason* is used in this book from now on, it means right Reason.

WHAT IS THE OTHER MOST BASIC WAY TO KNOW REALITY/GET TRUTH?

Reason is knowledge that comes from humans. We can also get knowledge from God, which is the other most basic way we know reality. In Math class, if we cannot figure out the answer on our own, the teacher reveals/shows the answer and how to get it, and then we trust/believe/ have faith in the teacher as someone who knows Math better than we do.

---

24 Synonyms for *logic* are *inference/inferring, argument/arguing, reasoning,* and *concluding*. The basic form of logic is: Because . . ., because . . ., therefore . . .

25 All academic subjects use logic—what makes them different is that they use different evidence. The logic that should be used in History is the same logic that should be used in Biology; but History uses different evidence than Biology does.

In life, there are things no human can figure out on his own until God reveals/shows the answer, and then we trust/believe/have faith in God. The name for this other most basic way to know reality is Faith in Divine Revelation.26

The word *Divine* comes from the Latin *Deus*, meaning "God." Divine Revelation is God's Revelation/the Revelation of God/ Revelation from God. 27 The word *revela-tion* comes from the Latin word *velum*, which means "veil" or "curtain," so *to reveal* means "to un-veil, un-cover, or pull the curtain back." Divine Revelation is God unveiling/ uncovering/showing/communicating Who He is and what He wants. The word *Revelation* means "Divine Revelation" when it is used by itself without the adjective *Divine* and is capitalized. Real Revelation can only come from the real God.

Religious Faith28 is accepting/trusting/saying Yes to Divine Revelation. Someone has true Faith ONLY by responding to a real/actual Revelation from the real God, e.g., belief in Zeus was NOT true Faith because Revelation could not come from Zeus because Zeus never existed.

Just as we know the answer after the Math teacher reveals it to us, we know reality after God reveals it to us. Faith in Divine Revelation is knowledge. "I believe in one God" really means NOT "I feel that there is one God" or "I imagine there is one God," BUT "I know that there is one God." When humans have true Faith, they get objective truth.

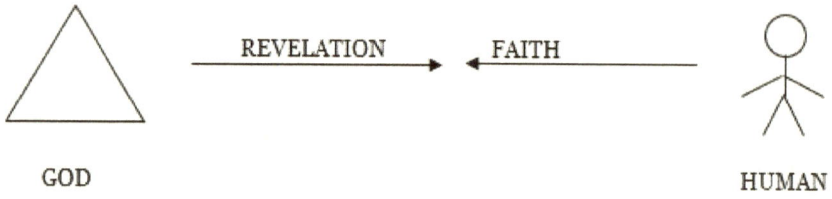

GOD   HUMAN

---

26 Practically, most of what we learn is revealed to us—by teachers and other sources—because we have NOT figured out the content for ourselves. Instead we believe our teachers and sources, all of which is still Reason when it does NOT involve getting knowledge from God.

27 *CCC*, 39-43, 50, 142-143.

28 *CCC*, 144-184.

The Fullness of Life

Revelation is what God freely does; Faith is what humans do in response. For the rest of this book, *Faith* (with a capital *F*) means (1) <u>religious</u> Faith and not faith in a Math teacher or someone less than God and (2) <u>true</u> religious Faith in real Divine Revelation.

NO human being can figure out reality by himself. Every human being turns to those whom he trusts know more than he does. If we do not put our trust in God and turn to Him for the meaning of life, we will put our trust/have "faith" in someone else to show us the meaning of life. We will give someone the role of God in our lives. We could even make ourselves that someone-playing-the-role-of-God. But no one knows more than God does.

WHAT IS THE RIGHT RELATIONSHIP BETWEEN FAITH AND REASON?

First, let's summarize: the two most basic ways humans know the truth about reality are Reason and Faith.29 Reason is all knowledge that does NOT come from Faith, and Faith is all knowledge that does not come from Reason. In the words of Saint John Paul II, "Faith and Reason are like two wings on which the human spirit rises to the . . . truth." Who is the better thinker? NOT the one who thinks whatever he wants to think, BUT the one who knows reality as it really is by using Faith and Reason. Who is the freer thinker? NOT the one who is "free" to think whatever he wants, BUT the one whose thought is free from error and falsehood.

Saint John Paul II best answers the subtitle question as he quotes Vatican I:

> [T]here can never be a true divergence between Faith and Reason since the same God who reveals the mysteries and bestows the gift of Faith has also placed in the human spirit the light of Reason. This God could not deny Himself, nor could the truth ever contradict the

---

29 Both Reason and Faith are both processes and products/results. Reason is both the process of figuring things out and the knowledge that results from figuring out. Faith is both the process of accepting Revelation and the knowledge that results from accepting Revelation.

truth.[30]

Reason and Faith (remember we mean *right Reason* and *true Faith in real Revelation*) do not contradict/disagree with each other. A person who values Faith can and should also value Reason (e.g., Science). A person who values Reason can and should also value Faith. Because Reason and Faith are in harmony, and because Catholicism values both Reason and Faith, it was the Catholic Church that invented the university, the first of which was the University of Bologna in 1088. The first free library was built by a Catholic cardinal, Federigo Borromeo, in 1609. Because Reason and Faith are in harmony, Catholic schools teach subjects other than Religion/Theology. Because Reason and Faith are in harmony, all of the following persons were Catholics:

- Founder of the Modern Scientific Method.
- Founder of heliocentric cosmology.
- Inventor of the first electrified musical instrument.
- Early anatomist whose discoveries were so important the Fallopian Tubes are named for him.
- Maker of the first electric motor.
- Creator of the first analog computer.
- Founder of Genetics.
- Founder of Acoustics.
- First person to transmit the human voice by a wireless machine.
- Discoverer of osmosis.
- Founder of Accounting.
- Founder of Geology.
- First person to successfully predict the trajectory of a hurricane.

---

[30] *Fides et Ratio*, 53.

- First American woman to win a Nobel Prize in science.
- Founder of Analytic Geometry.
- Founder of Embryology.
- Founder of Pneumatic Chemistry.
- Inventor of the battery.
- Founder of modern Algebra.
- Founder of modern Human Anatomy.
- Founder of the theory of the cellular structure of human organisms.
- Founder of Bacteriology.
- Founder of modern Physiology.
- Founder of modern Anatomical Pathology.
- Founder of modern Chemistry.[31]

On the other hand, Faith gives knowledge that is beyond Reason's ability to give. God gives knowledge that human beings can NOT figure out for themselves. Faith is NOT anti-Reason. It is NOT irrational/anti-rational, BUT it is supra-rational/beyond-rational. Faith is NOT a "blind faith" or a "take it or leave it" kind of faith without reasons for believing it, the classic expression of which is Tertullian's "Credo quia absurdum" ("I believe because it is absurd").

The proverbial "leap of Faith" is not that big a leap. There are reasons for believing Faith. Faith makes sense. While Faith is a leap from Reason, Faith never requires that we give up Reason or that we suspend Reason while we have Faith. When we say at Mass "I believe in God," we should NOT stop believing in Physics, Biology, and Chemistry, even as we are confident that God knows more than all the physicists, biologists, and

---

31 See http://www.ncregister.com/blog/astagnaro/a-short-list-of-lay-catholic-scientists and http://www.ncregister.com/blog/astagnaro/a-list-of-244-priest-scientists-from-acosta-to-zupi

chemists that ever have lived and ever will live put together.

Of course, there are also people who are *irrational in their disbelief*. All the philosophy in the world will not convince someone who is simply being emotional. There are many reasons people are irrationally hostile to Faith. Maybe they are rebelling against Faith because they hate their father or mother. Maybe they cannot get past that time when a priest or teacher was unfair to them. Maybe they are depressed. Maybe they simply want to get drunk or high, or they do not want to give up hook-ups and pornography. Maybe they are arrogant cannot admit that someone with Faith can be wiser than they are. Maybe they have been traumatized in some way.

Faith is not a substitute for Reason. Faith is not a substitute for knowing finance, medicine, plumbing, gardening, sports, time management, interpersonal skills, career discernment, sexuality, and all the other things we need to know in order to make the most of life. But Faith provides the context and the parameters for everything else. Faith provides balance to other things and prevents them from becoming too important or too unimportant.

Classic Philosophy[32] has given us the "Laws of Thought" which are the laws that thinking must obey in order to be good thinking. Both right Reason and true Faith must obey these Laws of Thought. Three of these have been implicit in this book:

1) The Law of Correspondence: A thought (or its spoken or written expression) is true ONLY when it corresponds to/agrees with/fits/matches/is in touch with reality; and so a thought (or its expression) is false when it does NOT correspond to/fit/match reality. E.g., *God exists* is true because it corresponds to reality.

2) The Law of Non-Contradiction: Any thought (or its spoken or written expression) cannot be both true and false at the same time in the same way.[33] E.g., *God exists* and *God does not exist* cannot

---

[32] The philosophy based on the philosophy of Aristotle (384-322 BC) and culminating in the philosophy of St. Thomas Aquinas (1225-1274 AD), which is opposed by Modernism and Postmodernism.

[33] A contradiction should NOT be confused with two other possible ways for two thoughts or their expressions to be opposite each other. *All dogs are brown.* – *Some dogs are not brown.* is a **contradiction** because **both statements cannot be true at the same time AND cannot be false at the same**. However, *All dogs are brown.* – *No dogs are brown.* is a **contrary** because both

both be true at the same time and in the same way. Either God exists, or He does not exist.

3) The Law of the Unity of Truth: A true thought or its expression in one subject (e.g., Science) never contradicts/disagrees with a true thought or its expression in another subject (e.g., Theology). E.g., *God exists* does not contradict Science, although Science by itself does not lead to knowledge of God.

Real Catholics are never afraid of the truth. Real Catholics always seek the truth. Everyone should go wherever the truth leads them. There is a long list of brilliant people who began as non-Catholics, even atheists, and became Catholics because they were committed to the truth.34

WHAT DOES *NOT* PUT US IN TOUCH WITH REALITY?

On September 11, 2001, the people in the Twin Towers of the World Trade Center *felt* safe one second before the first terrorist-piloted plane struck. Those people in the Twin Towers ***wanted*** to be safe one second before the first terrorist-piloted plane struck. But they ***were not*** safe one second before the first terrorist-piloted plane struck. Over 2,600 would soon die (excluding those who were casualties on that day at the Pentagon and in the planes and those who became casualties later).

Whether we are at work or home or anywhere, our emotions and desires tell us NOT about reality, BUT about ourselves. Emotions and desires are NOT bad in and of themselves. They make us human and not machines. It is psychologically healthy to be in touch with our emotions and desires. However, contrary to Subjectivism, we should NOT be governed by our emotions and desires. We should be very aware that emotions and desires can confuse or block Reason and Faith.

The Subjectivist spin on the Law of Correspondence is that "truth" corresponds to one's emotions or desires. That "truth" can be about God,

---

statements cannot be true at the same time but ***both statements can be false*** at the same time. And *Some dogs are brown. – Some dogs are not brown.* is a **subcontrary** because statements both cannot be false at the same time but ***both statements can be true*** at the same time.

34 To name some: St. Paul, St. Augustine, Blessed John Henry Newman, G. K. Chesterton, Evelyn Waugh, Edith Stein, J. R. R. Tolkien, Sigrid Undset, Jacques Maritain, Graham Greene, Alasdair MacIntyre, Mortimer Adler, Avery Cardinal Dulles, SJ, Fr. Richard Neuhaus, and Elizabeth Fox-Genovese.

morality, sexuality, or anything else. Something is "true to me" depending on "how I feel" or "what I want." Subjectivists have no use for the Law of Non-Contradiction. It does not matter to them if different beliefs or values contradict each other.

The attempt to harmonize Reason and Faith is under attack by Subjectivism and, more deeply, by Modernism and Postmodernism. Modernism is the philosophy that <u>one</u> thing is completely subjective but another thing is objective. Modernists disagree among themselves over what is subjective and what is objective. E.g., Karl Marx (1818-1883 AD) considered Morality to be objective, but David Hume (1711-1776 AD) considered Morality to be subjective; both considered Science to be objective; both considered traditional Religion to be objectively false. By now Modernism has a long history. It began with the Enlightenment and can be traced back to Rene Descartes (1596-1650 AD). The thrust of Modernism is to value Reason over Faith. Postmodernism is the philosophy that <u>everything</u> (even Math and Science) is completely subjective. It is as disenchanted with Reason as it is with Faith. Postmodernism can be traced back to Friedrich Nietzsche (1844-1900 AD) and can especially be found in the writings of Michel Foucault and Jacques Derrida.

WHAT SHOULD WE NOW REALIZE ABOUT BEING CATHOLIC?

What is obvious to most people is that there is a Catholic way of acting/doing things, which involves: Catholic morality, such as never choosing or supporting abortion; Catholic worship, such as the Mass; and Catholic prayer, such as the Rosary. What is probably less obvious to most people, but what we should now realize as a result of this chapter, is that there is a **Catholic way of thinking** that uses BOTH Reason AND Faith in order to know the objective truth about God and everything else.

To think the Catholic way is to think kat' holon/holistically/completely. To think without either Faith or Reason is to think incompletely. We need to avoid Fideism, which va-lues Faith without valuing Reason. We need to avoid Rationalism, which values Reason without valuing Faith. (The different versions of Modernism are all Rationalisms;

Post-modernism seeks to be neither Fideist nor Rationalist.)

The Catholic way of thinking is NOT simply the way any individual Catholic thinks. An individual Catholic, including a priest or bishop, might believe he is thinking the Catholic way when he is not actually thinking the Catholic way. It is possible to act the Catholic way (e.g., go to Mass) while not thinking the Catholic way about that action (e.g., thinking Mass is no better and no worse than any other way of worshipping). The Catholic way of acting makes much more sense when one understands the Catholic way of thinking. And let us remember that the judgment we should make about someone who disagrees with the Catholic way of thinking is NOT that he is automatically going to Hell or that he does not have human dignity and does not deserve human rights, BUT that he is objectively mistaken. It really is possible for people who disagree with each other to be friends.

Merely having an open mind is nothing.

The object of opening the mind, as of opening the mouth [to eat],

is to shut it again on something solid.

—G. K. Chesterton

PERSONAL FAITH RESPONSE

Check any statements below that describe you.

In order to LIVE FULLY:

1. _____I agree with the objective truth in this chapter.

2. _____I will use Reason to get the truth about reality.

3. _____I will use Faith to get the truth about reality.

4. _____I will keep Faith and Reason in the right relationship to each other.

5. _____I will use Faith and Reason to know when to properly be subjective.

6. _____I will be in touch with my feelings/emotions and wants/desires.

7. _____I will NOT let my feelings and wants cloud/block my efforts to know the truth about reality.

VOCABULARY

Truth: The match/fit/agreement/correspondence of a thought (or its expression) to reality.

Knowledge: Having the truth about reality.

Lie: Presenting to others as true what one knows is false.

Mistake: Honestly thinking something is true that is really false.

Evidence: Something concrete/specific/particular.

Logic: Putting together evidence/data in a way that makes sense; drawing a conclusion from premises; the safest way to be logical is to reason "Because . . ., because . . ., therefore . . ."

Reason: Knowledge that comes from the human ability to figure something out by using evidence and logic.

Divine Revelation: God unveiling/uncovering/showing/communicating Who He is and what He wants us to know.

Faith: Knowledge that comes from God by accepting His Revelation

Modernism: Subjectivism about some things and Objectivism about others.

Postmodernism: Subjectivism about all things.

Fideism: Valuing Faith without valuing Reason.

Rationalism: Valuing Reason without valuing Faith.

PART 2

HOW DO WE KNOW GOD?

Chapter I: DOES EVERYONE SEEK GOD?

Chapter II: HOW DO WE KNOW GOD BY USING ONLY REASON?

Chapter III: HOW DO WE KNOW GOD FROM HIS REVELATION?

Part 2: How Do We Know God?

Chapter I

DOES EVERYONE SEEK GOD?

WHAT DO WE WANT MORE THAN ANYTHING ELSE?

A fact of human existence is that we humans always want more than we already have, know, and experience. Everyone to one extent or another is dissatisfied and restless. And yet after we try new and what-we-hope-are-better things and experiences, we eventually are dissatisfied with them and we eventually are restless. Even celebrities with great wealth and success, who seem to have "everything," can be so restless that they try things like drugs that ruin their lives.

In a word, what we humans want more than anything else is transcendence, which comes from the Latin for "to climb (*scandere*) across (*trans*)" and which means "experiencing more than we already experience/going beyond usual limits." Sometimes we seek it subconsciously/unintentionally/indirectly. Sometimes frustration or disappointment discourage us from seeking transcendence; but even when we give up seeking it, we still wish that we had it.

In fact, not only do we humans tend to want more than we already have, know, and experience; but we also want the greatest/ultimate/absolute/supreme/perfect thing. Neither the most comfort and pleasure, nor the greatest accomplishments, nor the best friendships, nor the best family will end our restlessness and dissatisfaction. Even being religious and saintly will not end our restlessness and dissatisfaction.

There is nothing greater/more ultimate/more absolute/more supreme than the one true God. As St. Augustine famously said, "Our hearts are restless until they rest in You, O God." As Psalm 63 says,

God, You are my God whom I seek;

For You my flesh pines and my soul thirsts

Like the earth, parched, lifeless and without water.

Thus have I gazed toward You in the sanctuary

To see Your power and your glory.

We will ONLY find the ultimate transcendence and finally end our restlessness when we directly experience God Himself after this life. Have you ever had a religious "high" from a Mass, praying, a retreat, or a religious experience, and then felt disappointed when it didn't last? Now you know why. We cannot have the fullness of life until we directly experience God Himself after this life. Realizing that this life will never be perfect is an important part of maturity. BUT we can have a better or worse life, a more meaningful or less meaningful life. We can be more fully alive or less fully alive in the here and now. We can find a very good degree of transcendence and greatly reduce our restlessness as we await the ultimate adventure of meeting God face-to-face.

Throughout the great majority of history, the great majority of human beings have searched for transcendence by searching for God or some kind of spiritual/supernatural reality. The study of world history is incomplete without the study of world religion. It is human nature to believe in God or some kind of spiritual or supernatural reality.[35] It is natural to be on a spiritual quest.

The reason everyone seeks transcendence is because God made us to seek it. God made us to seek transcendence because God made us to seek Him.[36] God wants us to know Him and have a relationship with Him. The greatest adventure is knowing and having a relationship with God.

---

[35] *CCC*, 28.
[36] *CCC*, 1, 27, 1721.

WHAT IS NEW ABOUT THE HUMAN SEARCH FOR TRANSCENDENCE?

There are several things that are new about the human search for transcendence, although today's young people might think that what is "normal" to them has always been that way.

One is that atheism and agnosticism are gaining some ground. *Atheism* comes from the Greek prefix *a*, which means "no," and *theos*, which means "god," and so a-the-ism is literally "no-god-ism," the belief that there is no God.[37] *Agnosticism* comes from the Greek prefix *a* and *gnosis*, which means "know-ledge," and so a-gnostic-ism is literally "don't-know-ism," the belief that it cannot be known if God exists, and so it is neither belief in God nor unbelief in God.[38] It is new in history to have as many people as there are now who are searching for transcendence without searching for God or some kind of spiritual/supernatural reality.

Also new in history is that there are more people who believe in some kind of spiritual or supernatural reality without being involved in organized religion. It has become more common to hear "I'm spiritual, but I'm not religious" or words to that effect.

And, as we have already seen, it is also new in history to have as many people as there are now who are Subjectivists and so who believe that transcendence is completely subjective. "I have my religion, and you have your religion, and who's to judge?" God is "whoever" or "whatever" someone believes God to be. Subjectivists make God in their own image and likeness.

WHAT ABOUT THOSE WHO HAVE GIVEN UP ON GOD OR RELIGION?

God's existence is NOT self-evident/obvious. It is natural, at some point, to wonder/question/have doubts about God's existence and to seek reasons for believing in God.[39] But everyone has a most important thing in his life, an absolute value, a highest priority, an ultimate goal in his life, which is reflected in how he spends his time and his money. Everyone

---

37 *CCC*, 2123-2126.
38 *CCC*, 2127-2128.
39 *CCC*, 37.

worships something, even if it is himself. Human beings cannot not worship, cannot not have an absolute. So when people give up on finding the one true God, they find a substitute for God.

Just as some people seek transcendence unintentionally/indirectly, those who have given up on God or religion are actually seeking the one true God unintentionally/indirectly.[40] People seek the one true God unintentionally/indirectly whenever they sincerely seek truth, goodness, or beauty.

So, in this way, there are two kinds of people in the world: those who seek the one true God intentionally/directly and those who seek the one true God unintentionally/indirectly. What Saint Paul said to the pagans in Athens (Acts 17:23-27), he says to non-believers today:

> What therefore you unknowingly worship, I proclaim to you. The God who made the world and all that is in it . . . it is He who gives to everyone life and breath and everything . . . so that people might seek Him, even perhaps grope for Him, and find Him though He is not far from any one of us.

Who should have reasons for what he believes? The theist ("god-ist"/one who believes in God)? Yes. The atheist? Yes. The agnostic? Yes. Theism, atheism, and agnosticism cannot all be true; one must be true, and the others must be false. The rest of this part of the book will show in more detail how we know God is real. First, we will learn God is real by using only Reason. Then we will know God is real from His Revelation.

---

[40] *CCC*, 29-30.

PERSONAL FAITH RESPONSE

Check any statements below that describe you.

In order to LIVE FULLY:

1. _____I agree with the objective truth in this chapter.

2. _____I want more than I already have, know, and experience—I want transcendence.

3. _____I realize that this life will never be perfect.

4. _____I am now:

    1) _____A theist.

    2) _____An atheist.

    3) _____An agnostic.

5. _____I want to know whether God exists.

VOCABULARY

Transcendence: Experiencing more than we already experience/going beyond usual limits.

Atheism: Belief that there is no God.

Agnosticism: Belief that it cannot be known if God exists.

Theism: Belief in God/a Supreme Being.

Part 2: How Do We Know God?

Chapter II

HOW DO WE KNOW GOD BY USING ONLY REASON?

SOURCES

- St. Thomas Aquinas, *Summa Theologica*, I, Q. 2, art. 3.
- Peter Kreeft, *A Shorter Summa* (Ignatius Press, 1993).
- Jacques Maritain, *Approaches to God*, trans. Peter O'Reilly (Harper & Brothers, 1954).
- John F. Wippel, "Metaphysics," *The Cambridge Companion to Aquinas*, Norman Kretzmann and Eleonore Stump, eds. (Cambridge University Press, 1993).
- http://www.aquinasonline.com/Topics/5ways.html

WHAT ARE THE FIVE PROOFS?

St. Thomas Aquinas (1225-1274 AD) is arguably the greatest thinker in the history of the Catholic Church and even in the history of the world. St. Thomas has shown in his *Summa Theologica* that we can know God is real by using ONLY Reason in what are known as his "Five Proofs for the Existence of God," or "Five Proofs" for short, which is what we will cover in this chapter.

The following proofs for God's existence are not exact translations of St. Thomas' words but are paraphrases that rely on the sources cited above and that are intended to simplify and clarify without distorting St. Thomas' thought. Strictly speaking, St. Thomas' Five Proofs as they appear in the *Summa Theologica* are not proofs, but summaries of proofs. For example, what is presented here as the Second Proof takes only one paragraph in the *Summa Theologica* but takes thirty-one paragraphs in St. Thomas' *Summa contra Gentiles*. The Five Proofs appear in this chapter in a different order than they appear in the *Summa Theologica*. The order here is assumed to be more helpful for the reader.

If you want to try reading St. Thomas' proofs on your own, visit http://www.ccel.org/a/aquinas/summa/FP/FP002.html#FPQ2OUTP1

THE FIRST PROOF: FROM EFFECT TO CAUSE

- **Long version:**

Because things exist; and

because nothing that exists can cause itself to exist;[41]

∴[42] each thing ("Z") that did not cause itself to exist must be the effect of some other thing ("Y") which caused it.

We can diagram the above as: Y → Z

Because that other thing ("Y") cannot have caused itself; and

because that other thing ("Y") did exist, otherwise the currently existing thing that did not cause itself to exist ("Z") would not exist;

∴ that other thing ("Y") must have been the effect of yet another thing ("X") which caused it, and so on.

---

[41] The closest thing there is to something that SEEMS to cause itself to exist are virtual particles that SEEM to pop in and out of existence in a vacuum state. However, "Vacuum states—no less than giraffes or refrigerators or solar systems—are particular arrangements of *elementary physical stuff* . . . none of these poppings [of virtual particles]—if you look at them aright—amount to anything even remotely in the neighborhood of a creation from nothing [and thus from no cause]," physicist David Albert, as quoted by Trent Horn in *Why We're Catholic* (Catholic Answers Press, 2017).

[42] ∴ = therefore

The Fullness of Life

We can diagram the above as: . . . → X → Y → Z

Because this process of cause and effect cannot go back infinitely, otherwise it would have never started in the first place; and

because this process of cause and effect did start, otherwise nothing would exist;

∴ there must be an Uncaused Cause which itself had no cause and which began the process of cause and effect, to which everyone gives the name *God*.

We can diagram the above as: A → . . . → X → Y → Z

- **Short version:**

Because only if there is an Uncaused Cause, then are there other causes; and because there are other causes;

∴ there is an Uncaused Cause, to which everyone gives the name *God*.

By *God* in his conclusion, St. Thomas means a Supreme Being since that being which is the only Uncaused Cause is supreme/superior to every other being because every other being is caused. "God is the Uncaused Cause" means that God is the ONLY thing that always existed. God did NOT have a beginning.

Recall that Reason is essentially evidence and logic. Since St. Thomas uses only Reason in this Proof, where are the evidence and the logic? The logic is found (and will be found in the other Proofs) in "Because . . ., because . . ., therefore." Logic is having reasons for one's conclusion (which begins with "therefore").

In this and the other Proofs, St. Thomas uses not only evidence, but evidence that is common and undeniable. What evidence does St. Thomas use in this proof? (1) Things exist. (2) Nothing causes itself to exist.

This proof also provides an answer to the classic question, Why is there something rather than nothing?—which cannot be answered by atheists and agnostics. If an atheist asks a theist, "Why does God exist?" and the theist answers "Just because He does," then the theist has not really given a reason to the atheist. BUT if a theist asks an atheist, "Why is there something rather than nothing?" and the atheist answers "Just because there is," then the atheist has not really given a reason to the theist. Both theists and atheists should "play by the same rules"—if a theist should have reasons for believing in God (and he should), then an atheist should have reasons for why there is something rather than nothing.

THE SECOND PROOF: FROM CHANGE

- **Long version:**

Because in the world things change by going from having potential to actualizing that potential, as that which is cold has the potential to become hot; and because nothing can change itself;[43]

∴ whatever thing that changes must be changed by something else—a "changer"/catalyst[44]—as fire, which is actually hot, makes cold wood, which was potentially hot, become actually hot.

Because this changer cannot change itself;

∴ there must be yet another changer that changed it, and so on.

Because this process of change cannot go back infinitely or no change would have ever happened in the first place (as we saw in the First Proof from Effect to Cause);

∴ there must be an Unchanged Changer[45] to start the process of change, and this everyone understands to be God.

- **Short version:**

Because only if there is an Unchanged Changer, then there can be other (changed) changers; and

because there are other changers;

---

[43] Although one part of something can change a different part of that same thing. "I" do not change "myself"—one part of me changes a different part of me.

[44] Usually translated from the Latin as "mover," but the Latin means "that which causes every kind of change" and not just the changing of places.

[45] Usually translated as "Prime Mover." We could also call the Unchanged Changer the "Uncatalyzed Catalyst."

The Fullness of Life

∴there is an Unchanged Changer.

By *God* in his conclusion, St. Thomas means a Supreme Being since that being which is the only Unchanged Being is supreme/superior to all other beings that do change. God is the only being that is unchanging/never changes.

What common, undeniable evidence does St. Thomas use in this proof? (1) Things change. (2) Nothing changes itself.

This previous point is a good example of how we need to use the same word consistently.[46] If someone says, "But I can change me," "I" and "me" mean two different things. "I" is one part of me, e.g., my willpower or my hand, and "me" is another part of me, e.g., my weight or hair. So my willpower changed my weight—my weight did not change itself. My hand changed my hair by applying dye, combing, etc. One strand of hair does not change itself, even just by growing—it needs nutrition, etc.

This proof does not completely explain how things change, and it is not intended to. In other words, to completely understand how things change, we can also learn how they change chemically, historically, etc. But this Proof deals with change as movement from potentiality to actuality, which is the kind of change that is common to and the basis/foundation of all other processes of change such as chemical change, historical change, etc.

THE THIRD PROOF: FROM PREDICTABILITY

- **Long version:**

Because every unintelligent natural thing acts in a consistent/predictable way; and

because every unintelligent natural thing cannot act consistently/predictably unless it has been given a direction/purpose by some being with intelligence, as the arrow goes to its target because it was shot by the archer;

∴something intelligent exists that has given a direction/purpose to

---

[46] The inconsistent use of the same term to mean different things is called *equivocation*.

every unintelligent natural thing—there exists a Direction-giver of each natural thing, and this being we call *God*.

- **Short version:**

Because we find a watch;

and because a watch could not have given itself the purpose of telling time;

∴ there is a watchmaker.

By *God* in his conclusion, St. Thomas means a Supreme Being since that being which is the Direction-giver of each being is supreme/superior to every directed natural being.

What common, undeniable evidence does St. Thomas use in this proof? Every unintelligent natural thing acts consistently/predictably.[47]

This proof explains something about reality that an atheist or agnostic cannot explain—that natural things do not act completely randomly. If an atheist tries to argue that natural things act randomly in the universe and so God does not exist, you can give these replies:

- Natural things act with only <u>some</u> randomness, NOT <u>complete</u> randomness—there is enough predictability in order for Science and Math to work because Science and Math would not work in a universe of completely random natural things.

- If you believe natural things act with complete randomness, then you don't believe in Science and Math.

- Is that which you call random really random or only apparently random because we don't completely understand it?

If a theist asks an atheist, "Why does every unintelligent thing act in a consistent/predictable way?" and the atheist answers "Just because it

---

[47] Notice that St. Thomas is arguing from the predictability of individual things, NOT from the overall design of the universe, although good arguments can be made for the existence of a Supreme Being from the intelligent design of the universe, such as by the Discovery Institute at www.discovery.org.

The Fullness of Life

does," then the atheist is not really giving a reason to the theist.

THE FOURTH PROOF: FROM NECESSITY

- **Long version:**

    This proof often re-uses a point/statement/proposition, and so the points are numbered so that you can see more easily how they are re-used. This is the most difficult, mind-blowing proof so buckle your seat belt.

    Because (1) things both exist and do not exist at different times; and

    because (2) every possibility happens with infinite time;

    ∴ (3) one possibility is the simultaneous non-existence of all things.

    Because (4) time already is infinite if God does not exist and so did not create time/give time a beginning; and

    because (2) every possibility happens with infinite time;

    ∴ (5) every possibility has already happened if God does not exist.

    Because (3) one possibility is the simultaneous non-existence of all things; and

    because (5) every possibility has already happened if God does not exist,

    ∴ (6) the simultaneous non-existence of all things would have happened by now.

    Because (6) the simultaneous non-existence of all things would have happened by now; and

    because (7) that which does not exist only begins to exist by something already existing—nothing brings itself into existence (as we saw in the First Proof from Effect to Cause);

    ∴ (8) by now nothing still would exist.

    Because (9) things do exist now; and

because (7) that which does not exist only begins to exist by something already existing,

∴ (10) there exists something which cannot both exist and not exist at different times—

something which must exist at all times—a Necessary Being/a Must-Be Being/a Being That Needs to Exist, and this being all men speak of as *God*.

- **Short version:**

Because only if there is Something-That-Must-Exist-at-All-Times/a Necessary Being, then there can exist things which both exist and do not exist at different times/unnecessary beings; and

because there unnecessary beings;

∴ there is a Necessary Being.

- **Really Short version:**

If absolutely nothing needs to exist (if there is no Necessary Being), then nothing would exist.

Because things do exist, there is a Necessary Being.

Without the Necessary Being, there would be no universe. By *God* in his conclusion, St. Thomas means a Supreme Being since that being which is the Only Necessary Being is supreme/superior to all other beings since all other beings are unnecessary.

What common, undeniable evidence does St. Thomas use in this proof? (1) Things exist and do not exist at different times. (2) Nothing brings itself into existence.

THE FIFTH PROOF: FROM DEGREES

Because among things there are some things that are more beautiful, better (more good), etc. and some things that are less beautiful, less good, etc.—there are degrees/grades/scales/ranges of quality;

and because something is "more" or "less" only as it resembles something else which is the maximum/the "most," as a thing is said to be warmer as it more nearly resembles that which is warmest;

∴ there is something which is the most beautiful, the best (most good), etc.—a Perfect Being, and this we call *God*.

By *God* in his conclusion, St. Thomas means a Supreme Being since that being which is the Perfect Being is supreme/superior to every imperfect being.

What common, undeniable evidence does St. Thomas use in this proof? There are degrees of quality among things—everything is not of the same degree/quality.

Going beyond St. Thomas' Proof, we can add that just as a thing is said to be warmer as it more nearly resembles that which is warmest, the human person's openness to truth, beauty, moral goodness, and freedom resembles/reflects/suggests that there is a Being Who is perfect truth, perfect beauty, perfect moral goodness, and perfect freedom. E.g., St. Augustine wrote:

> Question the beauty of the earth, question the beauty of the sea, question the beauty of the air distending and diffusing itself, question the beauty of the sky . . . question all these realities. All of these respond: "See, we are beautiful." Their beauty is a profession. These beauties are subject to change. Who made them if not the Beautiful One who is not subject to change?[48]

WHAT DO WE KNOW FROM THE FIVE PROOFS?

St. Thomas shows that the First Vatican Council (1869-1870)—repeated by the *Catechism of the Catholic Church*—was right when it taught, "God, the first principle and last end of all things, can be known with certainty from the created world by the natural light of human reason."[49]

We know from the Five Proofs that there is only one God/Supreme Being because the Uncaused Cause, the Unchanged Changer, the Purpose-

---

[48] As quoted in *CCC*, 32.
[49] *CCC*, 31-36.

giver of Things, and the Only Necessary Being must all be the same Being as long as there is a Perfect Being. For example, in the case of the Uncaused Cause, because there is a Perfect Being, and because there is an Uncaused Cause, the Perfect Being must be the Uncaused Cause, since the "Perfect Being" would not be perfect if it were caused by another being which was uncaused.

From this what follows? Atheism is objectively false. Agnosticism is objectively false. Polytheism/belief in more than one god is objectively false.

We also know from the Five Proofs that God's essence/identity has five characteristics/attributes: (1) God is the Uncaused Cause, (2) God is the Unchanged Changer, (3) God is the Purpose-giver of each natural thing, (4) God is the Only Necessary Being, and (5) God is the Only Perfect Being.

The Five Proofs do NOT settle all issues about who the Supreme Being is and which religion is the truest, and St. Thomas never claimed that they do. The Five Proofs help us know God's existence and something, not everything, about God's essence/identity.

The Five Proofs do not remove all doubt about the existence of God/the Supreme Being because Reason is not a substitute for Faith in Divine Revelation. An encounter with God is needed to know He is real. But the Five Proofs are examples of how Reason supports Faith. St. Thomas shows that thinking that God is real can be highly intelligent and can rise above the level of childish belief in Santa Claus or pre-scientific belief in myths.[50]

What does God want us to do as a result of learning these proofs? Be confident that He exists, get to know Him better, and develop an ever better relationship with Him by being open to His Revelation.

Let's also take this opportunity to synthesize the Proof from Effect to Cause and the Proof from Necessity: Because God is the ultimate cause of everything, and because God is the only being that needs to exist, therefore God did not have to cause/create anything—the existence of anything (e.g., you and me) is a gift from God to that thing. Shouldn't we thank God for

---

[50] For more proofs for the existence of God, see Peter Kreeft and Ronald Tacelli, SJ, *Handbook of Christian Apologetics*, Chapter 3, "Twenty Arguments for the Existence of God" (InterVarsity Press, 1994).

the gift of our existence by developing an ever better relationship with Him, which includes knowing him better?

DOES EVIL DISPROVE THE EXISTENCE OF GOD?

Evil undeniably exists. The most common argument made by atheists is: Because evil exists, therefore God does not exist.

One problem for atheism is that when it makes this argument, it implicitly/indirectly accepts the Christian belief that there is one God and that He is perfectly good because atheists take for granted that there is not one Evil Supreme Being or many evil gods or one imperfect God, any of which could explain evil.

The **second problem** for atheism is that it cannot ultimately explain the evil which it uses to justify its unbelief in God. Just as a fish cannot know it is wet because it is never dry or, more seriously, someone blind from birth cannot know light or color, we can only know there is evil because we know there is good. Good undeniably exists. Yet there can only be good if there is a cause of goodness, which must be a good Uncaused Cause and thus a good Supreme Being. Atheism cannot explain the cause of goodness because it rejects a good Uncaused Cause. Atheism cannot answer the question: If there is no God, where does goodness come from?

So these problems for atheism show, from Reason, that the existence of evil does NOT disprove the existence of God. Faith will give us more answers to the question, Does evil disprove the existence of God?

PERSONAL FAITH RESPONSE

Check any statements below that describe you.

In order to LIVE FULLY:

1. _____I agree with the objective truth in this chapter.

2. _____I am now:

    1) _____A theist.

    2) _____An atheist.

    3) _____An agnostic.

3. _____My answer to the above is different from my answer at the end of the previous chapter.

4. _____My answer to the above is the same as my answer at the end of the previous chapter.

5. _____I am grateful to God for the gift of my existence.

6. _____I want to know God better and have a better relationship with Him.

VOCABULARY

The Five Proofs: St. Thomas Aquinas' proofs for the existence of God that use only Reason.

Uncaused Cause: The being which has no cause and which began the process of cause and effect.

Unchanged Changer: The being which is unchanged and which began the process of change.

Necessary Being: The being which must exist at all times so that other beings may exist.

Unnecessary being: A being which both exists and does not exist at different times because its existence is not necessary.

Supreme Being: The being which is supreme/superior to every other being.

Polytheism: Belief in more than one god.

Part 2: How Do We Know God?

Chapter III

HOW DO WE KNOW GOD FROM HIS REVELATION?

SOURCES

- The United States Conference of Catholic Bishops (hereafter, USCCB), http://www.usccb.org/catechism/general/q&a.shtml, especially the Questions 5, 10, 16, 19, and 44.

- Scott Hahn, Gen. Ed., *Catholic Bible Dictionary* (Doubleday, 2009), "Apostle," pp. 58-60, "Revelation, Divine," pp. 773-776.

WHY IS GOD'S REVELATION NOT OBVIOUS TO EVERYONE?

God wants us to know Him so that we can have a relationship with Him. So God is in constant communication with us. God is constantly revealing Himself to us.[51] Yet Revelation is not obvious to everyone.

When a great coach and the average spectator watch the same sporting event, who sees more of what is happening? When someone with a graduate degree in art history and the average person look at the same work of art, who sees more? It is clear that seeing includes *knowing what to look for*. And so it is with Revelation. One reason that someone does not see God revealing Himself through natural and supernatural phenomena

---

[51] *CCC*, 52.

is that he does not know what to look for.

A second reason someone does not see God's Revelation is because he is distracted from it. We have all lost something or not seen something that turned out to be right there in front of us. We have all not heard things said to us because we were concentrating on something else. God, too, is right in the middle of things and yet can be completely missed and unseen and unheard. The great poet T. S. Eliot wrote that we moderns are "distracted from distraction by distraction."[52] And he wrote that before TV, the internet, social media, and the 24-7 news cycle! One thing we especially need to make sure is not distracting us from Revelation is ourselves—our appearances, our feelings, our wants, our difficulties.

A third reason God's Revelation is not obvious to everyone is provided by the great Christian thinker and writer C. S. Lewis:

> [S]unlight, though it has no favourites, cannot be reflected in a dusty mirror as clearly as in a clean one. You can put this another way by saying that while in other sciences the instruments you use are things external to yourself (things like microscopes and telescopes), the instrument through which you see God is your whole self. And if a man's self is not kept clean and bright, his glimpse of God will be blurred—like the Moon seen through a dirty telescope.[53]

WHAT ELSE ARE REVELATION AND FAITH BESIDES KNOWLEDGE?

In a personal relationship, each gets to know the other. Besides knowledge of each other, there is interaction in the relationship. Knowledge affects interaction, and interaction affects knowledge. We need to

---

[52] T. S. Eliot, *Collected Poems 1909-1962*, "Burnt Norton," (Harcourt, Brace, and World, 1963).

[53] *Mere Christianity* (Collier Books, 1986).

know something about another person in order to choose how much we will interact with him. After becoming an acquaintance, do we want to go on to become friends or even best friends? The more we interact with him, the more we know him. The more we know him, the better we can interact with him. We interact through words and deeds. Relationships grow stronger as we share both communication and experiences.

So far we have emphasized that Faith is a form of knowledge—the knowledge we get from God—and Revelation is God's giving of that knowledge. Besides knowledge, Revelation and Faith are interaction between God and believers. God wants us to know Him so that we can have a relationship with Him. Revelation and Faith are the two sides of the whole relationship between God and us. In a relationship with God, the more we know Him, the better we can interact with Him. The better we interact with God, the more we come to know Him.

Faith is the acceptance of Revelation with more than one's mind. Faith is acceptance of Revelation with one's actions so that one responds to God with one's whole life. Likewise, God does not only reveal Himself through concepts, words, and knowledge. God also reveals Himself through actions and events.54 Our relationship with God grows stronger as we share both communication and experiences with Him.

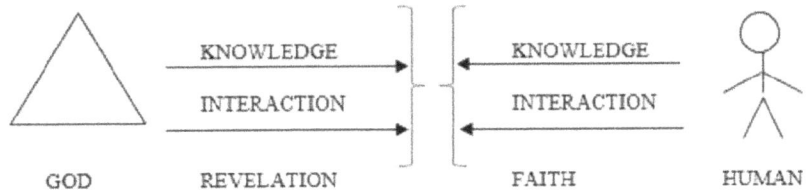

This sheds light on another reason that God's Revelation is not obvious to everyone. Just as two people at the same workplace, in the same neighborhood, on the same team, in the same classroom, in the same restaurant, etc.—even in the same family—can choose to ignore each other, we can choose to ignore God. This is especially true because God does not force us to have a relationship with Him, even though He constantly invites us to have a relationship with Him.

Reflecting on personal relationships can help us reflect on our

---

54 *CCC*, 53, 1147.

relationship with God. There is a wide spectrum of personal relationships in our lives. The spectrum starts with the overwhelming majority of the billions of people in the world who are and will remain strangers. There are others in our lives with whom our relationship has progressed from being strangers to becoming acquaintances—we get to know faces, names, characteristics. Some of our acquaintanceships progress to friendship, and from friendship sometimes to close relationships. Who is God to you? Stranger? Acquaintance? Friend? One to Whom you are close? The One to Whom you are closest?

There are two basic ways that God reveals Himself to us—two basic ways He communicates and interacts with us. One is Natural Revelation. The other is Supernatural Revelation.

WHAT IS NATURAL REVELATION?

Natural Revelation is God's Revelation of Himself <u>through</u> the objective good, truth, and beauty of non-religious things.55 Just as a mirror or water reflects a face by providing an image of that face, anything that is objectively good, true, or beautiful reflects God, Who is Perfect/Absolute Goodness, Truth, and Beauty. As the Book of Wisdom (13:2-5) in the Old Testament says,

> [E]ither fire, or wind, or the swift air, or the circuit of the stars, or the mighty water, or the luminaries of heaven . . . [the ignorant] considered gods.
>
> Now if out of their joy in their beauty they thought them gods, let them know how far more excellent is the Lord than these . . .
>
> Or if they were struck by their might and energy, let them realize from these things how much more powerful is the One Who made them.
>
> For from the greatness and beauty of created things their Original Author, by analogy, is seen.

Natural Revelation takes place when something non-religious becomes a window through which we see God, instead of when that non-religious thing is a wall between us and God, at which our vision stops and

---

[55] *CCC*, 32, 54.

behind which we do not see God. Any time we experience ANY degree of goodness, truth, or beauty, we experience a "little bit" of God. So we need to realize that our experience of God is often like the prophet Elijah's experience of God:

> [Elijah] came to a cave . . . Then [God] said [to Elijah], "Go forth, and stand upon the mount before the LORD." And behold, the LORD passed by, and a great strong wind tore the mountains, and broke in pieces the rocks before the LORD, but the LORD was not in the wind; and after the wind an earthquake, but the LORD was not in the earthquake; and after the earthquake a fire, but the LORD was not in the fire; and after the fire a still small voice. When Elijah heard it, he wrapped his face in his mantle and went out and stood at the entrance to the cave (1 Kings 19:9, 11-13).

Just as Elijah experienced God in the still small voice and not in the great strong wind, the earthquake, or the fire, our experience of God will often be in subtle and low-key ways, and not in dramatic ways with angelic choirs and trumpets. When we have the eyes of Faith, what we see as evidence in our use of Reason, e.g., St. Thomas Aquinas' evidence in his Five Proofs, become examples of Natural Revelation. Objectively good, true, and beautiful things and events are signs/signals/indications of God; they are media through which God communicates. Natural Revelation is God's sign language. Through non-religious things, God is saying: "The good, true, and beautiful things of the universe are signs that I love you. Use them to know and love Me better in this life so that you will be happy with Me in eternal life." When we allow our experience of things to be Natural Revelation, things brings us closer to God; but when we do NOT allow our experience of things to be Natural Revelation, things become substitutes for God and therefore take us farther from God. Other religious/theological terms for a non-religious thing when it is an experience of Natural Revelation are *blessing*, *grace*, and *gift*.

Where is God? Natural Revelation answers this question by answering that God is everywhere INDIRECTLY by being present THROUGH things. As Psalm 139:7-12 says:

Where can I go from You, Lord?

From Your presence, where can I flee?

If I ascend to the heavens, You are there;

If I lie down in the Underworld, there You are.

If I take the wings of dawn [go as far east as I can]

And dwell beyond the sea [as far west as I can],

Even there Your hand guides me,

Your right hand holds me fast.

If I say, "Surely darkness shall hide me,

And night shall be my light,"

Darkness is not dark for You

And night shines as the day.

As we Catholics say at Mass, "Holy, Holy, Holy Lord God of Hosts, Heaven AND EARTH are full of Your glory"; and so not just Heaven is full of God's glory, but so is earth full of God's glory. As C. S. Lewis said, "We may ignore, but we can nowhere evade, the presence of God. The world is crowded with Him. He walks everywhere incognito [i.e., unrecognized]."[56]

In the "Canticle of Brother Sun" (attributed to St. Francis of Assisi) below, those things the Canticle tells us God reveals Himself through are underlined:

Most High, all powerful, good Lord,
Yours are the praises, the glory, the honor, and all blessing.

---

[56] C. S. Lewis, *Letters to Malcolm: Chiefly on Prayer* (Mariner Books, 2002).

The Fullness of Life

*To You alone, Most High, do
they belong,
and no man is worthy to
mention Your name.*

*Be praised, my Lord, through <u>all
your creatures</u>,
especially through my lord
<u>Brother Sun</u>,
who brings the day; and you
give light through him.
And he is beautiful and radiant in
all his splendor!
Of you, Most High, he bears the
likeness.*

*Praised be You, my Lord, through
<u>Sister Moon and the stars</u>,*

in heaven you formed them clear and precious and beautiful.

*Praised be You, my Lord, through <u>Brother Wind</u>,
and through <u>the air</u>, cloudy and serene,
and <u>every kind of weather through which
You give sustenance to Your creatures</u>.*

*Praised be You, my Lord, through <u>Sister Water</u>,
which is very useful and humble and precious and chaste.*

*Praised be You, my Lord, through <u>Brother Fire</u>,
through whom you light the night*

and he is beautiful and playful and robust and strong.

*Praised be You, my Lord, through <u>Sister Earth</u>,
who sustains us and governs us*

and who produces varied fruits with colored flowers and herbs.

*Praised be You, my Lord,
through <u>those who are forgiving for Your love,
and bear infirmity and tribulation</u>.*

Blessed are those who endure in peace
for by You, Most High, they shall be crowned.

Praised be You, my Lord, through our <u>Sister Death</u>,
from whom no living man can escape.

Woe to those who die in mortal sin.
Blessed are those whom death will find in Your most holy will,
for the second death [i.e., Hell] shall do them no harm.

Praise and bless my Lord, and give Him thanks and serve Him with great humility.

Amen.

WHAT IS SUPERNATURAL REVELATION?

Supernatural Revelation is God's Revelation of Himself through religious/supernatural things, such as unique historical events, miracles, etc., as well as through those sacred writings that express this Revelation. Supernatural Revelation is more direct than Natural Revelation.

God most directly reveals Himself in Jesus Christ, Who is the first and last definitive Word of Revelation/the definitive Word of God/the definitive God event.[57] So the best way to know God is to know Jesus Christ.

After Jesus' time on earth, Jesus most directly reveals Himself in, and so the most important Supernatural Revelation is in:[58]

1) The Catholic Church's Sacred Scripture, which is also known as the Bible, the Word of God, the Word of the Lord, or simply Scripture; it is the only book written by God and the divinely inspired record of God's revelation in history.

2) The Catholic Church's Sacred Tradition, which is the sacred words and actions that were handed on/passed on outside of Sacred Scripture: the words and actions of Jesus experienced by the Twelve Apostles and the words and actions of the Twelve Apostles

---

[57] *CCC*, 50, 53, 65-66.
[58] *CCC*, 76, 79-81.

The Fullness of Life

that were inspired by God. And so Sacred Tradition ended when the last Apostle died.

Examples of Sacred Tradition that are commanded NOWHERE in the Bible and that are done by Christians today ONLY because the Apostles did them are:

- Moving the Lord's Day from Saturday to Sunday.[59]

- Reading the New Testament, which are the Bible books written after Jesus, during worship.[60]

Because Sacred Tradition began with the Revelation to the Apostles from Jesus Himself, who died, rose, and ascended about 30 AD, and because the first book of the New Testament was written about 50 AD, therefore Sacred Tradition existed about twenty years before the first book of the New Testament. Because the Church and its Faith existed from the time Jesus began His public ministry, and because all of the New Testament was not written until as early as 70 AD but maybe as late as 100 AD, therefore the Church and its Faith existed at least forty years before the New Testament as a whole and thus the Bible as a whole. The Bible itself affirms that God reveals Himself through Tradition.[61]

Sacred Tradition with a capital *T* is different from Church traditions with a small *t*.[62] Church traditions can and do change. They are not Revelation. They are part of the Faith; they are responses to Revelation. Sacred Tradition never changes. To worship God on Sunday is Sacred Tradition. To include Mass on the vigil of Sunday (on Saturday at 4:00pm or later) as Sunday Mass is an ancient tradition (discontinued for centuries but revived by Pope Pius XII in 1953) that considers the day to begin not at midnight or at sunrise but at sunset. Another example of tradition and not Sacred Tradition is the language used at Mass, e.g., the replacement of Latin with the vernacular/local language that was begun in 1964.

---

[59] *CCC*, 1166. In the Jewish calendar, the Lord's Day, or Sabbath, is the last day of the week, which in English is *Saturday*. The Apostles made the Jewish first day of the week, which in English is *Sunday*, the Lord's Day.

[60] *CCC*, 1349.

[61] See Acts 2:42, 20:35; 1 Cor 11:2, 15:3,11; 2 Thes 2:15, 3:6; 2 Tm 2:2, 3:14-15; Rom 10:17; 1 Pt 1:25.

[62] *CCC*, 83.

God reveals Himself equally in Sacred Scripture and Sacred Tradition.[63] And because God never contradicts/disagrees with Himself, Revelation in Sacred Scripture and Revelation in Sacred Tradition never contradict each other. The term for what God has revealed in Sacred Scripture and Sacred Tradition taken together is the *Deposit of Faith*. It could well be called the "Deposit of Revelation." Revelation and Faith go hand in hand. Without Revelation, there is no Faith.

WHO SHOULD INTERPRET REVELATION?

Neither Sacred Scripture nor Sacred Tradition is self-explanatory. Neither has meanings that are always obvious. Both need to be interpreted.[64]

Christ had many disciples/followers; but Christ Himself chose some of His disciples to be the leaders of the rest of His disciples, and these leaders were the Twelve Apostles.[65] All of the Apostles were disciples, but NOT all of the disciples were Apostles. The Venn Diagram below shows the relationship between Christ's disciples and the Twelve Apostles.

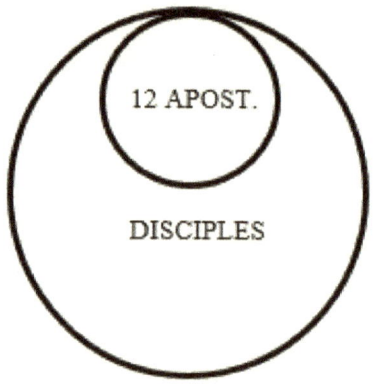

---

[63] *CCC*, 82.

[64] *CCC*, 85.

[65] *CCC*, 857-860. See Mt 10:1-4, Mk 3:13-19, and Lk 6:12-16. Jesus shares His authority and mission with the Twelve Apostles in Mt 10:1-15, 19:28, 28:16-20; Mk 6:7-13, 16:15-16, 19-20; Lk 9:1-5, 24:46-49; and Acts 1:8, 2:37-43. Jesus eats the Last Supper only with the Twelve Apostles (Mt 26:20, Mk 14:17, Lk 22:14). In Rev 21:14, the twelve Apostles are the foundation of the New Jerusalem/Kingdom of God.

The Fullness of Life

Christ also chose one of the Twelve Apostles to be the leader of the rest of the Twelve Apostles, and that was St. Peter. He is the rock on which Jesus builds His church (Mt 16:18). [66] The Twelve Apostles were the leaders of the disciples, and St. Peter was the leader of the leaders. The Venn Diagram below shows the relationship between the disciples, the Twelve Apostles, and St. Peter.

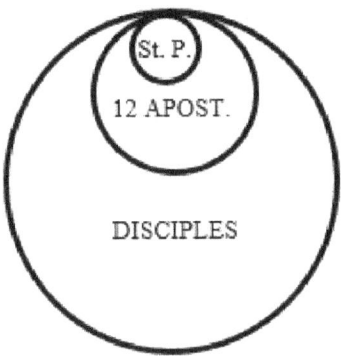

These Twelve Apostles knew Jesus personally both before and after His Resurrection. They knew Jesus better than anyone else in history. With their knowledge of Jesus and under the inspiration of the Holy Spirit given to them by Jesus, the Twelve Apostles chose men to be their successors/continue their work, who are the bishops, each of whom governs an area of the Church called a diocese. Every current bishop was ordained/made a bishop by a bishop who was ordained by a bishop who was ordained in a line of succession by a bishop who was ordained by one of the Twelve Apostles in a process called Apostolic Succession.[67]

---

[66] In Mt 16:13-20, Peter is the one who speaks for the Twelve Apostles, and Christ gives Peter the keys of the Kingdom of God just as the kings of ancient Israel gave the keys of their kingdom to their second-in-command/right-hand man/"prime minister." Peter also speaks for the Apostles in Mk 8:29/Lk 9:20, Mt 15:15/Lk 12:41, Mt 16:22/Mk 9:32, Mt 18:21, Mt 19:27/Mk 10:28/Lk 18:28, Mk 11:21, Lk 8:45, Jn 13:6-9, Jn 13:24, Acts 2:14-36, Acts 3:12-26, 4:8-12, Acts 5:29-32, and Acts 10:34-43. In Mt 14:22-33, Mk 1:36, and Jn 18:10, Peter is the one who takes action when the other Apostles do not. In Lk 24:34, Jn 20:1-8, and 1 Cor 15:5, Peter is the first of the Twelve Apostles to see that Jesus rose from the dead. In Lk 22:31-32, it is only to Peter that Jesus gives the job of strengthening the other Apostles. In Jn 21:15-17, Jesus, the Risen Lord, makes only Peter the shepherd of Jesus' flock. The disciple whose name is mentioned in the Gospels more frequently than any other disciple is Peter.

[67] *CCC*, 85, 860-862, 880. Apostolic Succession is documented by Clement in

APOSTLE → BISHOP → BISHOP … BISHOP → CURRENT BISHOP
2000+ YEARS

St. Peter chose a man to be his successor/continue his work, who is the pope. Just as St. Peter was one of the Twelve Apostles, the pope is one of the bishops. Some years after the Ascension, St. Peter left Jerusalem and ended up in Rome, and so he was the first Bishop of Rome and was eventually put to death there by the Roman emperor Nero on the hill the Romans called Vatican Hill; and so every pope is the Bishop of Rome. St. Peter's tomb is directly under the altar in St. Peter's Basilica in Vatican City, which is the church where the pope usually says Mass. Just as St. Peter was the leader of the Twelve Apostles, the pope is the leader of the Bishops, a position called Papal Primacy (*papal* = the pope's, and *primacy* = first place of importance).[68]

In terms of leadership, the Pope is to the bishops what St. Peter was to the Twelve Apostles. In terms of succession, the Pope is to St. Peter what the bishops are to the Twelve Apostles.

The name for the pope and the bishops together is the Magisterium. Because Christ gave the authority to interpret Revelation ONLY to the Twelve Apostles under Peter's leadership, and because ONLY the Magisterium is the successor of the Twelve Apostles under Peter's leadership, therefore ONLY the Magisterium has the authority to interpret Revela-

---

96 AD, Ignatius of Antioch in 107 AD, Hegesippus in 180 AD, Irenaeus in 189 AD, Tertullian in 200 AD, Cyprian of Carthage in 253 AD, Jerome in 396 AD, and Augustine in 397 AD. See www.catholic.com/library/Apostolic_Succession.asp.

[68] *CCC*, 85, 862, 881-885. Papal Primacy is documented by Hermas in 80 AD, Clement in 96 AD, Dionysius of Corinth in 170 AD, Irenaenus in 189 AD, Tertullian in 200 AD, Cyprian of Carthage in 251 AD, Firmilian in 253 AD, Eusebius of Caesarea in 312 AD, Pope Julius I in 341 AD, the Council of Sardica in 342 AD, Optatus in 367 AD, Epiphanius of Salamis in 375 AD, Jerome in 396 AD, Ambrose of Milan in 388 AD, Augustine in 412 AD, the Council of Ephesus in 431 AD, Peter Chrysologus in 449 AD, and the Council of Chalcedon in 451 AD. See www.catholic.com/library/Authority_of_the_Pope_Part_1.asp and also this page www.catholic.com/library/Peter_Successors.asp.

tion.[69] No priest, no deacon, no nun, no Theology teacher or professor, no campus minister, no youth minister, no DRE, no other Catholic, and no one else has the authority to interpret Revelation.

God designed Sacred Scripture, Sacred Tradition, and the Magisterium to go together.[70] No one of them makes sense without the other two. Scripture, Tradition, and the Magisterium are like the 3 legs of a stool. One leg needs the other two legs in order for the stool to stand.

WHERE DO REVELATION AND FAITH MEET?

Revelation is God's communication not only of Who He is and how He interacts with us, but also of how He wants us to interact with Him. Faith is acceptance not only of knowing God as He wants to be known, but also of interacting with Him as He wants to be interacted with.

Revelation and Faith meet in doctrine, which is a teaching by the Magisterium that makes either Revelation or Faith clearer and that is true for all times and places. To be Catholic is to be faithful to Catholic doctrine. If a person is not faithful to a particular doctrine, that person cannot accurately claim to be Catholic on the issue covered by that doctrine. As recent popes have said:

> It has to be noted that there is a tendency on the part of some Catholics to be selective in their adherence to the Church's moral teaching. It is sometimes claimed that dissent from the Magisterium is totally compatible with being a "good Catholic," and poses no obstacle to the reception of the Sacraments. This is a grave error...

—Pope John Paul II, 1987

> Dear brothers and sisters, how necessary it is today at the dawn of the third millennium for the entire Catholic community to proclaim, teach, and witness to the entire truth of Catholic faith, doctrine, and morals in a unanimous and harmonious manner!

—Pope Benedict XVI, 2005

---

[69] *CCC*, 85-87, 888-892.
[70] *CCC*, 95.

> Since the faith is one, it must be professed in all its purity and integrity. Precisely because all the articles of faith are interconnected, to deny one of them, even those that seem least important, is tantamount to distorting the whole.
>
> —Pope Francis (*Lumen Fidei*, 48), 2013

A good Catholic is orthodox—NOT Eastern Orthodox, but "right-believing," which is the original meaning of *orthodox*. A good, orthodox Catholic is a Catholic who is trying to be faithful to all Catholic doctrine. The opposite kind of Catholic, although baptized in the Catholic Church, is a:

- Cafeteria Catholic who picks and chooses what he wants to believe and practice from the "menu" of doctrines;

- Cultural Catholic who is Catholic out of habit and feels comfortable in Catholic places or with other Catholics without really caring to know and practice the Catholic Faith;

- Nominal Catholic who is Catholic in name while knowing and practicing the Faith in a superficial way; or

- Heretic who presents as Catholic that which is not really Catholic. A material heretic commits heresy without intending to do so. A formal heretic stubbornly presents as Catholic doctrine what he knows to be a contradiction of Catholic doctrine.[71]

The best single place to find Catholic doctrine is the *Catechism of the Catholic Church*. The *Catechism* describes the Catholic Faith as having Four Pillars, which are four ways of knowing and interacting with God. Revelation and Faith meet in the Four Pillars because they express how God wants us to know Him and interact with Him. The Four Pillars are:

1) Creed, which is doctrine about God and supernatural things.

2) Morality, which is making our actions faithful to God.

---

[71] *CCC*, 2089.

3) Worship, where we encounter God in sacred rituals as we are assembled with others.

4) Prayer, where we encounter God in our own personal ways.

The actions of morality, worship, and prayer are interacting with God as He wants to be interacted with as long as they are in harmony with Catholic doctrines of morality, worship, and prayer.

WHY DOESN'T GOD REVEAL HIMSELF DIRECTLY? WHY IS HE BEHIND A CURTAIN/VEIL?

Our eyes need light in order to see, BUT our eyes are not able/not "equipped" to take in too much light at one time. Just as too much light would overpower our eyes, too much of God/the Supreme Being/the Only Absolute and Perfect Being/the Lord of the Cosmos/the Creator of Heaven and Earth would overpower us.

We need to be "equipped" to see God face-to-face/to know God directly/to experience God fully. We need to be transformed. Only death or the Second Coming of Christ can transform us in this way. But this is only half of the answer. We will learn the other half when we study the Book of Genesis in Sacred Scripture.

SUMMARY: WHAT IS THE FULLNESS OF REVELATION AND FAITH?

God made us to know Him and have a relationship with Him.

God gave us Reason to know Him. God also reveals Himself so that we can know Him.

God will NOT reveal Himself directly/fully/face-to-face/with no "veil" or "curtain" between us and God until we are transformed by either death or the Second Coming of Christ.

God reveals Himself more indirectly through non-religious things, which is Natural Revelation.

God reveals Himself less indirectly through religious things, such as miracles, which is Supernatural Revelation, which is clearest in Jesus Christ, Who most directly reveals Himself in the Sacred Scripture and Sacred Tradition of the Catholic Church as they are interpreted and clarified in the doctrines taught by the Magisterium. (Jesus, the Holy Spirit, the Magisterium, and the Four Pillars will be explained at greater length later in the book.)

The acceptance of Divine Revelation is Faith. Faith is knowledge that comes from God.

Catholic Faith is the acceptance of the one true God's Natural Revelation and Supernatural Revelation, especially acceptance of the doctrines taught by the Magisterium, which results in a personal relationship with God based on true knowledge of Him.

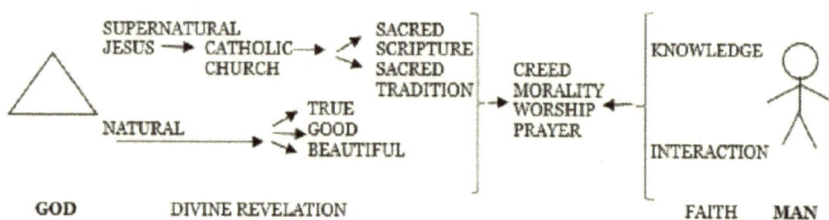

Because Faith is the acceptance of Revelation, and because this chapter and the rest of the book present Revelation, the PERSONAL FAITH RESPONSE to it is now a response of Faith or a rejection of Faith.

PERSONAL FAITH RESPONSE

Check any statements below that describe you.

In order to LIVE FULLY:

1. _____I agree with the objective truth in this chapter.

2. _____I will know and have a relationship with God through non-religious things.

3. _____I will know and have a relationship with God through Jesus Christ.

4. _____I will know and have a relationship with God through Sacred Scripture.

5. _____I will know and have a relationship with God through Sacred Tradition.

6. _____I will know and have a relationship with God through the Four Pillars of the Catholic Faith.

7. _____I will use the *Catechism of the Catholic Church* to know the doctrine taught by the Magisterium.

8. _____I will not contradict Catholic doctrine.

VOCABULARY

Natural Revelation: God's Revelation of Himself through the objective good, truth, and beauty of non-religious things.

Supernatural Revelation: God's Revelation of Himself through religious/supernatural things.

Sacred Scripture: The divinely inspired record of God's revelation in history; also known as the Bible/the Word of God/the Word of the Lord/Scripture.

Sacred Tradition: The words and actions of Jesus experienced by the Twelve Apostles and the inspired words and actions of the Twelve Apostles that were handed on/passed on outside of Sacred Scripture.

Deposit of Faith: What God has revealed in Sacred Scripture and Sacred Tradition taken together.

Disciple: Follower.

Twelve Apostles: The disciples of Christ that He chose to be the leaders of the rest of His disciples.

St. Peter: One of the Twelve Apostles that Christ chose to be the leader of the Twelve Apostles; the one Christ chose to be the leader of the leaders.

Successor: One who continues the work of another.

Bishop: A successor of the Twelve Apostles.

Diocese: An area of the Church governed by a bishop.

Pope: A successor of St. Peter who is the leader of the bishops and so the leader of the Church; also the Bishop of Rome.

Magisterium: The pope and the bishops together.

Doctrine: A clarification of Revelation or definition of the Catholic Faith, made by the Magisterium, that and that is true always and everywhere for everyone.

Orthodox Catholic: A "right-believing" Catholic who is trying to be faithful to all Catholic doctrine

Cafeteria Catholic: Someone baptized in the Catholic Church who picks and chooses what he wants to believe and practice from the "menu" of doctrines.

Cultural Catholic: Someone baptized in the Catholic Church who is Catholic out of habit and feels comfortable in Catholic places or with other Catholics without really caring to know and practice the Catholic Faith.

Nominal Catholic: Someone baptized in the Catholic Church who is Catholic in name only.

Heretic: Someone baptized in the Catholic Church who is presents as Catholic that which is not really Catholic. A **material heretic** commits heresy without intending to do so. A **formal heretic** stubbornly contradicts what he knows to be Catholic doctrine.

Catechism of the Catholic Church: The best single place to find Catholic doctrine.

Four Pillars: Creed, Morality, Worship, and Prayer, the four ways of knowing and interacting with God where Revelation and Faith meet because they express both Revelation and Faith.

Creed: Doctrine about God and supernatural things.

Morality: Making our actions faithful to God.

Worship: Encountering God in sacred rituals as we are assembled with others.

Prayer: Encountering God in our own personal ways.

PART 3:

HOW SHOULD WE READ SACRED SCRIPTURE?

Chapter I: WHAT ARE IMPORTANT BASICS ABOUT SACRED SCRIPTURE?

Chapter II: WHAT LANGUAGE AND MEANINGS ARE IN SACRED SCRIPTURE?

Chapter III: WHAT DOES GOD REVEAL THROUGH GENESIS 1-3?

Part 3: How Should We Read Sacred Scripture?

Chapter I

WHAT ARE IMPORTANT BASICS ABOUT SACRED SCRIPTURE?

SOURCES

- Scott Hahn, Gen. Ed., *Catholic Bible Dictionary* (Doubleday, 2009), "Bible," "Hebrew Language," "Septuagint," "Versions of the Bible."
- S. J. Rafe, *Where Did the Bible Come From?* (St. Michael's Media, 2007).

WHY IS SACRED SCRIPTURE IMPORTANT?

First and foremost, Scripture is the only book written by God.[72] It is, along with Sacred Tradition, one of the two ways God most directly reveals Himself after Jesus Christ. As St. Jerome said, "Ignorance of the Scriptures is ignorance of Christ."[73]

Scripture is the account of how God originally revealed Himself to and had a relationship with real people. And it is a way for God to reveal Himself to and have a personal relationship with anyone who reads Scripture.

---

[72] *CCC*, 105.
[73] Quoted in *CCC*, 133.

Scripture is important in the life of the Catholic Church.[74] The first basic part of Mass, and usually of all the Sacraments, is the Liturgy of the Word, during which Scripture is read aloud. If someone went to Mass every day over the 3-year cycle according to which Scripture is read at Mass, he would hear about 27% of the Bible read. Scripture is an essential part of the Liturgy of the Hours, which is the formal prayer required of priests, deacons, brothers, and nuns that is said every day at designated times. The Magisterium encourages us to study Scripture. Reading and reflecting on Scripture is a common way for both individuals and groups to pray. Reading and reflecting on Scripture is a bond Catholic Christians have with Eastern Orthodox Christians and Protestant Christians.

WHAT ARE THE PARTS OF THE BIBLE?

Scripture is divided into two main parts:

- The Old Testament, which expresses Revelation before the time of Jesus Christ, and which is still sacred to the Jews, the people who first received Supernatural Revelation.

- The New Testament, which expresses Revelation during and after the time of Jesus Christ.

Each testament is divided into books, each of which has a name, e.g., the first book of the Old Testament is the Book of Genesis. Each book name has an abbreviation, e.g., in the New American Bible Revised Edition the abbreviation for Genesis is Gn. Not every book has a title that begins with the "Book of . . ."

There are 46 books in the Old Testament[75] which are usually grouped into:

- The Pentateuch, which begins with the Book of Genesis and ends with the Book of Deuteronomy. *Pentateuch* means the "Five Books" from the Greek *penta*, "five," and *teuchos*, "book." Judaism calls the Pentateuch the *Torah*, which is Hebrew for "The Law."

---

[74] *CCC*, 103-104, 131-133.
[75] *CCC*, 120.

- The Historical Books, which begin with the Book of Joshua and include all the books thereafter up to and including the Book of Esther and then also include the First and Second Books of Maccabees.

- The Wisdom Books, which begin with the Book of Job and end with the Book of Sirach.

- The Prophetic Books, which begin with the Book of Isaiah and end with the Book of Malachi.

There are 27 books in the New Testament[76] which are grouped into:

- The Gospels, which begin with Matthew and end with John.

- The Acts of the Apostles, a book which is in a group by itself.

- The Letters or Epistles, which begin with Romans and end with Jude.

- The Book of Revelation, a book which is in a group by itself.

Each book is divided into chapters, each of which is numbered; and its number appears in its title, e.g., Chapter 1, Chapter 2, etc. Each chapter is divided into verses, each of which is numbered; and each verse's number appears at the beginning of the verse. A verse or set of verses considered by itself is called a *passage*.

The above is true of all Christian Bibles in general. However, there are more books in the Catholic Old Testament than in the Protestant Old Testament, which will be explained later. Also, different Bibles use different systems of numbering verses. The system used in this book is the system used in the New American Bible Revised Edition.

The Jewish Bible includes only the Old Testament because they do not recognize that there has been Revelation through Christ in a New Testament. What Christians call "The Old Testament" Jews call "The Bible."

---

[76] *CCC*, 120.

HOW DID THE BIBLE COME TO BE?

No book in Sacred Scripture dropped down from the sky. The human author of each Biblical book did NOT write it with the intention of its becoming part of the Bible.

Some books of Scripture, e.g., Genesis, were written in a 3-stage process:

1) A real person experienced God's Revelation/had a personal relationship with God.

2) Stories and reflections about his experience/relationship were handed on by word of mouth in oral traditions, sometimes for centuries as in the case of the oldest Old Testament books.

3) The stories and reflections were finally put down in writing by one or more persons other than the person who had the actual experience/relationship. In some cases there might have been different written traditions as well as different oral traditions. The final form of a book is sometimes the work of an editor.

Some books of Scripture, e.g., St. Paul's Letter to the Galatians, were written in a 2-stage process:

1) A real person experienced God's Revelation/had a personal relationship with God.

2) The experience was written down by that very person, although again sometimes edited by someone other than the author.

Both the writing of a book and the process of its reaching its final form—oral tradition, written tradition, editing—are inspired by God.[77] Just as God could have "authored" the human race in a quick act of special creation or in a long process of evolving humans from non-humans, God did author all of Sacred Scripture—both through the 3-stage process and the 2-stage process.

Scripture does NOT say which books/writings should be in Scripture. The books in Scripture had to be chosen.

---

[77] *CCC*, 106-107.

At the time of Jesus, all the books of the Old Testament had been put in their final written form; but there were two different collections of Jewish Sacred Scripture in two different languages: the collection in the Hebrew language and the collection in the Greek language, which included all the books in the Hebrew collection plus seven other books.[78]

After Jesus, the Church was roughly divided into the Latin-speaking Church in the western Mediterranean world and the Greek-speaking Church in the eastern Mediterranean world. Everyone in the Latin-speaking Church agreed that the Greek collection is the true Old Testament. There were minor disagreements in the entire Church about which orthodox books/books with right belief should be in the New Testament until a canon/official list was formulated at the Council of Carthage in the year 397 AD.[79] There was also complete agreement in the entire Church to reject certain heretical books/books with false beliefs, e.g., "The Gospel of Peter" and "The Gospel of Thomas."

And so it was Sacred Tradition that decided which books should be in Sacred Scripture. It was probably Melito of Sardis (died c. 180) who coined the terms *Old Testament* and *New Testament*. Around the year 400 AD, the books of the New Testament were published together for the first time as one volume with the entire Old Testament, and so the Bible as we know it made its first appearance.[80]

In the Latin-speaking Church, there was no disagreement about the canon for over 1,100 years after the Council of Carthage until Martin Luther, originator of the Protestant Reformation, published his version of the New Testament in 1522. Luther considered the Letter to the Hebrews, the Letter of James, the Letter of Jude, and the Book of Revelation to be less sacred than the other books of the New Testament; but his followers later went back to the Catholic canon of the New Testament. Luther also changed the Old Testament canon by going back to the Jews' Hebrew collection, and his followers kept this change. In response, the Council of

---

[78] The books in Greek collection that are not in the Hebrew collection are: 1 and 2 Maccabees, Tobit, Judith, Sirach, Wisdom, Baruch, and some additions to Esther and Daniel.

[79] There were several local canons/official lists with minor variations from at least 170 AD until the Council of Carthage.

[80] St. Jerome was the first to do so. He wrote his one-volume Bible in Latin, which he translated from individual Hebrew and Greek books. He finished his translation in 405 AD.

Trent in 1546 settled the issue for the Catholic Church by reaffirming the canon of the Council of Carthage and rejecting Luther's revisions.

Protestant Bibles and Catholic Bibles now have the same New Testament books, but Protestant Bibles (the Hebrew collection) have seven less Old Testament books than Catholic Bibles (the Greek collection). Another difference between Catholic and Protestant Bibles is that Catholic Bibles tend to have much more commentary/explanation for the actual words of Scripture, which is found in introductions, footnotes, and appendixes.

So, in one sense, the Bible is a library of books written by different human authors at different times. In another sense, the Bible is one book because all of its book are united as a primary way, along with Sacred Tradition, for God to reveal Himself.[81]

In 1205, Stephen Langton divided the Bible into chapters. In 1528, Santes Pagninus divided the Old Testament into verses. In 1551, Robert Etienne divided the New Testament into verses.

The translation of the Bible into English began with the translation of parts of the Bible into Old English as early as the 600s. The first time the entire Bible was translated into English was the 1300s. The first time the entire Bible was printed in English was 1535 by the Protestant Miles Coverdale. The first time the entire Catholic Bible was printed in English was 1609.

There are two basic ways to translate the Bible. "Formal equivalence" is word-for-word translation of the Bible so that the English version is as close as possible to the original languages even if the translation does not flow in English very well. "Dynamic equivalence" is keeping the meaning of the original languages in eloquent/fluent/well-written English that is not word-for-word from the original languages. Both approaches have their pros and cons. The true student of the Bible (who has not learned Hebrew and Greek) will have Bibles translated both ways.

There are many versions of the Bible. The version referenced in this book is the New American Bible Revised Edition, because it is the version used at Mass. For a list of versions approved by the U. S. Conference of Catholic Bishops, see the site at http://www.usccb.org/bible/approved-

---

[81] *CCC*, 121-123, 128-130, 134.

translations/index.cfm.

HOW DOES BIBLICAL NOTATION WORK?

Biblical notation allows us to note/cite/refer to a passage by noting its book, chapter, and verse in that order, e.g., Lk 18:8. *Lk* refers to the book (in this case the Gospel of Luke). *18* refers to the chapter. *8* refers to the verse. The part of the Bible that is NOT included in biblical notation is the testament that a passage is in. When you do not know which testament a passage is in or which book is being abbreviated in a particular biblical notation, there might be a list of book abbreviations at the beginning of the Bible.

There are things common to all biblical notation.

- A number that comes ***right BEFORE a colon*** (:) represents a chapter, e.g., in *Lk 5:1* the chapter is 5.

- A number that comes ***right AFTER a colon*** represents a verse, e.g., in *Lk 5:1* the verse is 1.

- A ***hyphen*** (-) means "through" or "up to and including."

    o When there is **no colon**, the hyphen refers to chapters, e.g., *Lk 5-7* means Chapter 5 through Chapter 7 of Luke, which is a total of 3 chapters.

    o When the hyphen appears **after a colon**, the hyphen refers to **verses**, e.g., *Lk 5:1-11* means verse 1 of Chapter 5 of Luke through verse 11 of Chapter 5 of Luke.

    o When the hyphen appears in notation **with 2 colons**, the number before the hyphen is a verse and the number after the hyphen is a chapter, e.g., *Lk 5:1-6:11* means Chapter 5, verse 1 of Luke through Chapter 6, verse 11.

- ***No colon***, such as in *Lk 18*, means an entire chapter, e.g., *Lk 18* means Chapter 18 of Luke.

- A ***semi-colon*** (;) excludes everything between what comes before the semi-colon and what comes after the semi-colon, e.g., *Dn 5; 11* represents only Chapter 5 and Chapter 11 of Daniel and excludes Chapters 6 through 10 of Daniel.

PERSONAL FAITH RESPONSE

Check any statements below that describe you.

In order to LIVE FULLY:

1. _____ I agree with the objective truth in this chapter.

2. _____ I will make Sacred Scripture important to my personal prayer and reflection.

3. _____ I will listen carefully to Sacred Scripture during worship.

4. _____ I will be good at using biblical notation so that I can use Scripture more easily.

VOCABULARY

Testament: One of the two main parts into which the Bible is divided.

Old Testament: Expresses Revelation before the time of Jesus Christ.

New Testament: Expresses Revelation during and after the time of Jesus Christ.

Book: What each testament is divided into.

Chapter: What each book is divided into.

Verse: What each chapter is divided into.

Passage: A verse or set of verses considered by itself.

3-Stage Process: How some books of Scripture were written: 1) A **real person** experienced God's Revelation, 2) stories and reflections about his experience were handed on in **oral traditions**, and 3) the oral traditions were finally **put down in writing** down by one or more persons other than the person who had the actual experience.

2-Stage Process: How some books of Scripture were written: 1) A **real person** experienced God's Revelation and 2) stories and reflections about his experience were **put down in writing** by that person.

Orthodox: Right-believing.

Canon: Official list.

Heretical: False-believing.

Martin Luther: Originator of the Protestant Reformation who disagreed with the 1,100-year old traditional canon of the Bible.

Council of Trent: The council of the Catholic Church that reaffirmed the traditional canon of the Bible and rejected Luther's revisions.

Formal Equivalence: Word-for-word translation of the Bible so that the English version is as close as possible to the original languages.

Dynamic Equivalence: Translation keeping the meaning of the original languages in eloquent English.

Biblical Notation: Notation of a passage's book, chapter, and verse.

Part 3: How Should We Read Sacred Scripture?

Chapter II

WHAT LANGUAGE AND MEANINGS ARE IN SACRED SCRIPTURE?

SOURCES

- Scott Hahn, Gen. Ed., *Catholic Bible Dictionary* (Doubleday, 2009) "Interpretation of the Bible."

USING SCRIPTURE WITH THIS BOOK

We are about to begin our study of Sacred Scripture. It will take us several chapters to cover the Old and New Testaments. By the end of our last chapter on the New Testament, we will have covered enough key passages so that you will be very familiar with Scripture.

In each chapter you have the option of reading a Scripture passage that is explained before it is explained. Doing so can deepen your relationship with God. If you chose to do so, **look for the biblical notation in bold font** to know what to read in Scripture before you continue reading in this book. On the other hand, God understands how busy and tired we are with our many commitments. Reading Scripture along with this book is not necessary in order to understand this book. It might be more prudent to read at a later date the Scripture passages explained in this book.

If you read a passage explained in this book, do NOT expect to understand every word in a passage. Because each passage will be explained in this book, it is not necessary to understand every word in order to understand the substance of the passage. It also is not necessary to read footnotes and commentary provided in your Bible. Of course, whether now or later, it is a blessing to continue to grow in our understanding of Scripture. We are blessed to live at a time when there have never been so many excellent resources available for understanding Scripture.

WHAT ARE THE FOUR SENSES OF SCRIPTURE?

The Magisterium teaches that Scripture has four senses/meanings.[82]

One sense is the Literal Sense. In this case *literal* means *original* so the "Literal Sense" is the original meaning of the words of Scripture—what the words of Scripture meant to their human authors. The Literal Sense is discovered by exegetes/Scripture scholars and other experts (e.g., archeologists) who know ancient languages, literary forms and genres, history, culture, etc. The Literal Sense is a good source of historical truth, but not of scientific truth.

There are three other senses. The Allegorical Sense is how events in the Old Testament are related to Jesus Christ, e.g., how the manna in the desert foreshadows the Eucharist. The Moral Sense is what Scripture teaches about good behavior. The Anagogical Sense is what Scripture teaches about eternal realities (from the Greek *anagoge* meaning "elevation"). These three Senses of Scripture are based on the Literal/Original Sense.

The Senses of Scripture are more reasons for appreciating that the Bible is NOT just another piece of literature. No other literature has as much allegorical, moral, and anagogical meaning that is true for all people at all times.

---

[82] *CCC*, 115-119.

WHAT IS A KEY TO READING SCRIPTURE?

The interpretation of Scripture can get very complicated. A simple key to reading Scripture is knowing when its language is literal and when its language is figurative.

1) Literal language which is language that does NOT need to be interpreted/ language that should be taken at face value/language that means exactly what it says.

2) Figurative language which is language that DOES need to be interpreted because it uses symbols and metaphors.

An example of literal language is *It is raining very hard*. An example of figurative language is *It is raining cats and dogs*.

1 Mc (Maccabees) 1:1-7 says that Alexander the Great had a great empire which he divided when he realized that he was going to die. **Prv (Proverbs) 31:30** says that charm is deceptive and beauty is fleeting. **Mk (Mark) 15:15** says that Pilate had Jesus scourged and handed Him over to be crucified. These passages are examples of literal language.

Mt (Matthew) 5:29-30 says that if your right eye causes you to sin, tear it out and throw it away; if your right hand causes you to sin, cut it off and throw it away. **Lk (Luke) 6:29-30** says that to the person who strikes you on one cheek, offer the other one as well; give to everyone who asks of you, and from the one who takes what is yours do not demand it back. **Lk 14:12-13** says that when you hold a lunch or a dinner, do not invite your friends or relatives; but rather, when you hold a banquet invite the poor, the crippled, the lame, the blind. These passages are examples of figurative language.

So in Scripture there is both literal and figurative language. Scripture itself does NOT say that Scripture should always be taken literally. So to take all of Scripture literally in order to be true to Scripture is NOT being true to Scripture. Just as humans communicate through both literal and figurative language, God reveals Himself and communicates through both literal and figurative language.

WHY IS SOME OF SCRIPTURE'S LANGUAGE FIGURATIVE?

God gave the human writers of Scripture the gift of inspiration. God inspired the human writers to put into Scripture what God wanted to reveal so that we humans can find salvation. Scripture is inerrant, which means that the human writers made no errors in matters of Revelation and Faith. So Scripture is the Word of God.

On the other hand, God allowed the human writers to be themselves and to use their own powers and abilities, and so God worked through the human writers and NOT around them, just as in Natural Revelation when God reveals Himself through non-religious things and NOT around them. That makes Scripture the words of men. The human writers of Scripture were still men of their own times, e.g. none of them knew nuclear physics. And each human writer still had his own personality, writing style, culture, and purpose.

God is the primary author of Scripture, but the human writers did not passively write down only what God told them to. Scripture is the Word of God in the words of men.[83]

There are several reasons why some of Scripture's language is figurative. Sometimes the figurative language was intended by its human writer to be figurative. Sometimes the language that its human writer intended to be literally true turns out to be figuratively true. Sometimes the human author communicated more of Revelation than he was aware he was communicating.

When reading Scripture, we need to give attention BOTH to what the human authors intended to say AND to what God reveals to us through the human authors' words.

HOW DO WE KNOW WHEN SCRIPTURE IS LITERAL OR FIGURATIVE?

Scripture itself is NOT always clear when its language is literal or figurative.

One way we know when Scripture's language is literal and when it is

---

[83] *CCC*, 101-111.

figurative is by using Reason, which never contradicts Faith. So we should take Scripture literally when its language does NOT contradict the truth we have discovered in other subjects, such as history, archeology, science, etc. And when taking Scripture literally contradicts true history, true archeology, true science, etc., then we should take Scripture figuratively.

However, we should realize that supernatural and miraculous things do NOT contradict the truth/knowledge we get from Reason. Supernatural things are beyond what we can know from Reason and beyond what naturally happens. There are indeed "more things in heaven and earth, Horatio, than are dreamt of in your philosophy," as Hamlet instructs.

Sometimes those passages of Scripture that tell us something miraculous or supernatural happens are clearly literally true. Sometimes it is not so clear if they are literally true. We need to be open to all such passages being literally true because God Almighty can do anything.[84] Not only can He part the Red Sea if He wants to, but He can also part the Pacific Ocean. We should admit that we may never know whether some passages are literally or figuratively true until we meet God face-to-face. We do know that miracles have happened throughout history. We know miracles happen today. Those who try to reduce Scripture to a purely natural or secular level are to be pitied—they are limiting themselves to what is dreamt of in their philosophies.

The other way we know when Scripture's language is literal and when Scripture's language is figurative is when we are told which it is by the Magisterium, who alone has been given by God the authority to interpret Scripture. Important Magisterial documents are *Divino Afflante Spiritu* by Pope Pius XII in 1943; *Dei Verbum* by Vatican II in 1965; and *Interpretation of the Bible in the Church* by the Pontifical Biblical Commission in 1993.

We need to make sure that we read and interpret Scripture in the light of the same Holy Spirit by Whom it was written.[85] In order to do so the Catechism gives us three criteria:[86]

---

[84] *CCC*, 268-274.

[85] *CCC*, 111-114.

[86] *CCC*, 112-114. For a brief but masterful critique of the strengths and weaknesses of the "historical-critical" method of interpreting Scripture, see the

1) We need to read and interpret each part of Scripture in light of the entire Bible. Other parts of Scripture shed light on each part of Scripture.

2) We need to read Scripture within the Church, not as an outsider.

3) We need to be attentive to the *analogy of faith*, which is the unity that exists in the Catholic Faith. One part of the Faith does NOT contradict other parts of the Faith because God's Revelation in Sacred Scripture NEVER contradicts His Revelation in Sacred Tradition. God NEVER contradicts Himself.

IS SCRIPTURE'S FIGURATIVE LANGUAGE OBJECTIVELY TRUE OR SUBJECTIVELY TRUE?

Our previous example of figurative language, "It is raining cats and dogs," is what when it actually is raining very hard? Subjectively true, because it can be raining very hard for me while at the same time and in the same way it is not raining very hard for you? No, "It is raining cats and dogs" is objectively true because it corresponds to the reality of a hard rain. We can be subjective about the hard rain—it might not bother you as much as it bothers me.

Figurative language can be objectively true. As the great Catholic thinker, G. K. Chesterton, said, "Fairy Tales are more than true. Not because they tell us that dragons exist, but because they tell us that dragons can be beaten."

Likewise, those passages in Scripture that are figurative are also objectively true. Many examples of this will be provided in later chapters.

We are now ready to encounter God in Sacred Scripture.

"Foreword" of Pope Benedict XVI's *Jesus of Nazareth: From the Baptism in the Jordan to the Transfiguration* (Doubleday: 2007).

PERSONAL FAITH RESPONSE

Check any statements below that describe you.

In order to LIVE FULLY:

1. _____I agree with the objective truth in this chapter.

2. _____Now that I have a better understanding of the rich and profound complexity of Scripture, I will be more open than ever to God's Revelation in it.

VOCABULARY

Literal Sense: The original meaning of the words of Scripture.

Allegorical Sense: How events in the Old Testament are related to Jesus Christ.

Moral Sense: What Scripture teaches about good behavior.

Anagogical Sense: What Scripture teaches about eternal realities.

Literal language: Language that does NOT need to be interpreted/language that should be taken at face value/language that means exactly what it says.

Figurative language: Language that DOES need to be interpreted because it uses symbols and metaphors.

Inspiration: The gift God gave the human writers of Scripture so they could to put into it what God wanted to reveal.

Inerrancy: Scripture having no errors in Revelation and Faith.

Analogy of Faith: The unity that exists in the Catholic Faith so that God's Revelation in Sacred Scripture never contradicts His Revelation in Sacred Tradition.

Part 3: How Should We Read Sacred Scripture?

Chapter III

WHAT DOES GOD REVEAL THROUGH GENESIS 1-3?

SOURCES

- Scott Hahn, Gen. Ed., *Catholic Bible Dictionary* (Doubleday, 2009) "Adam," "Creation," "Genesis, Book of."
- Stephen M. Barr, "Untangling Evolution," *First Things*, December 1997.
- http://firstthings.com/blogs/evangel/2011/01/thomas-fowler-discusses-the-evolution-controversy/
- http://firstthings.com/blogs/evangel/2010/08/multiple-constituencies-in-the-science-and-religion-debate/

IS GENESIS 1-3 LITERAL OR FIGURATIVE?

In **Gn (Genesis) 1-3**,[87] we find some of the most important words ever written in human history.[88] Gn 1-3 is a great example of how, according to God's design, Scripture does not make sense without Tradition and the Magisterium.

Below are 5 examples of language from Gn 1-3 that **must be literally**

---

[87] If you read the passage, keep in mind *the LORD* in Scripture is another name for God.
[88] *CCC*, 289.

true in order for the Catholic Faith to be objectively true. These passages provide Revelation from God about the origin of the universe and the origin of humanity. To accept this Revelation is to have knowledge from God, which is what Faith is, about the origin of the universe and the origin of humanity.

1) **1:1**: God created the heavens and the earth.[89]

2) **1:27**: The human being was the only creature God made in His image.[90]

3) **1:27**: Male/masculinity and female/femininity were created by God.[91]

4) **1:31**: God found everything He made to be very good.[92]

5) **2:3**: God made the 7th day (called the Sabbath) holy.[93]

Notice that God reveals Himself through His actions, such as the examples above, as well as through His words, just as we humans communicate and express ourselves through our actions as well as our words.

Keeping in mind that God reveals Himself through both literal and figurative language in Scripture, and keeping in mind that those passages in Scripture that are figurative are also objectively true, we see below examples of language from Gn 1-3 that **could be figuratively true** without affecting the objective truth of the Catholic Faith.

---

[89] *CCC*, 279-282, 286-288.
[90] *CCC*, 342-343, 355-368.
[91] *CCC*, 369-373.
[92] *CCC*, 299-301, 339-342.
[93] *CCC*, 345-349.

PASSAGE:	GN 1-3 LANGUAGE:	GOD REVEALS:
1:2-2:1	The universe was created in six 24-hour days.	God created the universe from nothing—God reveals that He is the Uncaused Cause![94]
2:2-3	God rested on the 7th day.	God made the Seventh day holy.[95]
2:8-9	God planted a garden in Eden and placed there the man and made grow a tree that was delightful and good.	At first, humans had perfect existence.[96]
2:16-17	God gave the man this order: You are free to eat from any of the trees except the tree of knowledge of good and evil.	God knows better than we humans know what is good for us.[97]
2:20-24	A woman was made from the man's rib to be the man's helper which is why a man leaves his father and mother and clings to his wife.	Gender is created by God and NOT by humans;[98] and God made marriage to be between one man and one woman.[99]
3:6	The woman and the man ate the forbidden fruit.	Humans have free will and can misuse it to sin, which is disobeying God.[100]

---

[94] *CCC*, 296-298.
[95] *CCC*, 345-349.
[96] *CCC*, 54, 374-378.
[97] *CCC*, 398.
[98] *CCC*, 369-373.
[99] *CCC*, 1601-1617.
[100] *CCC*, 385-390, 396-401.

3:15	The woman's offspring will strike at the snake's head.	God will send a savior to completely defeat evil.[101]
3:16-19	To the woman and the man, God said that their sin of disobedience had caused their existence from then on to involve toil, pain, and death.	Sin brought evil into the world—God does not create evil, but He allows evil because He gives free will to humans (and angels), and their bad choices have consequences.[102]
3:23	God banished Adam and Eve from the Garden of Eden.	The first humans, and all humans after them, lost perfect existence.[103]

So some parts of Gn 1-3 must be literally true, and some parts of Gn 1-3 could be figuratively true, which we will understand better by the end of this chapter.

WHAT IS THE DOCTRINE OF ORIGINAL SIN?

Regardless of how exactly Gn 1-3 is literal or figurative, Gn 1-3 affirms an event that actually happened at the very beginning of human history. This event is summarized in one of the most important doctrines of the Catholic Faith—the Doctrine of Original Sin, also known as the Fall from Grace or, more simply, the Fall. The Doctrine of Original Sin has several parts. What follows summarizes the paragraphs of the *Catechism* already footnoted in this chapter.

Before the first humans sinned, they had perfect human existence because they lived only in the state of grace/sharing God's life. They were in harmony with God. They were in harmony with each other. They were

---

[101] *CCC*, 55, 410-412.
[102] *CCC*, 302-314, 385-386, 413.
[103] *CCC*, 379, 402-409.

The Fullness of Life

in harmony with Nature. They had inner harmony between their minds, wills, emotions, and bodies. They had the fullness of life.

The first humans had free will and used it to disobey God/commit the Original Sin/fall from grace because they wanted to be equal to God. (The same was true of some of the angels before them, who then became devils/ demons.[104])

Rejection of God's will/sin had catastrophic results. Sin brought evil into the universe, which had been only good before sin entered it. Sin brought disharmony between humans and God, man and woman, and humans and Nature.

Humans cannot have perfect existence until God sends a Savior to make our existence perfect again.

Until we humans are completely saved from the Fall, every one of us has a fallen human nature that includes a weakened will, a weakened mind, weakened emotions, and a weakened body. Our weakened will is inclined/leans to sin; our weakened mind makes knowing truth difficult; our weakened emotions both under-react and over-react; and our weakened body gets tired, gets sick, gets injured, gets old, and dies.

Until we humans are completely saved from the Fall, the universe will be imperfect and Creation/Nature will be dangerous.

Until we humans are completely saved from the Fall, none of us can have the fullness of life that humans had before the Fall.

There is no better explanation than Original Sin for why we human beings are so restless and constantly searching for transcendence. We are restless because we miss the Garden of Eden. We search for transcendence because we search for the perfect existence we had in the Garden of Eden.

There is no better explanation than Original Sin for how both a good God and evil can exist at the same time. God does not create evil but He allows it to enter the universe because He gives humans free choice to accept or reject Him.

---

[104] *CCC*, 328-333, 391-395, 397, 407-409.

There is no better explanation than Original Sin for what is wrong with the world and why counseling, medicine, technology, social justice, and all other human effort will NOT completely save us (although all of them can be very helpful).

So the event at the dawn of human history described in Gn 1-3, sometimes literally and sometimes figuratively, was so important, so cataclysmic, so momentous that if we do not understand it, we do not understand the rest of human history. As C. S. Lewis put it:

> What Satan put into the heads of our remote ancestors was the idea that they could "be like gods"—could set up on their own as if they had created themselves—be their [own] masters—invent some sort of happiness for themselves outside God, apart from God. And out of that hopeless attempt has come nearly all that we call human history—money, poverty, ambition, war, prostitution, [economic] classes, empires, slavery—the long terrible story of man trying to find something other than God which will make him happy.
>
> The reason it can never succeed is this. God made us: invented us as a man invents an engine. [When a] car is made to run on gasoline, . . . it would not run properly on anything else. Now God designed the human machine to run on Himself. He Himself is the fuel our spirits were designed to burn, or the food our spirits were designed to feed on. There is no other . . .[105]
>
> That is the key to history. Terrific energy is expended—civilizations are built up—excellent institutions devised; but each time something goes wrong. Some fatal flaw always brings the selfish and cruel people to the top and it all slides back into misery and ruin. In fact the machine conks. It seems to start out all right and runs a few yards, but then it breaks down. They are trying to run it on the wrong juice. That is what Satan has done to us humans.

To reject God's Revelation in Sacred Scripture is to be like Adam and Eve with the forbidden tree in the Garden of Eden—it is to think we know what is good for us better than God knows what is good for us.

---

[105] *Mere Christianity* (Collier Books, 1986).

WHAT ABOUT EVOLUTION?

We should accept the truth no matter what its source is. We should accept truth that comes from both Faith and Reason. The science of evolution is an example of Reason. We should always accept true science, including true science about the origin of humanity.[106]

What does SCIENCE say about the origin of humanity? All science is NOT equally settled/proven/conclusive. E.g., the science about the origin of the earth is more settled than the science about the origin of the first life on earth and the science about the origin of humanity. The science about evolution within the same species (sometimes referred to as "micro-evolution"), e.g., evolution of one kind of dog from another kind of dog, is more settled than the science about evolution of one species from another species (sometimes referred to as "macro-evolution"), e.g., evolution of the dog from a non-dog ancestor. There are many scientific problems with the theory of evolution, which are usually not taught in high school-level or even college-level biology courses. E.g., high school and college students are usually not taught how the scientific experts disagree with each other on the roles of natural selection, random mutation, and genetic drift in evolution. The evolution of humans from non-humans should be considered NOT a fact absolutely supported by evidence, BUT a very good theory with very good evidence supporting it that answers some questions about the origin of humanity but does not answer other questions about the origin of humanity, e.g., how many original humans were there?

What does FAITH say about the origin of humanity? God has revealed THAT He created the human race, NOT HOW He created the human race. Because God can do anything, God might have created humans through the slow process of evolution from non-humans OR God might have created humans in a special act of creation and NOT through evolution from non-humans—the story of Adam and Eve might be literally true to some degree.

If humans evolved from non-humans, the Doctrine of Original Sin IS still true. The Doctrine of Original Sin does NOT depend on whether or not humans evolved from non-humans. If humans evolved from non-humans, God DOES exist. The existence of God has NOTHING to do with whether or not humans evolved from non-humans.

---

[106] *CCC*, 283-285.

If we ever get absolutely convincing evidence that humans evolved from non-humans, Scripture IS still the Word of God/Divine Revelation. The story of Adam and Eve will turn out to be figuratively true while also being objectively true.

Despite all the efforts of Reason and Faith to understand the origin of humanity, the origin of humanity remains a great mystery. It could well remain that way until we meet God face to face. One can believe in the evolution of humans from non-humans and remain a good Catholic as long as one still believes in God, His creation of the universe, Original Sin, and the entrance of a soul into each human body at the moment of conception.

Catholic doctrine uses the names *Adam and Eve* for the first humans whom God created EITHER through the process of evolving humans from non-humans OR through a special act of creation that did not involve evolution from non-humans, much like that described in the Book of Genesis.

EXAMPLES OF HOW TRUE FAITH AND TRUE SCIENCE SUPPORT EACH OTHER:

- Stephen M. Barr, *Modern Physics and Ancient Faith*.
- Michael J. Behe, *The Edge of Evolution*.
- Michael J. Behe, *Darwin's Black Box*.
- Michael J. Behe, William Dembski, and Stephen M. Barr, *Science and Evidence for Design in the Universe*.
- Discovery Institute Center for Science and Culture, available at http://www.discovery.org/id/
- Etienne Gilson, *From Aristotle to Darwin and Back Again*.
- Fr. Stephan Horn, *Creation and Evolution*.
- Thomas Howard, *Chance or the Dance: A Critique of Modern Secularism*.
- Fr. Stanley L. Jaki, OSB, *The Limits of a Limitless Science and Other Essays*.
- Fr. Stanley L. Jaki, OSB, *Bible and Science*.
- Fr. Stanley L. Jaki, OSB, *The Only Chaos and Other Essays*.
- Fr. Stanley L. Jaki, OSB, *Miracles and Physics*.
- Stephen C. Meyer, *Darwin's Doubt: The Explosive Origin of Animal Life and the Case for Intelligent Design*

- Fr. Robert Spitzer, SJ, *New Proofs for the Existence of God: Contributions of Contemporary Physics and Philosophy.*

HOW DOES ORIGINAL SIN HELP US UNDERSTAND REVELATION?

The fact that God is not obvious to us humans and that He therefore reveals/"unveils" Himself is due to the fact that He is "veiled" from us/that there is a "curtain" between God and us. It was Original Sin, and NOT God, that pulled the curtain/veil between us humans and God and that gave us a fallen/weakened human nature which is not able/not "equipped" to see God face-to-face/to know God directly/to experience God fully.[107]

So God pulls back the curtain between us and Him by means of Natural Revelation and Supernatural Revelation. God pulls back the curtain between us and Him in order to save humanity from the Fall.

So great is the distance that Original Sin puts between God and humans that a radical transformation of human nature is needed in order for us to see God face-to-face/to know God directly/to experience God fully.

---

[107] *CCC*, 37, 402-406.

PERSONAL FAITH RESPONSE

Check any statements below that describe you.

In order to LIVE FULLY:

1. _____I agree with the objective truth in this chapter.

2. _____I will respect God's Creation/Nature.

3. _____I will respect all human beings as made in the image and likeness of God.

4. _____I will respect marriage and gender as God made them.

5. _____I will keep holy the Sabbath by worshipping God on that day.

6. _____I agree that God knows what is good for me better than I or anyone else knows what is good for me, and I will try to avoid Adam and Eve's mistake of wanting to be God's equal.

7. _____I will look at myself and everyone else as having a fallen human nature in need of salvation.

8. _____I will appreciate the seriousness of sin/rejecting God.

9. _____I will appreciate that all human actions, including my own, have consequences.

10. _____I will respect the mystery of human origins, and I will respect whatever truth I can get from Faith and from Reason.

11. _____I will NOT give up seeking the fullness of life that can only come from living in the state of grace/sharing God's life: being in harmony with Him, being in harmony with others, being in harmony with Nature, being in harmony with my own mind, will, emotions, and body.

VOCABULARY

Grace: Sharing God's life.

Sin: Rejection of God's will.

Original Sin: The first sin of the first humans that had catastrophic results.

The Fall: The Fall from Original Grace; another name for Original Sin.

PART 4:
WHAT DOES GOD REVEAL THROUGH THE OLD TESTAMENT?

Chapter I: WHAT DOES GOD REVEAL THROUGH GENESIS 4-11?

Chapter II: WHAT DOES GOD REVEAL TO AND THROUGH THE PATRIARCHS?

Chapter III: WHAT DOES GOD REVEAL TO AND THROUGH MOSES?

Chapter IV: WHAT IS THE HISTORY OF THE CHOSEN PEOPLE?

Chapter V: WHAT DOES GOD REVEAL THROUGH THE HISTORY OF THE CHOSEN PEOPLE?

Chapter VI: WHAT ARE OTHER KEY PASSAGES IN THE OLD TESTAMENT?

Part 4: What Does God Reveal through the Old Testament?

Chapter I:

WHAT DOES GOD REVEAL THROUGH GENESIS 4-11?

SOURCES

- Scott Hahn, Gen. Ed., Catholic Bible Dictionary (Doubleday, 2009), "Abel," "Babel, Tower of," "Cain," "Flood," "Genesis, Book of," "Noah."

Whether it is Genesis 4-11 or any other passage we study in this book, space does not permit us to go beyond identifying what God reveals through it. There are many excellent sources for gaining a more in-depth understanding of Scripture. What we are focusing on is the most important thing to focus on: What does God reveal? What is God communicating? What does God want us to know? Knowing more than that is fascinating but not imperative for us, although Catholic Doctrine has needed the work of scholars to clarify God's Revelation in Scripture.

In **Gn (Genesis) 4**, Cain, a son of Adam and Eve, murders his brother, Abel, because God looked with favor on Abel's offering. In **Gn 6:5-22; 7:11-23; 8:6--9:18**, Noah builds an ark in which he, his family, and two of every kind of animal are saved from the Flood, which kills all living things except those on the ark. In **Gn 11:1-9**, men try building a tower to the sky at Babel.

The stories in Gn 4-11 are probably figuratively true. But remember that God reveals Himself through Scripture's figurative language, which is objectively true. Gn 4-11, like the rest of Scripture, will ultimately make sense only when it is taken together with Sacred Tradition and interpreted by the Magisterium, which expresses its interpretations of Revelation as doctrines that define the Catholic Faith. These passages, as does Scripture as a whole, show that God reveals Himself through both words and actions.

One way to understand God's Revelation in Gn 4-11 is, to borrow words from St. Augustine that we used in an earlier chapter: God hates sin[108] but loves sinners.[109] St. Augustine himself only said that WE should hate sin but love sinners. St. Augustine's insight into being Christian suggests an insight into GOD Himself.

How does God reveal that He hates sin in terms of the plots of these stories? After Cain murders Abel, God makes Cain a constant wanderer.[110] In order to wipe out the wickedness and corruption on the earth, God sends the Flood. Because the builders of the Tower of Babel are beginning to think they can do anything and therefore are beginning to think of themselves as equal to God, God makes them speak different languages and scatters them throughout the earth.[111]

How does God reveal that He still loves sinners in terms of the plots of these stories? God puts a mark on Cain so no one would kill him. God promises/makes a covenant with Noah that He will never send a flood to destroy all His creatures.[112] Through Noah's sons—Shem, Ham, and Japheth—God allows the earth to be repopulated. After Babel, God calls Abram, as we shall see.

Gn 4-11 begins the long story, told throughout the rest of Scripture, of how God saves humanity from the Fall even while sin multiplies.

---

[108] *CCC*, 208, 1077, 1850, 2259-2260.
[109] *CCC*, 1, 30, 51-52, 210-211, 218-221, 410, 457-458.
[110] *CCC*, 401, 2259-2260.
[111] *CCC*, 57.
[112] *CCC*, 56, 58, 71, 1080.

PERSONAL FAITH RESPONSE

Check any statements below that describe you.

In order to LIVE FULLY:

1. _____I agree with the objective truth in this chapter.

2. _____I will realize that God hates sin, both my sin and the sins of others.

3. _____I will realize that God always loves sinners, both me and others.

VOCABULARY

Cain: The son of Adam and Eve who murdered his brother.

Abel: The son of Adam and Eve who was murdered by his brother .

Noah: The man who built an ark in which he, his family, and two of every kind of animal were saved from the Flood.

Babel: The place where men tried building a tower to the sky.

Part 4: What Does God Reveal through the Old Testament?

Chapter II:

WHAT DOES GOD REVEAL TO AND THROUGH THE PATRIARCHS?

SOURCES

- Scott Hahn, Gen. Ed., Catholic Bible Dictionary (Doubleday, 2009), "Abraham," "Circumcision," "Covenant," "Genesis, Book of," "Hebrew," "Isaac," "Jacob," "King," "Patriarch," "Priest, Priesthood," "Prophet."
- https://www.britannica.com/biography/Abraham.
- Fr. William Most, *Free from All Error: Authorship, Inerrancy, Historicity of Scripture, Church Teaching, and Modern Scripture Scholars*, "Ch. 26: Biblical Archaeology," www.catholicculture.org.

WHAT IS ESSENTIAL BACKGROUND FOR THE PATRIARCHS?

The first major character of the Bible whom we can date and about whose time and place there is some documentation with sources outside the Bible,[113] and so whom we know is a real/historical person, is Abraham, who at first is called Abram. He lives about 1800 BC. He is one of the most

---

[113] For example, the Mari Tablets, Nuzi Tablets, and Amarna Letters.

important people to ever live because of the crucial role he plays in the history of salvation and in the history of the human race.

Since Faith is the response to God's Revelation that results in knowledge of God and a personal relationship with Him, Abraham is the Model of Faith. Abraham comes to know God. Abraham has a close personal relationship with God. The *Catechism*, echoing St. Paul, calls Abraham "the father of all who believe."[114]

Abraham is the first of the Patriarchs, a term which comes the Greek words *patri*, which means "father" and *arch* which means "ruler"; and so they are father-rulers/rulers who are fathers. Their society is a tribal society.[115] The patriarchs had three offices, which in this context means positions of authority:

1) They spoke for God to the people, and thus they had the office of prophet, which in the Old Testament means "spokesman-for-God's-Will-in-the-present" much more than "predictor-of-the-future."

2) They conducted worship, especially offering sacrifice, and thus had the office of priest.

3) They ruled their people, and thus had the office of king.

The Patriarchs had these offices naturally/informally. These offices describe what they did, NOT what they were called in their own time.

---

[114] *CCC*, 144, 146, 1080, 2569, 2572.

[115] For some people, *patriarchy* has become a dirty word. In reality, throughout history, human society was organized as tribes under father-rulers until agriculture was developed and strong government was in place. Even with agriculture and government, the roles of men as warriors and providers for the family and women as home-makers and child-raisers remained fairly constant throughout history until the second half of the Twentieth Century when for the first time in history (1) there were effective natural family planning and artificial birth control and (2) much work outside the home no longer needed physical strength due to the development of technology. History is being described here, not morally analyzed. Whether there is some kind of conspiratorial "patriarchy" in place today, sex roles changed as quickly as they should have, or changing sex roles have always been good, especially for children, are matters on which Catholics are free to disagree. These issues will be dealt with in a later chapter.

The Fullness of Life

It is with the Patriarchs that the one true God begins to enter human history in a dramatic way by revealing Himself more directly than He had done before. What God revealed TO the Patriarchs God then reveals THROUGH the Patriarchs to anyone who reads about them in Scripture.

Just as we look to the great athletes in order to play sports better, the great thinkers in order to think better, the great musicians in order to play music better, etc., we look to the great real people in the Bible, like Abraham, who actually experienced God in order to experience God better in our own lives.[116] We look to the great real people in the Bible, like Abraham, who actually had a great relationship with God in order to have a better relationship with God in our own lives. As we study the real people in the Bible, we need to avoid the temptation to be a snob toward the past. Yes, the events of this real story took place a few thousand years ago, and so times were different then; but the essential issues of human existence remain the same from one historical era to another.

HOW DOES ABRAHAM RESPOND TO GOD?

n **Gn 11:31-12:9**, God reveals to Abram that He wants him to leave his land and the house of his father (depicted here by József Molnár, 1850). The land he originally leaves, along with his father, is Ur. They journey to Haran, where his father dies and where he receives God's call. Abram leaves the house of his father with his wife, Sarai, and his brother's son, Lot. From Haran he travels to Canaan. The journey from Ur to Haran is a distance of about 600 miles. The journey from Haran to Canaan is about 500 miles.

In **Gn 15**, God and Abram form a covenant. The importance of covenant cannot be overstated. The word *testament* comes from the Latin that was

---

[116] *CCC*, 147, 165.

used to translate the Hebrew and Greek words for *covenant*, and so Sacred Scripture is actually divided into the Old Covenant and the New Covenant. In order to understand Scripture, in order to understand Jesus Christ, in order to understand God and His plan for us, we must understand covenant.

A covenant is an agreement to establish a binding family-like relationship in which two previously unrelated parties are committed to doing their parts. Covenants were widespread throughout the ancient Near East and Mediterranean world. The establishment of a covenant involved sacred rituals and oaths/promises. A covenant is more profound than a contract in our society, which is limited to the business being transacted and has nothing explicitly sacred about it. The family-like relationship established by a covenant is far more than a business transaction.

So in order for God and Abram to make a covenant, they must be two previously unrelated parties. Why are God and Abram unrelated before their covenant? The Fall. Because of Original Sin, humans had made themselves strangers to the God Who had made them to share His life with them. It is with Abram that God and humans begin to re-establish a close relationship with each other. Momentous!

God formalizes His covenant with Abram when He reveals Himself as a smoking fire pot and a flaming torch, which pass between pieces of heifer, goat, and ram that Abram had split in two and placed opposite each other. In what becomes God's first promise to Abram, God reveals that His part of their covenant is that He will give Abram (1) descendants as numerous as the stars of the sky and the sands of the seashore and so make Abram the father of a nation and (2) the land of Canaan, which is thus the "Promised Land." Abram's part of the covenant is to leave his native land.

In **Gn 17:1-17**, as God's part of their covenant, God makes a second promise to Abram: that kings, and thus a dynasty, will stem from Abram, in spite of Abram's advanced age. Abram's part of the covenant is (1) to change his name to Abraham and to change his wife's name to Sarah and (2) to circumcise himself and every male of his people.[117]

---

[117] "Circumcision of the flesh symbolized the spiritual circumcision of the heart: the cutting away of the heart's stubborn resistance to the Lord and His commandments" (*Catholic Bible Dictionary*, p. 153).

The Fullness of Life

In **Gn 21:1-8; 22:1-18**, Sarah, at a very old age, becomes pregnant and gives birth. The name of Abraham and Sarah's son is Isaac. When God calls Abraham, he responds, "Here I am." Abraham loves his long-awaited son very much, yet God reveals to Abraham His Will is that Abraham is to sacrifice Isaac in the land of Moriah. At the moment that Abraham is about to sacrifice his beloved son in obedience to God's will (depicted here by Rembrandt, 1634), God tells him not to do so. So what was also required of Abraham by the covenant was complete trust in God. God makes His third promise to Abraham as His part of their covenant: all nations, and not just his own people, will find blessing in Abraham.

WHAT DOES GOD REVEAL TO AND THROUGH ABRAHAM?

In the middle of religions that believed in many false gods, God reveals that He is the one true God. Abraham experienced the one true God.[118]

God reveals that His Will is more important than anything else. And He reveals that He is totally trustworthy and should be totally trusted and obeyed.[119]

God makes a covenant with Abraham that gives Abraham a crucial role in God's salvation of humanity from the Fall[120] which God will accomplish through three promises He makes to Abraham:

1) Abraham's descendants, to be as numerous as the stars of the sky and the sands of the seashore, will be given the Promised Land.

2) Kings, and thus a dynasty, will stem from Abraham.

---

[118] *CCC*, 200-201.
[119] *CCC*, 145-146, 2570-2572.
[120] *CCC*, 59, 72, 762, 1080.

3) All nations will find blessing in Abraham by being able, like Abraham, to know God and have a relationship with Him.

God also reveals that human sacrifice is against His Will even though other peoples, such as the Canaanites, were committing it.[121] God's Revelation to Abraham begins the long process of humans realizing that they have a dignity that only comes from being created in God's image and likeness.[122]

WHAT DOES GOD REVEAL TO AND THROUGH THE OTHER PATRIARCHS?

In **Gn 26:1-5**, God reveals to Isaac after Abraham dies that He is renewing the covenant with Isaac. In **Gn 28:10-15**, God reveals that He is renewing the covenant with Isaac's son, Jacob. In **Gn 32:23-31**, when Jacob is alone, he wrestles until dawn with a man who gives him the new name of *Israel*, which means "he who wrestled (*Isra*) with God (*el*)." So the "man" is an angel representing God. Jacob has twelve sons, and these twelve sons are the fathers of the Twelve Tribes of Israel.

In **Gn 49:10**, one of Jacob's sons is Judah, from whom the scepter shall never depart until tribute comes to him. Scepter and tribute belong to a king. This passage reveals that the tribe of Judah is to be the tribe from which God wants the kings of His people to come.

In **Gn 41: 39-41**, another one of Jacob's sons, Joseph, is put in charge of Egypt by Pharaoh/Egypt's king. In **Gn 46:5-7**, as a result of Joseph's position, Jacob and all his descendants settle in Egypt.

The descent of the Patriarchs:

Abraham

Isaac

---

[121] *CCC*, 2270-2275, 2373-2379.
[122] *CCC*, 356-357, 1929, 2258.

Jacob

Twelve sons, including Judah and Joseph

Twelve Tribes

The Age of the Patriarchs begins with Abraham and ends with Joseph and his brothers. By the end of the Age of the Patriarchs, God and humans have significantly begun to grow in closer relationship with each other. A covenant has been established. Abraham is indeed the Father of Faith.

There are more key passages about the Patriarchs in the last chapter on the Old Testament in this book.

WHAT ARE THE NAMES OF THE PEOPLE DESCENDED FROM ABRAHAM?

During the time of Abraham and Isaac, the people were only called the *Hebrews*.

Beginning with Jacob and from then on, the people are also sometimes called *Israel*, which therefore is the name of Jacob's people as well as the name of Jacob himself. They are also called the *Israelites* or the *Twelve Tribes of Israel*—while they continue to be called the *Hebrews* sometimes.

About 8 centuries after Jacob, when the people call their country *Judah* (which the Greeks and Romans call *Judea*), they are also called the *Jews* because *Jew* is derived from *Judah*—while they continue to be called the *Hebrews* and *Israel/the Israelites* sometimes.

Because the people descended from Abraham were chosen by God to be the people through whom He saves the world from the Fall, they can be called the *Chosen People* at any time in their history.[123]

---

[123] *CCC*, 60.

WHAT ARE THE LANGUAGES OF THE PEOPLE DESCENDED FROM ABRAHAM?

The language of the Patriarchs was Hebrew, which was used by the Chosen People until they were exiled to Babylonia (586-537 BC). This is why most of the Old Testament was written in Hebrew.

Beginning with the Babylonian Exile (586-537 BC), the Chosen People used the Aramaic language, which was to that era of the Middle East what English is to the world today—the most commonly spoken language. Hebrew became a language only used by Jewish scholars.

Jesus preached and taught in Aramaic.

PERSONAL FAITH RESPONSE

Check any statements below that describe you.

In order to LIVE FULLY:

1) _____I agree with the objective truth in this chapter.

2) _____I will realize that God is revealing Himself to me.

3) _____As best as I can, I will grow in my knowledge of the one true God and His Will for me.

4) _____I will develop a personal relationship with God, which is the greatest adventure of all.

5) _____I will trust and obey God; I will make God's Will more important to me than anything else in my life.

6) _____I will not "sacrifice human life," but I will respect all human life from conception to natural death.

VOCABULARY

Patriarch: The father-rulers of the Chosen People from Abraham to the sons of Jacob.

Abraham: The first Patriarch and the Father of all who believe, with whom God made an important covenant.

Sarah: The wife of Abraham.

Covenant: A binding/committed relationship.

Canaan: The land God promised to the Chosen People and so the land where they settled. Also known as the **Promised Land**.

Isaac: The son of Abraham, and Sarah.

Moriah: The place where Abraham was going to sacrifice Isaac.

Jacob: The son of Isaac.

Israel: The name given to Jacob by God, and so also a name of Jacob's people/the Chosen People.

Twelve Tribes of Israel: The tribes fathered by the twelve sons of Jacob/Israel and so also a name of the Chosen People.

Judah: The son of Jacob from whose tribe God wants Israelite kings to come.

Joseph: The son of Jacob whom Pharaoh put in charge of Egypt, the result of which is that the Chosen People settle in Egypt for a while.

Office: A position of authority/job/responsibility   .

Prophet: One who speaks for God.

Priest: One who conducts worship, especially by offering sacrifice.

Hebrew: The earliest name of the Chosen People, and the name of the language they spoke from Abraham until the Babylonian Exile.

Jews: The latest name of the Chosen People.

Chosen People: The descendants of Abraham chosen by God to be the people through whom He saves the world from the Fall.

Aramaic: The language the Chosen People spoke from the time of the Babylonian Exile.

Part 4: What Does God Reveal through the Old Testament?

Chapter III

WHAT DOES GOD REVEAL TO AND THROUGH MOSES?

SOURCES

- Scott Hahn, Gen. Ed., Catholic Bible Dictionary (Doubleday, 2009), "Exodus," "Exodus, Book of," "God," "Law," "Manna," "Moses," "Passover," "Sinai," "Ten Commandments."

WHAT IS ESSENTIAL BACKGROUND FOR MOSES?

The next major Old Testament figure whom we will study is Moses, who lived about 1200 BC—about 600 years after Abraham and about 400 years after Joseph. Moses is another real person to whom God revealed Himself. More than that, Moses is the greatest human figure in the Old Testament, greater even than Abraham, which is why he will be studied more in this book than any other Biblical figure besides Jesus. Moses has a greater friendship with God than anyone else in the Old Testament. He is a bridge between the Patriarchs and the kinds of leaders the Chosen People have after him. He is the greatest Patriarch, the greatest prophet, the greatest priest, and the greatest king in the Old Testament. Moses is the most important person in human history before Christ.

Again, just as we look to those who are great in order to get better at something, we look to the great real people in the Bible who actually experienced God and had a relationship with Him, like Moses, in order to experience God better and have a better relationship with Him in our own lives. What God revealed TO Moses God then reveals THROUGH Moses to anyone who accepts His Word in Scripture.

HOW DOES MOSES RESPOND TO GOD?

In **Ex (Exodus) 1:1-2:22**, the Chosen People, by the time of Moses' birth, are still in Egypt, where they have been made slaves. Pharaoh (not a personal name, but the title of every ancient Egyptian king) commands that every Hebrew baby boy should be killed. Moses' mother puts him in a basket to float on the river so that he might escape. Moses is found by Pharaoh's daughter, who adopts him. Moses flees to Midian after he kills an Egyptian in outrage at the Egyptian striking a Hebrew.

In **Ex 2:23-3:14; 4:10-17**, God reveals Himself to Moses in the form of a burning bush. When God calls Moses, Moses responds, "Here I am," just as Abraham had done. God is so holy that the ground of the burning bush is holy. Moses takes off his sandals because he is on holy ground. God is so holy that he hides his face because he is afraid to look at God.

God tells Moses that He is sending Moses to bring the Chosen People out of Egypt. God reveals His name as "I am who I am" or, more simply, as "I AM," which in the Hebrew language is *Yahweh*. When Moses is not confident that he is able to do God's Will, God gives him Aaron, his brother, to be his spokesman.

In **Ex 6:1-6:13**, God tells Moses to tell the Chosen People that the covenant He made with Abraham, Isaac, and Jacob He is also establishing with them. God's part is to free the Israelites from slavery in Egypt and to give them Canaan/the Promised Land. This covenant keeps God's first promise to Abraham.

In **Ex 7:8-13**, God reveals to Pharaoh that he should obey Him by turning Moses' staff into a serpent. When Pharaoh's sorcerers turn their staffs into serpents, Moses' serpent swallows those of Pharaoh's sorcerers. Then God, by sending nine plagues, reveals to Pharaoh that He should be obeyed.

In **Ex 11:1-8; 12:21-42**, God sends the tenth plague, which is the death of every first-born. On the night of the tenth plague, every Israelite family eats a lamb. The name of (1) the event when the Israelites were saved from the tenth plague and (2) the meal eaten that night and every year after that to commemorate it is *Passover* because God passed over the houses of the Israelites, which spared the Israelites from the tenth plague. The Egyptians suffered the tenth plague because God did not pass over their houses. The sign that a house should be passed over is lamb's blood on the door frame, and thus the Israelites are saved from the tenth plague by the blood of a lamb. During the meal the Israelites eat bread that is unleavened/without yeast/flat.

In **Ex 13:17-14:31**, Pharaoh lets the Israelites go. Moses takes the bones of Joseph with him. God goes before the Israelites by means of a pillar of cloud by day and a pillar of fire by night. Pharaoh changes his mind about freeing the Israelites, pursues them with his chariots and army, and catches up with them as they camp by the Red Sea. The Israelites escape when God divides the Red Sea with the water as a wall to the Israelites' right and left so that they can pass through the sea on dry land. Once the Israelites are safe on the other side, God makes the water flow back so that the Egyptians, who have also begun to pass through the sea, drown in it instead.

In **Ex 15:22-16:15, 16:35**, God provides water to the people at Marah. In the evening, God provides quail. In the morning, He provides manna, which tastes like wafers made with honey. The only morning God does not provide it is the morning of the Sabbath. The Israelites eat the manna for 40 years until they finally come to Canaan/the Promised Land.

In **Ex 19:1-8, 16-20; 20:1-17**, Moses goes up Mount Sinai. God comes down to Moses to now make a covenant with the Chosen People that He had started making with Moses when He appeared in the Burning Bush. The Chosen People as a whole, not one person representing them, become the other party of the covenant. God now reveals that the Chosen People's part of the covenant is to obey the Ten Commandments.

In **Ex 24:12-18; 25:10-22**, Moses goes back up Mount Sinai, where he stays for 40 days. God tells Moses to have the Israelites build an ark to hold the Ten Commandments, which are the tangible expression of the covenant; and so it is called the Ark of the Covenant (depicted here in a gilded bas relief from the Auch Cathedral). An ark is a vessel/something that carries things, which is a boat in the case of Noah and a chest in this case.

In **Ex 32**, when Moses is delayed from coming down from Mount Sinai, the Israelites have Aaron make a golden calf, which they worship and which has become the classic example of an idol/false god. God does not approve of the Israelites' worshipping the golden calf.

The name of the whole event of the Israelites being freed from Egypt is the Exodus, which means "leaving/departure." And so the book of the Bible in which this event takes place is the Book of Exodus.

In **Numbers 20:2-13**, the Israelites once again need water. God tells Moses to provide it by striking the rock once, but Moses strikes it twice. Because Moses does not have confidence in God, God does not allow Moses to enter the Promised Land. This might be a good example of something Jesus says, "Much will be required of the person entrusted with much, and still more will be required of the person entrusted with more" (Luke 12:48).

In **Leviticus 8:1-13**, the first official/formal/professional priest the Chosen People ever have is Aaron, and joining him are his sons. Moses ordains Aaron by putting vestments on him and anointing him by pouring oil on his head, which makes his priestly work sacred. The job of the priests is to lead the worship of God by sacrificing victims, which in this case are a bull, two rams, and unleavened bread, on an altar as an offering to God.

Aaron also holds the office of prophet. After Aaron, being a priest is all that priests do. There is beginning to be a "division of Patriarchal labor." After Aaron, those who have the one office of priest usually do not have the other offices of prophet and king.

WHAT DOES GOD REVEAL TO AND THROUGH MOSES?

By revealing His name is *Yahweh*, which means in English "I Am Who I Am" or more simply "I AM," God shows that He is NOT whoever or whatever someone might believe BUT that He has an objective identity.[124] Just like different perceptions about something are better or worse

---

[124] *CCC*, 203-213.

depending on how close they come to the reality of that thing, beliefs about God are better or worse depending on how close or far they are to the reality of God.

By saving the Israelites from slavery to the most powerful empire in the world at that time and by giving them the Promised Land, God keeps His first promise to Abraham that he will be the father of a people and he will be given the Promised Land.[125]

By revealing that He wants the Ten Commandments obeyed, God reveals that the greatest slavery is slavery to sin and the greatest freedom is freedom from sin.[126] God shows that religion involves morality. For all other ancient peoples, religion tended to be much more about trying to get the gods and goddesses to help you—grow a successful crop, win a battle, become fertile, be healthy, etc. The gods and goddesses themselves were often immoral.

WHAT IS NEW ABOUT THE CHOSEN PEOPLE'S FAITH RESPONSE TO GOD BECAUSE OF HIS REVELATION THROUGH MOSES?

Through the mediation of Moses, the relationship between God and humans becomes profoundly closer. The covenant made at Mount Sinai through Moses is not a different covenant from the covenant made by Abraham but greater fulfillment of the promises God made to Abraham. There is one covenant that is being made in different steps.[127]

Notice that there is more to the Faith of the Chosen People as a result of Moses' encounter with God.

- One response the Chosen People make to God's Revelation through Moses is that they begin to have Sacred Scripture— Revelation that is written down. They have the tablets on which God had written the Ten Commandments. They have the writing begun by Moses.[128]

---

[125] *CCC*, 62.
[126] *CCC*, 387, 549.
[127] *CCC*, 62-64.
[128] There is enough evidence to know that Moses wrote some of the Book of Exodus (and other parts of the first five books of the Old Testament), but there is

- The Chosen People now have the Ark of the Covenant, in which they carry the Ten Commandments.

- The Chosen People have a more defined code of behaving the way God wants them to, which includes the Ten Commandments but is much more than the Ten Commandments,[129] all of which they call the *Law*.[130]

- The Chosen People have priests, who are the only ones with the job of leading the worship of God by sacrificing animal or plant victims on an altar as an offering to God.[131]

From the time of Abraham until the time of Moses—the first six hundred years of their history—the Chosen People did not have Sacred Scripture, the Ark of the Covenant, the Law, or priests.

---

not enough evidence to know how much.

[129] E.g., Ex 20:23-23:19, Ex 34:10-26, Lv (Leviticus) 1-16, Lv 17-27; Deuteronomy 12-26.

[130] *CCC*, 1961-1964, 2056-2063.

[131] *CCC*, 1539-1543.

The Fullness of Life

PERSONAL FAITH RESPONSE

Check any statements below that describe you.

In order to LIVE FULLY:

1. _____I agree with the objective truth in this chapter.

2. _____I will obey God's commandments in order to experience the greatest freedom.

   The Ten Commandments have been translated in different ways from their original version in the Hebrew language. Here is the definitive version from the *Catechism of the Catholic Church*:[132]

   1. I am the Lord your God: you shall not have strange gods before me.
   2. You shall not take the name of the Lord your God in vain.
   3. Remember to keep holy the Lord's Day.
   4. Honor your father and your mother.
   5. You shall not kill.
   6. You shall not commit adultery.
   7. You shall not steal.
   8. You shall not bear false witness against your neighbor.
   9. You shall not covet your neighbor's wife.
   10. You shall not covet your neighbor's goods.

3. _____I will help to free other people from current forms of slavery by practicing the Corporal

Works of Mercy in whatever way is appropriate.

- To feed the hungry;

---

[132] *CCC*, between 2051 and 2052.

- To give drink to the thirsty;
- To clothe the naked;
- To visit and ransom the captive;
- To shelter the homeless;
- To visit the sick;
- To bury the dead;
- To care for Creation.

4._____I will help to free other people from current forms of slavery by practicing the Spiritual

Works of Mercy in whatever way is appropriate.

- To admonish the sinner;
- To instruct the ignorant;
- To counsel the doubtful;
- To comfort the afflicted;
- To bear wrongs patiently;
- To forgive injuries;
- To pray for the living and the dead.

VOCABULARY

Moses: The greatest of God's spokesmen in the Old Testament who has a greater friendship with God than anyone else in the Old Testament.

Pharaoh: The title of every king of ancient Egypt.

Yahweh: God's name in the Hebrew language which He revealed to Moses and which means "I am who I am" or "I AM."

Aaron: Moses' brother and the first official priest of the Chosen People.

Passover: (1) The event when the Israelites were saved from the tenth plague and (2) the meal eaten that night and every year after that to commemorate it.

The Fullness of Life

Red Sea: The body of water divided by God so the Israelites could escape the Egyptians.

Manna: The wafers provided by God to feed the Israelites in the desert.

Mount Sinai: Where God revealed His name and made a covenant with the Chosen People.

Ten Commandments: What the Chosen People must obey as their part of the covenant.

Ark of the Covenant: The vessel in which the Ten Commandments are carried.

Golden Calf: The idol worshipped by the Chosen People when Moses was on Mount Sinai.

Idol: False god.

Exodus: (1) The name of the whole event of the Israelites being freed from Egypt and (2) the book of the Bible in which this event takes place.

Priest: The one who leads the worship of God by sacrificing victims on an altar as an offering to God.

Anoint: To pour oil on to bless or make sacred.

The Law: The Chosen People's code of behaving the way God wants them to.

Part 4: What Does God Reveal through the Old Testament?

Chapter IV

WHAT IS THE HISTORY OF THE CHOSEN PEOPLE?

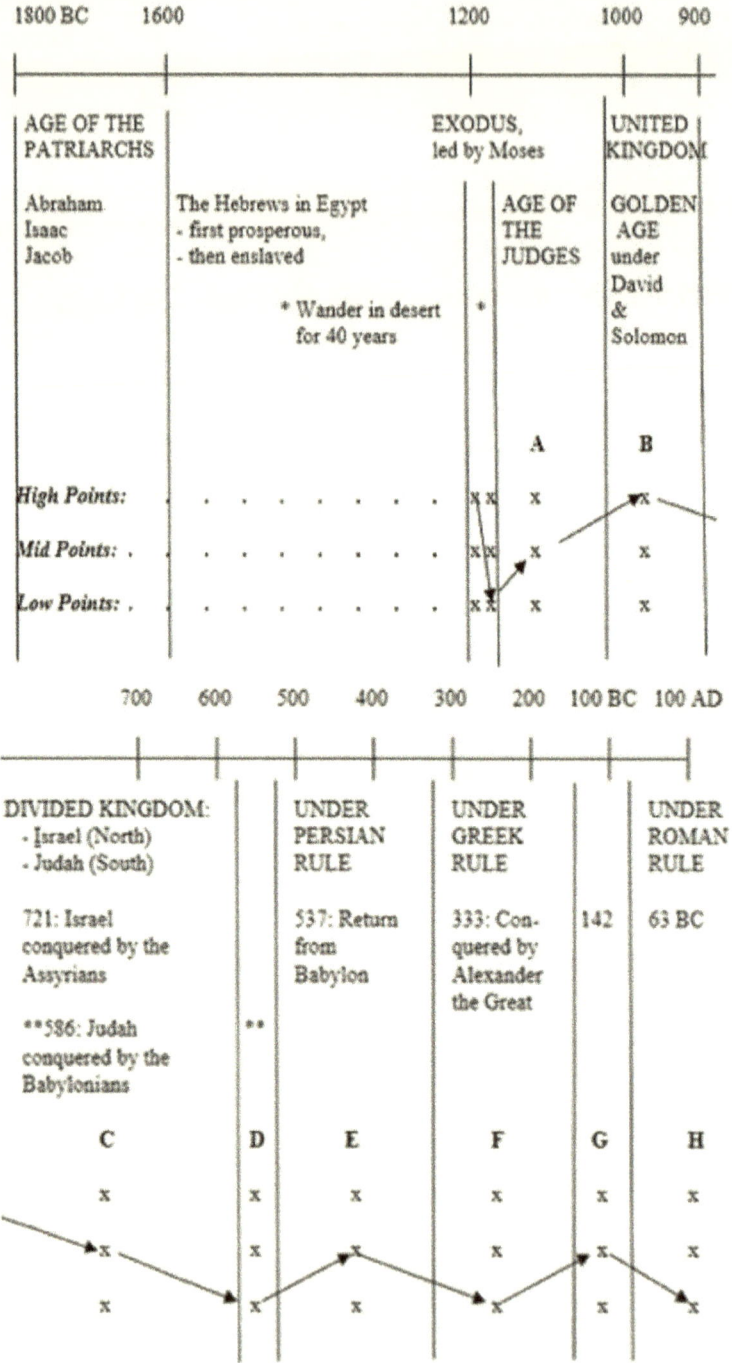

The Fullness of Life

Passage:	Passage Summary:	Timeline:
Jos (Joshua) 1:1-10	Moses is succeeded by Joshua, who leads the settlement of the Promised Land.	A
Jgs (Judges) 3:7-31	Whenever the Israelites are in trouble, God raises up temporary saviors—mostly military leaders—who are called "Judges" (and so they are not charged with settling legal disputes as we think of a judge in a court room), such as Othniel, Ehud, and Shamgar.	A
Jgs 13:1-5, 24; 15-16	The most famous of the Judges is Samson, who had great strength, was eventually captured by his enemies, and died by destroying the pagan temple that he and his enemies were in.	A
1 Sm (Samuel) 3	God calls prophets, such as Samuel, to be His spokesmen and to tell the Chosen People what He wants in the present much more than to predict the future, which represents a further "division of Patriarchal labor."	A
1 Sm 9:26-10:1; 10:17-24	God gives the Israelites their first king, who is Saul, after Samuel anoints him by pouring oil on his head, just as Moses had done to Aaron when Aaron was made a priest. This is the final "division of Patriarchal labor."	B
1 Sm 17:12; 2 Sm 5:1-12	David, from Bethlehem in Judah, becomes the second king, and makes Jerusalem (also called Zion and the City of David) the capital.	B
2 Sm 7:1-17	God makes a covenant with David that his royal "house"/dynasty will last forever, which keeps God's second promise to Abraham—another significant step in the one covenant between God and the Chosen People.	B
1 Kgs (Kings) 8:1-21	Solomon, the son of David, is the third king, builds the Temple on Mt. Moriah, where Abraham was told to sacrifice Isaac; the Ark of the Covenant is placed in the Temple which becomes the only place where God can be	B

		worshipped by sacrifice offered to Him.	
1 Kgs 11:41-12:20		After the death of Solomon, the kingdom divides into the Southern Kingdom ruled by Rehoboam, which calls itself Judah, and the Northern Kingdom ruled by Jeroboam, which calls itself Israel.	C
Is (Isaiah) 6:1-8		Isaiah is called by God to be His prophet while he is in the Temple where two seraphim/angels say words that we Catholics repeat at Mass ("Holy, holy, holy . . . glory") and who warns both Israel and Judah to return to God or face ruin.	C
2 Kgs 17:1-18		In 721 BC, Israel, the Northern Kingdom, is conquered by Assyria and destroyed forever, the ten Tribes that had lived there are scattered, and from then on those tribes are known as the "Ten Lost Tribes of Israel."	C
Jer (Jeremiah) 9:16; 9:22; 10:1		The prophet Jeremiah says in each of these verses, "Thus says the LORD," which is another example of how prophets are God's spokesmen who tell what He wants in the present much more than they predict the future.	D
2 Kgs 24:18-25:21		The "Chaldeans"/Babylonians conquer Assyria; and then in 586 BC, conquer Judah, the Southern Kingdom, destroy the Temple, and take the Chosen People into exile in Babylonia to begin the Babylonian Exile; the Ark of the Covenant is lost forever.	D
Ezr (Ezra) 1		In 537 BC, the Babylonian Exile ends when Persia under Cyrus conquers Babylonia, and he allows the Chosen People to return to the Promised Land, which is now part of the Persian Empire.	E
Ezr 3		The Second Temple is built, so Solomon's Temple is now called the First Temple.	E
1 Mc (Maccabees)		In 333 BC, Persia is conquered by the "Greeks"/Macedonians/Hellenists who now	F

1:1-2:27	rule the Chosen People. The Chosen People suffer horribly and so revolt in 142 BC under the leadership of Mattathias and his sons, who together are called the Maccabees.	
2 Mc 15:17-37	Led by Judas Maccabeus, greatest of the Maccabees, the Jews are free until 63 BC, when they are conquered by the Romans; so 142-63 BC is the last time there is a free Jewish land until the U. N. creates Israel in 1948 AD.	G

There are more key passages about the Chosen People in the last chapter on the Old Testament in this book.

VOCABULARY

Joshua: The successor to Moses who leads the settlement of the Promised Land.

Judges: Temporary saviors of the Chosen People between Joshua and Saul.

Samson: The most famous of the Judges; he had great strength.

Prophet: God's spokesmen who tell the Chosen People what He wants in the present much more than they predict the future. Once there are "full-time" prophets, the office of prophet is separated from the office of king.

Samuel: The first prophet who is also the last Judge and also acts as priest, and so he is a transitional figure in the leadership of the Chosen People. He anoints Saul king.

Saul: The first king of the Chosen People.

David: The second king, who makes a covenant with God.

Bethlehem: The city that David is from.

Jerusalem: The city David makes the capital of the Promised Land.

Judah: The name the Southern Kingdom called itself.

Isaiah: Prophet whose call by God includes angels' words we repeat at Mass.

Israel: The name the Northern Kingdom called itself.

Assyria: The empire that conquers and completely destroys the Northern Kingdom.

Jeremiah: Prophet, who exemplifies that the prophets were God's spokesmen who tell what God wants in the present much more than predictors of the future.

Babylonia: The empire that conquers Assyria and the Southern Kingdom, destroys the Temple, and takes the Chosen People into exile.

Babylonian Exile: The exile of the Chosen People in Babylonia.

Persia: The empire that conquers Babylonia.

Cyrus: The Persian emperor who allows the Chosen People to return to the Promised Land from Babylonia, although the Chosen People remain subjects of the Persian Empire.

Maccabees: The family that leads the revolt against the "Greeks"/Hellenists.

Judas Maccabeus: The greatest of the Maccabees.

Part 4: What Does God Reveal through the Old Testament?

Chapter V

WHAT DOES GOD REVEAL THROUGH THE HISTORY OF THE CHOSEN PEOPLE?

SOURCES

- Scott Hahn, Gen. Ed., Catholic Bible Dictionary (Doubleday, 2009), "Covenant," "Messiah."

HOW DOES THE "VINEYARD SONG" SUMMARIZE THE HISTORY OF THE CHOSEN PEOPLE?

Recall that God reveals Himself not only through words, but also through actions and events, just as we get to know someone not only by what they say, but also by what they do, just as they get to know us.

In **Is (Isaiah) 5:1-7**, God's Revelation through the historical events experienced by the Chosen People is summarized in the "Vineyard Song," which is an allegory, i.e., a story in which characters and events symbolize a deeper meaning. The "vineyard owner" symbolizes God. The "vineyard" symbolizes the Chosen People. The action of the vineyard owner—"He spaded it [the vineyard], cleared it of stones, and planted the choicest vines; within it he built a watchtower and hewed out a wine press"—symbolizes that God was always faithful to the covenant He made with the Chosen People by giving them the following (which will serve as a review of our Old Testament study):

- The Patriarchs—Abraham, Isaac, Jacob—who functioned as prophets, priests, and kings.

- The Promised Land, which provided for the Chosen People's security and material needs.

- The Exodus from slavery in Egypt after saving them from the Tenth Plague (the death of their first born) by means of the blood of a lamb on their door frames.

- Moses, the greatest figure in the Old Testament, through whom God freed the Chosen People from the Egyptians; made the covenant at Mount Sinai that gave His Law, especially the Ten Commandments; and began Sacred Scripture.

- Sacred Scripture, which could provide to all the Revelation experienced by real persons such as Abraham, the other Patriarchs, Moses, Joshua, the Judges, David and other kings, the prophets, and sometimes the whole people.

- Manna that fed the Chosen People as they wandered in the desert on their way from Egypt to the Promised Land.

- Priests, such as Aaron, who became the only people after Moses who could offer sacrifice to God.

- The Judges, such as Samson, to provide temporary leadership from the time of Joshua until the time the Chosen People had kings.

- Kings, such as Saul, David, and Solomon, to provide political leadership.

- Prophets, such as Samuel, Isaiah, and Jeremiah, to speak for God about God's will in the present much more than to predict the future.

The Fullness of Life

- The Temple, where God's presence was made more obvious, where the Ark of the Covenant was kept until the Babylonian Exile, and the only place where sacrifice was offered after it was built.
- Return from the Babylonian Exile so the people would once again have the Promised Land and the Temple.
- Freedom from idol-worshipping foreigners (the "Greeks") due to the leadership of the Maccabees.

The fact that the space for the vineyard needed to be spaded, cleared of stones, and planted with the choicest vines—the fact that the space was wild and needed cultivating—symbolizes the state of humanity after the Fall/Original Sin and its need for salvation. As the "vineyard owner" asked (rhetorically[133]), "What more could be done for my vineyard that I did not do?" God always loved His Chosen People in superabundance. The bulleted examples above are examples of God's love, God's action to save humanity from the Fall/Original Sin, God's faithfulness to the covenant, and God's Revelation through events—which are all different ways of saying the same thing.

The result of all of the "vineyard owner's" loving efforts was "rotten grapes," which symbolize the sin on the part of the Chosen People, even though God was always faithful to the covenant. Sin is lack of faithfulness to the covenant.

One way to understand the history of the Chosen People and that which God reveals through it is to once again draw upon the wisdom of St. Augustine: Hate the sin, but love the sinner. In terms of this instruction from St. Augustine, the "Vineyard Song" means that God reveals through the Old Testament that He remains faithful to the Chosen People by hating their sins but loving them.[134]

HOW DID THE COVENANT MAKE THE CHOSEN PEOPLE DIFFERENT FROM ALL OTHER ANCIENT PEOPLES?

It was to Abraham and his descendants that God chose to reveal Him-

---

[133] A rhetorical question is really a statement in the form of a question. The vineyard owner is really saying here, "There is nothing more I could have done for my vineyard."

[134] *CCC*, 59-64, 702-710.

self more directly than to any other people. There is no one in any other ancient religion to compare with Abraham and the other Patriarchs; Moses; Joshua and the Judges; Solomon and David; and Samuel, Isaiah, Jeremiah, Ezekiel, and the other prophets.

The Chosen People were the only ancient people to make a covenant with the one true God, the three most important steps of which were with Abraham, Moses, and David.

The Faith of the Chosen People corresponds to the objectively real God and His objectively real Revelation, and so Old Testament Faith is the objective truth.

The Faith of the Chosen People has the most literal truth of all the ancient religions, the rest of which have myths that are mostly figuratively true even though these myths often profoundly express the constant human search for transcendence and can often express objective truths. The Chosen People were the only ancient people to begin harmonizing Faith and Reason, which they did in the Wisdom Books of the Old Testament.

The Chosen People were the only ancient people to directly worship and pray to the one true God. Other ancient worship at times profoundly expressed the constant human search for transcendence and at other times expressed the depths of human depravity, e.g., infant sacrifice and orgy.

More than any other ancient people, the Jews learned that religion involves morality. For all other ancient peoples, religion tended to be much more about trying to get the gods and goddesses to help you. The gods and goddesses themselves were immoral. No other religion's god or goddess said, "Be holy, for I, the LORD, your God, am holy (Leviticus 19:2)."

The world would be a very different place if ancient religion, culture, and morality had not been challenged by the Faith of ancient Israel and the Reason of the ancient Greeks. It was these two peoples, more than any other ancient people, who discovered the most important truths that transcend all human culture and history. In order to live as fully as we can, we need the most important transcendent truths.

The Fullness of Life

HOW DOES THE OLD TESTAMENT EXPRESS THAT GOD WILL REVEAL HIMSELF <u>BEYOND</u> THE OLD TESTAMENT?

The Old Testament itself expresses that God will reveal Himself beyond the Old Testament.[135]

Remember that kings and priests (and sometimes prophets) were anointed with oil when they were installed in their office. In **Is 61:1-3**,[136] God reveals that He will send someone whom He has anointed to save the Chosen People. The Hebrew word for this person is *Messiah*, which means "the Anointed One," and which in effect means "The Savior." In the Messiah, the offices of king, priest, and prophet will be reunited. Also recall that God made a covenant with David that his dynasty would last forever.

In **Jer (Jeremiah) 31:31**,[137] God reveals that He will make a new covenant with the house of Israel and the house of Judah.

In **Is 11:1-2**,[138] God reveals that He will send a new Spirit.

In **Is 66:18, 23**,[139] God reveals that He will reveal Himself to the Gentiles/those who are not Jews.

We are now ready to encounter Jesus Christ!

---

[135] *CCC*, 711-716.

[136] And also in Hosea 3:4-5; Jer 23:5-6, 30:9, 33:15; Ezek 37:24-27; Is 11:1-10; Zech (Zechariah) 3:8, 9:9-10; Amos 9:13-15; Mic (Micah) 4:1-8.

[137] And also in Is 55:1-3, 59:20-21, 61:3-4, 8-9; Ezek 20:23-28, 34:25, 37:26.

[138] And also in Ezek 11:19, 36:25-28, 37:1-14; Joel 3:1-5.

[139] And also in Is 2:2-4; Jer 3:14-18; Mic 4: 1-5; Zech 8:20-23.

PERSONAL FAITH RESPONSE

Check any statements below that describe you.

In order to LIVE FULLY:

1. _____I agree with the objective truth in this chapter.

2. _____I will be grateful to God for His love and faithfulness throughout the centuries to save humanity, including me, from the Fall.

3. _____I will appreciate the Faith and the distinctiveness of the Chosen People.

4. _____I will be different from others to whatever extent my relationship with God calls me to be different.

5. _____I will encounter Jesus Christ as best as I can in the upcoming chapters.

VOCABULARY

Vineyard Song: A passage in the Book of Isaiah that summarizes God's faithfulness to the covenant.

Messiah: The "Anointed One"/Savior in whom the offices of king, priest, and prophet will be reunited.

Gentile: Non-Jew.

Part 4: What Does God Reveal through the Old Testament?

Chapter VI

WHAT ARE OTHER KEY PASSAGES IN THE OLD TESTAMENT?

WHAT ARE OTHER KEY PASSAGES ABOUT THE PATRIARCHS?

- Gn (Genesis) 16; 21:1-21: Ishmael.

- Gn 18:1-19:29: Sodom.

- Gn 25:19-26: The birth of Esau and Jacob.

- Gn 19:27-34; 27:1-40: Jacob's moves against Esau.

- Gn 33:1-17: The reconciliation of Esau and Jacob.

- Gn 37, 39-45: Joseph.

WHAT ARE OTHER KEY PASSAGES ABOUT IMPORTANT WOMEN?

- Judges 4-5: Deborah.

- The Book of Ruth.

- The Book of Judith.

- The Book of Esther.

WHAT ARE OTHER KEY PASSAGES ABOUT DAVID?

- 1 Sm (Samuel) 9:1-4, 17-19; 10:1: God chooses David.

- 1 Sm 17: Goliath.

- 1 Sm 18:6-9; 19:1-7; 24:3-21; 2 Sam 1-27: The relationship between David and Saul.

- 2 Sm 11:1-12:25: David's sin.

WHAT ARE OTHER KEY PASSAGES ABOUT THE PROPHETS?

- Jer (Jeremiah) 1:4-10, 20:7-13: The call of Jeremiah.

- Jer 20:7-13: What it is like to be a prophet.

- Ez (Ezekiel) 1:1-3:16: The call of Ezekiel.

- Ez 13:1-16: Against false prophets.

- 1 Kings 18:16-46: Elijah and the prophets of Baal.

- Is (Isaiah) 1:1-20: Call to justice.

- Is 55:1-13: Come to the Lord for life.

- Hos (Hosea) 4:7-14: Idolatry is like prostitution.

- Hos 11: God's love for His People.

WHAT ARE OTHER KEY PASSAGES OF WISDOM LITERATURE?

- Job 1-3, 38-39, 42: The suffering of Job.

- Job 28:12-28: The greatness of wisdom.

- Ps (Psalm) 1: "The law of the Lord is one's joy."

- Ps 8: "What is man . . .?"

- Ps 22: "My God, my God, why have You abandoned me?"

- Ps 23: "The LORD is my shepherd."

- Ps 51: "Have mercy on me, God."

- Ps 63: "For You my soul thirsts."

- Ps 84: "Better one day in Your courts than a thousand elsewhere."

- Ps 104: "LORD, You are great."

- Ps 115:3-8: "Their idols are the work of human hands."

- Ps 138: "I thank You, Lord, with all my heart."

- Ps 144: "Blessed be God, Who trains my hands for battle."

- Proverbs 8: No treasures can compare with Wisdom.

- Ecclesiastes 1-3: All is vanity.

- Wisdom 7:7-21: The greatness of wisdom.

WHAT ARE OTHER KEY PASSAGES ABOUT THE DIFFERENT WAYS GOD REVEALED HIMSELF?

- Gn 28: 10-19: God reveals Himself in dreams.

- Dt (Deuteronomy) 11:2-7: God reveals Himself in events.

- Dt 20:1-4: God reveals Himself in justified battle.

- Dt 31:9-13: God reveals Himself in His law.

- 1 Kgs 17:7-16: God reveals Himself in miracles.

- Ps. 7:4-18: God reveals Himself in the reward of good and punishment of evil.

- Ps 8: God reveals Himself in the human person.

- Ps 104: God reveals Himself in nature.

- Ps. 113: God reveals Himself in the poor being helped.

- Is 41:17-20: God reveals Himself in needs being met.

- Lamentations 3:1-33: God reveals Himself in suffering.

PART 5:

WHAT DOES GOD REVEAL THROUGH THE NEW TESTAMENT?

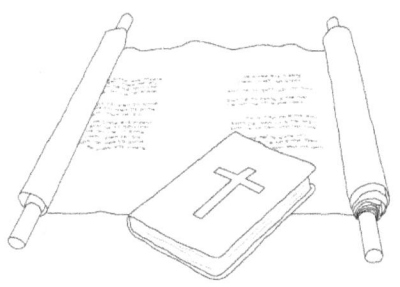

Chapter I: WHAT IS ESSENTIAL BACKGROUND FOR THE NEW TESTAMENT?

Chapter II: HOW DID THE GOSPELS COME TO BE?

Chapter III: WHAT DO THE SYNOPTIC GOSPELS REVEAL ABOUT JESUS?

Chapter IV: WHAT DOES THE GOSPEL OF JOHN REVEAL ABOUT JESUS?

Chapter V: WHAT IS REVEALED ABOUT JESUS IN ALL FOUR GOSPELS?

Chapter VI: DOES REASON SUPPORT FAITH IN THE RESURRECTION?

Chapter VII: WHAT IS THE NEW COVENANT?

Chapter VIII: WHAT ARE OTHER KEY PASSAGES IN THE NEW TESTAMENT?

Part 5: What Does God Reveal through the New Testament?

Chapter I
WHAT IS ESSENTIAL BACKGROUND FOR THE NEW TESTAMENT?

SOURCES

- Pope Benedict XVI, *Jesus of Nazareth*, Volumes 1-3, Doubleday.
- Scott Hahn, Gen. Ed., *Catholic Bible Dictionary* (Doubleday, 2009), "Jesus Christ," "Testament," "Texts of the Bible."

WHAT ARE THE BOOKS OF THE NEW TESTAMENT?

The New Testament expresses Revelation during and after the time of Jesus Christ, Who lived about:

- 1,800 years after Abraham.
- 1,200 years after Moses.
- 1,000 years after David.
- 550 years after the Babylonian Exile.
- 140 years after Judas Maccabeus.

The New Testament has 27 books that belong to four different categories/kinds of books:

1) Occupying the central place in the New Testament and all of Sacred Scripture are the 4 Gospels, which are the books that record the life and saving work of Jesus.

2) Letters, also called Epistles. These books were written by some of the first Christians, e.g., St. Paul. They were written either to a local church, e.g., "the Romans," or to persons, e.g., Timothy.

3) An account of the activities of some of the first Christians, especially St. Peter and St. Paul, of which there is only one book, called the Acts of the Apostles.

4) Apocalyptic literature, which is literature about the end of the world, of which there is only one book, called the Book of Revelation.

WHAT IS THE RELATIONSHIP BETWEEN THE OLD TESTAMENT AND THE NEW TESTAMENT?

The word *testament* serves as a synonym for that hugely important Old Testament word *covenant*—an agreement to establish a binding family-like relationship in which two previously unrelated parties are committed to do their parts. The *Old Testament* is really another way of saying the *Old Covenant*, and the *New Testament* is really another way of saying the *New Covenant*.

In **Matthew 5:17**, Jesus says that He has come not to abolish the law and the prophets but to fulfill them. "The law and the prophets" was what the Jews of Jesus' time, including Jesus Himself, called the Old Testament. Therefore Jesus, in effect, is saying in this passage that He has come to fulfill the one covenant God had made successively with Abraham, Moses, and David, which is expressed in the Old Testament.

In **Luke 22:20**, Jesus explicitly says that He brings a New Covenant. It is by bringing a New Covenant that Jesus fulfills the Old Covenant. Jesus is making the relationship between God and humans even better and closer. Jesus is doing even more to counteract the Fall—in fact, as we shall see, Jesus does the most that can be done to reconcile God and humanity.

The Fullness of Life

All of the books of the New Testament, in one way or another, are centered/focused on Jesus Christ as the definitive/final/greatest Revelation of God.[140] St. Augustine has given the classic way of understanding the relationship between the Old Testament and the New Testament: "The New Testament lies hidden in the Old Testament, and the Old Testament is unveiled/revealed in the New Testament." The NT lies hidden in the OT much in the OT foreshadows/prefigures/anticipates/implies what is in the NT. The OT is unveiled in in the NT because the meaning of the OT is clearer after we read the NT.

God intends the Old and New Testaments to be treated as one unified book.[141] The Sacred Scripture that expresses the New Covenant, which is the New Testament, completes the Sacred Scripture that expresses the Old Covenant, which is the Old Testament. There is one Sacred Scripture. The Old Testament is no less sacred than the New Testament. Some people mistakenly call the Old Testament the "Hebrew Scriptures" and the New Testament the "Christian Scriptures." The Magisterium does not do this because the Old Testament is Christian Scripture.

WHAT WILL BE THE FOCUS OF OUR NEW TESTAMENT STUDY?

Our focus will be the Gospels because they are the books of the New Testament that most reveal Jesus. The Gospels occupy the central place in not only the New Testament, but also all of Scripture,[142] which is why Catholics do something when the Gospel is read at Mass that they do NOT do for the other readings from Scripture—they stand.

You are about to participate in the greatest adventure that a human being can have, the adventure for which God began preparing you and every other human being since the Fall of the first humans: encountering Jesus Christ in order to become His follower and even His friend.

CAN WE BE SURE THAT JESUS EXISTED?

No serious historian who is accomplished in the study of ancient

---

[140] *CCC*, 65-66, 101-104
[141] *CCC*, 128-129, 134, 140, 522.
[142] *CCC*, 124-125, 139.

history doubts that Jesus existed. The historical methods that establish the existence of Socrates, Alexander the Great, Julius Caesar, and every other ancient person are the same historical methods that establish the existence of Jesus. If one doubts the existence of Jesus, then one should doubt the existence of Socrates, Alexander the Great, Caesar, and every other ancient person in history books.

Especially good evidence for the existence of Jesus is that there are ancient ANTI-Christian sources OUTSIDE the New Testament that document His existence. There are ancient authors who dislike and even despise Jesus and yet admit that He did exist.[143] There were many people living at the same time as Jesus. Those who did not become His followers never accused those who did become His followers of following a mythical person. There were many ridiculous accusations made against the first Christians, e.g., that they were cannibals because they ate Jesus' Body and drank His Blood, but following a mythical person was never one of them.

And if Jesus did not exist, how can Christians themselves be explained? Their number grew rapidly after Jesus was put to death. Their origin can NOT have been due to conspiracy since there was no worldly gain from becoming Christian for almost the first two hundred after Christ (i.e., until 311 AD with the Edict of Toleration). During that time, Christians were often scorned, hated, persecuted, imprisoned, tortured, exiled, or executed in horrible ways (stoned, burned, crucified, stabbed, beheaded).

We can be sure that Jesus existed. The real question about Jesus is NOT, Did Jesus exist? The real question about Jesus IS, WHO is Jesus?

HOW TRUSTWORTHY IS THE NEW TESTAMENT FOR KNOWING THE REAL JESUS?

The trustworthiness of the New Testament is important. It is our most important source for knowing Jesus. And over the centuries people have tried to change New Testament teaching about Jesus.

There were a number of "gospels," "acts," "epistles," and "apocalypses" written 100-400 years after Christ. Although many were lost to history

---

[143] Suetonius, Tacitus, Pliny the Younger, Josephus, Thallus, Mara bar Serapion, Lucian of Samosata, and the Babylonian Talmud.

until they were re-discovered in the 20th Century, they were known to the Church at the time they were written and rejected for being fake. There was no conspiracy to hide them. There were very few people who considered them worth preserving.

There have been people who have tried to change traditional, orthodox teaching about Jesus for any number of reasons. Some have wanted to justify their particular belief or, rather, lack of belief. Some have done so out of sincere but misguided or misinformed efforts to try to explain mysteries about Jesus or Revelation. Some have not liked what Jesus taught or did. Some find His Resurrection too good to be true, so much has the evil in the world gotten the better of them. In modern times, there have been individuals and groups who have tried to explain in natural, scientific terms the miracles of Jesus, thus undermining His Divinity.

The New Testament is very trustworthy for knowing the real Jesus.

Everything in the entire New Testament, including the Gospels, was written either by people who personally knew Jesus or by people who knew people who knew Jesus—2 degrees of separation!

There is NO writing from ancient times that has survived as well as the New Testament. It is important to know that we have the original manuscript of NO known ancient author. (We have a fair number of original anonymous writings in clay and stone.) All that we have for any known ancient author, Sacred or otherwise, are copies of copies of copies.

However, the evidence that the words we now have for the New Testament are indeed the original words of the New Testament authors is better than the evidence that the words we now have for any other ancient author are indeed the original words of that author.[144]

The New Testament is also trustworthy because the New Testament

---

[144] There is better evidence that the words of our New Testament are the actual words of the New Testament authors due to the age, quality, and quantity of surviving manuscripts. E.g., the oldest surviving manuscript of Julius Caesar's *The Gallic Wars* is from the Ninth Century—900 years after he wrote it—and there are only 12 manuscripts on which scholars base current translations. The oldest manuscript for the Gospels (a fragment from John's Gospel) dates to 125 AD—less than 100 years after Jesus. The oldest manuscript of the complete Gospels dates to the Fourth Century—300 years after Jesus. There are over 5,800 Greek manuscripts of the New Testament that date before the printing press. They are almost identical, having only very minor differences.

writers are trustworthy people. First Century people (both Christians and non-Christians) knew the difference between myth and fact. Luke (Lk 1:1-4), John (Jn 21:24-25), Peter (2 Pt 1:16), and Paul (Galatians 1:11-12; 1 Timothy 1:3-7; 2 Tm 4:3-4) explicitly affirm that they are telling facts and not myths. And there was no motive for the New Testament writers to write the New Testament other than to write the truth. As we have already seen, followers of Christ were treated horribly during the time the New Testament was written.

The New Testament will make sense when we realize that God equally reveals Himself through Sacred Tradition and that only the Magisterium has the God-given authority to interpret it.

PERSONAL FAITH RESPONSE

Check any statements below that describe you.

In order to LIVE FULLY:

1. _____I agree with the objective truth in this chapter.

2. _____I will be confident that Jesus existed.

3. _____I will honestly try to know the truth about WHO Jesus is Jesus and go wherever that truth leads me.

4. _____I will realize that the New Testament is very trustworthy for knowing the real Jesus.

VOCABULARY

Gospel: A New Testament book that records the life and saving work of Jesus.

Testament: (1) The most basic part of the Bible and (2) a synonym for covenant.

"The Law and the Prophets": What the Jews of Jesus' time, including Jesus Himself, called the Old Testament.

Part 5: What Does God Reveal through the New Testament?

Chapter II:
HOW DID THE GOSPELS COME TO BE?

SOURCES

- Pope Benedict XVI, *Jesus of Nazareth*, Volumes 1-3, Ignatius Press.

- Scott Hahn, Gen. Ed., *Catholic Bible Dictionary* (Doubleday, 2009), "Gospel," "John," "John, Gospel of," "Luke," "Luke, Gospel of," "Mark," "Mark, Gospel of," "Matthew," "Matthew, Gospel of."

HOW WERE THE GOSPELS WRITTEN?

LIKE much of the Old Testament, the Gospels came to be in three stages:[145]

> • 1st: There was a real person to whom and through whom God revealed Himself. In the case of the Gospels, this real person was Jesus, who wrote nothing about His words and actions.

---

[145] *CCC*, 126.

- 2nd: The words and actions of Jesus were handed on by word of mouth in oral traditions, and possibly in written traditions that have not survived.
- 3rd: Jesus' words and actions were finally written down, and even edited, by men who had their own emphases and their own limitations, and so the Gospels, like all of Scripture, are the Word of God in the words of men.[146]

UNLIKE much of the Old Testament, the final form of the Gospels/3rd Stage was put down in writing quickly after the life of the real person/Jesus/1st Stage. The time of oral tradition/2nd Stage was short. For much of the Old Testament, the 2nd Stage of oral tradition took CENTURIES between the 1st Stage of a real person experiencing Revelation and the 3rd Stage of writing and editing. For the Gospels, the 2nd Stage of oral tradition took DECADES between the 1st Stage of real people experiencing Jesus and the 3rd Stage of the final written form.

The final forms of Acts of the Apostles, Letters/Epistles, and Book of Revelation are basically the same as they were originally written by their authors.

Most, if not all,[147] of the New Testament was originally written in Greek, which was the common language of the eastern Mediterranean world after the conquests of Alexander the Great around 325 BC.

WHY ARE THERE FOUR GOSPELS?

There are four Gospels because the Gospels were written by different authors at different times and in different places to meet the needs of different local churches. As **John 21:25** says, no one Gospel could contain everything that could be written about Jesus. The Gospels do not contradict each other but complement/complete each other. Here is a summary of current scholarship (thus Reason, NOT Revelation) on the

---

[146] And so a Gospel might have been put in its final form not by the Gospel writer but by an editor who was very close to the writer, e.g. the Gospel of John might not have been put into its final form by John himself, but by someone who knew John very well. So "The Gospel According to . . ." can mean "The Gospel True to the Witness of . . ."

[147] There is good but inconclusive evidence that the Gospel of Matthew was originally written in Hebrew or Aramaic.

The Fullness of Life

background of the four Gospel writers.

St. Matthew was one of the Twelve Apostles. Also called Levi, he was a tax collector before he joined Jesus, which means he was a Jew who collected taxes from the Jews for the Romans, who had conquered the Jews, and so was viewed by his fellow Jews as a traitor. Because Matthew's Gospel does not explain features of the Jewish religion, he seems to have written his Gospel for Christians who had been Jews and/or for converting Jews to Christ. Those for whom Matthew originally wrote most likely lived in Palestine. He especially wrote his Gospel to show Jews who wanted to follow Jesus that Jesus is the fulfillment of the Old Covenant, e.g., Matthew quotes the Old Testament more than the other three Gospel writers. His Gospel was put in its final form as early as 50 AD and maybe as late as 90 AD.

St. Mark was not one of the Twelve Apostles; but he was at times a companion of two Apostles, St. Paul and especially St. Peter. There is some evidence that he knew Jesus personally. Because Mark's Gospel does explain the Jewish religion, Mark seems to have written for Gentile Christians and/or for converting Gentiles to Christ. Those for whom he originally wrote most likely lived in Rome. He especially wrote his Gospel to show that Jesus is the Son of God. Most of the evidence is that his Gospel was put in its final form before 70 AD.

Although St. Luke did not know Jesus, he knew people who knew Jesus (Lk 1:1-4), e.g., he was a companion of St. Paul. Because his Gospel has much more about St. Mary and the other women who were disciples, he seems to have known one or more of them very well. Because Luke's Gospel does explain the Jewish religion, he also seems to have written for the same kind of people as Mark, Gentile Christians and/or for converting Gentiles to Christ. Those for whom he originally wrote most likely lived in Greece. He especially wrote his Gospel to show that Jesus came to save everyone, especially the poor and all in need of mercy, as well as to show the important role played by women and the importance of prayer to Jesus. His Gospel was put in its final form as early as 60 AD and maybe as late as 72 AD.

St. John was one of the Twelve Apostles and part of Jesus' inner circle along with Peter and James. Because John's Gospel does not explain the Jewish religion, he seems to have written for the same kind of people as Matthew, Christians who had been Jews and/or for converting Jews to Christ. Those for whom he originally wrote most likely lived in Ephesus, a city on the Mediterranean Sea in what is now Turkey. John wrote his Gospel to show Jews who wanted to follow Jesus that Jesus is God. His Gospel was put in its final form as early as 60 AD and maybe as late as 100 AD.

The Gospels of Matthew, Mark, and Luke are very similar to each other; and so these three Gospels are called the Synoptic Gospels since *synoptic* means "same view." The Gospel of John is noticeably different from the others.

PERSONAL FAITH RESPONSE

Check any statements below that describe you.

In order to LIVE FULLY:

1. _____I agree with the objective truth in this chapter.

2. _____Just as each Gospel writer had a different perspective on Jesus without distorting the real Jesus, I will develop my own friendship with Jesus without distorting His true identity.

VOCABULARY

The 3-Stage Process: The process by which the Gospels were written: (1) Jesus, (2) Traditions, (3) Writing.

Gentile: A non-Jew.

Synoptic Gospels: Matthew, Mark, and Luke's Gospels, which are more similar to each other than they are to John's Gospel.

Part 5: What Does God Reveal through the New Testament?

Chapter III:

WHAT DO THE SYNOPTIC GOSPELS REVEAL ABOUT JESUS?

SOURCES

- Pope Benedict XVI, *Jesus of Nazareth*, Volumes 1-3, Ignatius Press.
- Scott Hahn, Gen. Ed., *Catholic Bible Dictionary* (Doubleday, 2009), "Jesus Christ," "Kingdom," "Messiah."

WHAT ARE IMPORTANT POINTS ABOUT JESUS' BIRTH?

In **Lk (Luke) 1:26-38**, Mary, who lives in the town of Nazareth, is told by the angel Gabriel that God has chosen her to conceive His Son.[148] Mary freely choses/consents to cooperate with God.[149] Gabriel tells Mary that she is to name her son Jesus, which means "God saves,"[150] and that God's covenant with David will be fulfilled in Him.

---

[148] *CCC*, 495.
[149] *CCC*, 494.
[150] *CCC*, 430-435.

Mary is a virgin,[151] although she is promised in marriage to Joseph, who belongs to the house/family of King David. God is Jesus' father and Joseph is Jesus' legal father but NOT Jesus' biological father. Jesus is thus a legal descendant of King David.

The event described in this passage is called the Annunciation, which means "Announcement," because it is when Gabriel announces to Mary that God has chosen her to be the mother of His Son.[152] The Annunciation is simultaneously the event at which Mary conceives Jesus by the power of the Holy Spirit, which is why it is celebrated every year in the Catholic Church on March 25 nine months before Christmas since, of course, the average pregnancy is 9 months long.

Catholics regularly quote the angel Gabriel. The first two lines of the "Hail Mary" are from verse 28. The Nicene Creed at Sunday Mass quotes verse 33, "and His Kingdom will have no end."

In **Lk 2:1-19**, Joseph has to be enrolled (in a census) decreed by the Roman Emperor Augustus because the Promised Land has been part of that empire since 63 BC. Jesus is probably born between 6 and 4 BC.[153] Jesus is born in Bethlehem, which is called the "City of David" because King David was also born there.

Jesus' birth is announced by angels to shepherds, who find Jesus thanks to the signs given to them: He is wrapped in swaddling clothes (clothes so tight that a baby cannot move his arms and legs) and lying in a manger (a box-like object out of which animals eat). The first two lines of the "Gloria" said at Sunday Mass quote the angels in verse 14.

In **Mt (Matthew) 1:18-2:23**, notice that ancient Jewish betrothal

---

[151] *CCC*, 496-497.

[152] *CCC*, 484-486, 494.

[153] *BC* means "Before Christ." Of course, Jesus was not born before Himself. The BC-AD way of numbering years was devised in 525 AD by Dionysus Exiguus. We do not know how he made his calculation. We now have enough evidence to know that he was slightly off, but we do not have enough evidence to know exactly by how many years he was off.

was not marriage, and so Joseph and Mary have not gone through a wedding, do not live together, and are not having sexual relations.¹⁵⁴ But betrothal was like marriage in that Mary is Joseph's wife and breaking betrothal meant getting divorced, which Joseph at first intends to do since she is pregnant and he knows he is not the father.

Jesus is paid homage by magi (astrologer-priests) from the east, who are thus the first Gentiles to whom Jesus is revealed, an event which is celebrated every year on the Feast of the Epiphany, which is a synonym for *Revelation*.¹⁵⁵ They give Jesus gifts of gold, frankincense, and myrrh. They are guided by a star but get further guidance from King Herod¹⁵⁶ and the priests and scribes in Jerusalem.

When they do not return to Herod, he has all the boys who are two and younger in Bethlehem and its vicinity massacred.¹⁵⁷ Jesus escapes because Joseph takes Him and Mary to Egypt. After the death of Herod, Joseph takes Jesus and Mary back to Nazareth.

Joseph gets guidance at key times from an angel in a dream.

Since the ancient Jews did not have the system of first names and last names, during Jesus' lifetime He would have been called "Jesus of Nazareth," since that was where He grew up, and "Jesus, Son of Joseph."

---

¹⁵⁴ *CCC*, 496-507. Mt 1:25 does NOT contradict Catholic doctrine. The word *until* (and the Greek word it translates) can also mean "and not after, either." Fr. John Echert provides other examples of this meaning of *until* in Scripture at www.ewtn.com/v/experts/showmessage_print.asp?number=339819&language=en.

¹⁵⁵ *CCC*, 528.

¹⁵⁶ Remember that the Promised Land is part of the Roman Empire. Although a "king," Herod was under the complete authority of the Roman emperor and so only had as much power as the emperor delegated to him.

¹⁵⁷ *CCC*, 530.

DID JESUS SIN?

In **Mt 4:1-11**, after Jesus has fasted for 40 days and 40 nights, He is tempted to sin by the devil/Satan three times. Jesus does not give in to temptation. As we read in **Hebrews 4:14-15**, our great high priest is Jesus, Who is like us in all ways except He never sinned.[158]

WHAT DOES JESUS TEACH IN THE SYNOPTICS?

In **Mt 4:17, 23; 9:35; Mk (Mark) 1:14-15**; and **Lk 4:43**, Jesus reveals that His purpose is to announce the good news of the Kingdom of God/Heaven.[159] Matthew is the only Gospel writer who follows the Jewish tradition that it is disrespectful to use the word *God*, so instead he substitutes "Kingdom of Heaven" for "Kingdom of God." *Kingdom of God* and *Kingdom of Heaven* mean the same thing.

The theme/topic of all Jesus' preaching and teaching is the Kingdom: either what it is or what it takes to be able to enter it. Jesus wants everyone to whom He preaches to agree with Him and become His follower. Where Jesus calls everyone to follow Him to is the Kingdom.

As in **Mt 13:24-30, 31-32**, and **44-50**, when Jesus teaches about the Kingdom, he often tells parables, which are very descriptive stories that teach a lesson or give an insight by using a clever simile or metaphor and so are easy to remember.

WHEN THE JEWS HEAR JESUS PREACH THE KINGDOM, WHAT DO THEY THINK HE MEANS?

The Jews of Jesus' time are well aware that God made a covenant with David that his "house"/dynasty would last forever. Because the Jews expect a dynasty of kings that will last forever, they expect a kingdom that will last forever. They are waiting for the Messiah to come who will bring

---

[158] *CCC*, 538-540.
[159] *CCC*, 541-546.

The Fullness of Life

the Davidic Kingdom.

Jesus claims to be the Messiah. In **Lk 4:16-21**, after Jesus reads a passage from the Book of Isaiah that describes the Messiah, He says, "This Scripture passage has been fulfilled in your hearing." In **Mt 11:2-6**, John the Baptist's disciples ask Jesus if Jesus is "he who is to come ," which is a reference to the Messiah. Jesus answers by describing what He does by using a description of the Messiah.

When the Jews hear Jesus preach that the Kingdom is near at hand, they think He means an everlasting kingdom that will be much like what their ancestors had experienced during the reign of King David. The Jews are not expecting that the Messiah bringing this Davidic kingdom will be God because before Jesus, God had not revealed that the Messiah would be God.

WHAT DOES JESUS *NOT* MEAN ABOUT THE KINGDOM?

Heaven is where souls that are separated from their dead bodies go to be with God. In **Mt 6:10**, Jesus teaches that God's ("Thy") Kingdom will come when God's ("Thy") will is done on Earth as it is currently being done in Heaven, which means that the Kingdom will be on Earth. We all well know that Earth is NOT Heaven.

When Jesus talks about the *Kingdom of God*, He does NOT mean Heaven, where souls that are separated from their dead bodies go to be with God. When Jesus talks about the *Kingdom of Heaven*, He does NOT mean Heaven, where souls that are separated from their dead bodies go to be with God. *Kingdom of God* and *Kingdom of Heaven* mean the same thing, but NEITHER means the same thing as *Heaven*.

Kingdom of God = Kingdom of Heaven ≠ Heaven

WHAT DOES JESUS DO IN THE SYNOPTICS?

We can understand better what Jesus means by the Kingdom when we realize that the Kingdom is the theme not only of Jesus' words, but also of Jesus' actions. Jesus' most distinctive action is performing miracles, which is when something supernatural happens that cannot be explained by Reason, e.g., Science, but can only be explained by Faith as the work of God.

Jesus performs miracles in order to give examples/signs of what life in the Kingdom is like.[160] Here are just a few of the many examples in the Gospels. In **Mt 9:27-31**, Jesus reveals that in the Kingdom no one will be blind. In **Mk 2:1-12**, Jesus reveals that in the Kingdom no one will be paralyzed. In **Lk 4:40**, Jesus reveals that in the Kingdom no one will be no sick. In **Lk 9:10-17**, Jesus reveals that in the Kingdom no one will be hungry. In **Mk 4:35-41**, Jesus reveals that in the Kingdom no one will be in danger from nature. In **Lk 7:11-17**, Jesus reveals that in the Kingdom no one will die. In **Mt 17:1-8**, the Transfiguration reveals what life in the Kingdom is like.[161]

So, in general, life in the Kingdom will mean, among other things, perfect physical health, which is another reason that when Jesus talks about the Kingdom, He is not talking about Heaven, where there are only souls and no bodies.

DOES JESUS FULFILL THE OLD TESTAMENT REVELATIONS ABOUT THE MESSIAH?

Before Jesus was born of Mary, God revealed several things about the Messiah.

- In **Is (Isaiah) 7:14** that the Messiah will be born of a young woman, who is therefore unmarried and therefore a virgin.

---

[160] *CCC*, 547-550.
[161] *CCC*, 554-556.

- In **Is 11:1-5** that the Messiah will "sprout from"/descend from Jesse, who is the father of David.

- In **Genesis 49:8-10** that the Messiah will be a descendant of Judah, from whose tribe (of the Twelve Tribes of Israel) David was descended.

- In **Micah 5:1** that the Messiah will come from Bethlehem.

- In **Is 35:5-6** that the Messiah will perform miracles.

- In **Is 26:19** that the Messiah will raise the dead.

All of the above prophecies are true about Jesus. Jesus fulfills the Old Testament prophecies about the Messiah. To know the Old Testament and to know Jesus Christ is to come to the same conclusion as Philip (told to Nathanael), "We have found the one about whom Moses wrote in the law, and also the prophets: Jesus, son of Joseph, from Nazareth" (John 1:45).

Christ is the English version of the Greek word (*Christos*) for the Hebrew word Messiah. Both the Greek and Hebrew words mean "the Anointed One."[162] So *Christ* is originally NOT a last name BUT a title, which is why Jesus is also called throughout the New Testament "the Christ" or "Christ Jesus." The ancient Romans gave the world the system of first name and last name, and so eventually due to their influence *Christ* became treated like a last name and so Jesus came to be called "Jesus Christ."

---

[162] *CCC*, 436-440.

PERSONAL FAITH RESPONSE

Check any statements below that describe you.

In order to LIVE FULLY:

1. _____I agree with the objective truth in this chapter.

2. _____I will celebrate the Annunciation every year.

3. _____I will celebrate the Birth of Christ every year.

4. _____I will celebrate the Epiphany every year.

5. _____I will take St. Joseph as my model if I become a husband and father.

6. _____I will do my best to resist temptation.

7. _____I will follow Jesus to the Kingdom of God.

VOCABULARY

Mary: The mother of Jesus.

Nazareth: The town where Mary lives when she is told God has chosen her to be the mother of Jesus.

Gabriel: The angel who tells Mary that God has chosen her.

Joseph: The husband of Mary and legal father of Jesus.

Annunciation: (1) The event when Mary is told God has chosen her to be the mother of Jesus and (2) the annual feast day celebrating this event.

Augustus: The Roman emperor at the time of Jesus' birth.

Bethlehem: (1) The town in which Jesus is born, which is also (2) the City of David.

Swaddling: Tightly wrapping.

Manger: Box-like structure out of which animals eat.

Betrothal: In ancient Judaism, being promised in marriage but not living together, not having sex, and not having gone through a wedding, yet needing divorce to break it.

Magi: Astrologer-priest from the East.

Epiphany: (1) The event when the magi paid homage to the newborn Jesus and (2) the annual feast day.

Herod: King of the Jewish people when Jesus is born.

Kingdom of God/Kingdom of Heaven: (1) The fulfillment of God's covenant with David, and which is (2) the theme of Jesus' words and actions.

Parables: Very descriptive stories Jesus told usually about the Kingdom.

Heaven: Where souls that are separated from their dead bodies go to be with God.

Miracles: Something supernatural that cannot be explained by Science, but can only be explained by Faith as the work of God.

Christ: Both a title and last name for Jesus which means the "Anointed One" or Messiah.

Part 5: What Does God Reveal through the New Testament?

Chapter IV:

WHAT DOES THE GOSPEL OF JOHN REVEAL ABOUT JESUS?

SOURCES

- Pope Benedict XVI, *Jesus of Nazareth*, Volumes 1-3, Doubleday.
- Scott Hahn, Gen. Ed., *Catholic Bible Dictionary* (Doubleday, 2009), "John, Gospel of."

WHAT IS IMPORTANT ABOUT THE PROLOGUE OF JOHN'S GOSPEL?

Jn 1:1-18 is called the "Prologue," which means it is the introduction for the Gospel. "The Word" and "he/him" in reference to "the Word" mean Jesus (so not "he/him" in verses 7-8, which refer to John the Baptist). A good exercise is to read this passage and every time you get to "the Word" and "he/him" (except in v. 7-8), say *Jesus*.

The first few words of John's Gospel were chosen by him to echo the first few words of the Book of Genesis. The beginning of the Book of Genesis reveals that God created the universe. John's Gospel reveals that God re-creates the universe by sending His Word to take on flesh. The Word-taking-on-flesh is Jesus. [163] The Word/Jesus has existed as long as

---

[163] *CCC*, 241, 291, 456-460.

God has existed, which is always.

Verses 9-11 and 14 reveal that Jesus is human. But every verse of the prologue profoundly and eloquently reveals that Jesus is God, which is a major theme of John's Gospel. While the divinity of Jesus is also revealed in the Synoptic Gospels, John emphasizes the divinity of Jesus more than the other Gospel writers.

DOES JESUS CLAIM TO BE GOD IN JOHN'S GOSPEL?

John claims that Jesus is God, but does Jesus claim that He is God?

In **Jn 8:48-59**, Jesus calls God "My Father." Jesus said that Abraham rejoiced to see His day and that "before Abraham came to be, I AM," which, remember, is the name of God. In **Jn 17:1-5**, Jesus says that the Father has given Him authority over all people so that Jesus may give eternal life to all. Jesus calls the Father the only true God who has sent Him/Jesus and asks the Father to glorify Him with the glory He had with the Father before the world began.

So, yes, Jesus claims to be God in John's Gospel.[164] He claims to be God in the Synoptic Gospels, too.[165]

WHAT DOES JESUS TEACH IN JOHN'S GOSPEL?

In John's Gospel, Jesus does not use the term *Kingdom* as much as He does in the Synoptic Gospels. He teaches about the Kingdom/ salvation by using synonyms. In **Jn 8:12**, Jesus teaches that He is the light of the world, and throughout John's Gospel "being in the light" and "seeing" are ways of being saved (in the Kingdom). In **Jn 10:10**, Jesus teaches that He has come so that people might have life more abundantly/to the full, and throughout John's Gospel "life" is a synonym for the Kingdom. In **Jn 14:6** Jesus teaches that He is our salvation. In the Synoptic Gospels, Jesus' message/good news is the Kingdom. In John's Gospel, Jesus' message/good news is Himself, which is appropriate because He is God.

---

[164] See also Jn 5:22-25, 7:35-39, 10:22-39.
[165] See Mt 11:4, 11:25-27, 12:6-8, 12:41, 10:37, 14:33, 16:13-18, 20:28, 26:26-28; Mk 2:7-12, 6:50, 8:38, 11:35-37, 14:61-65; Lk 10:21-22, 12:1-9, 14:25.

The Fullness of Life

In **Jn 6**, there is one very important example of Jesus' teaching. This chapter begins with Jesus feeding a crowd of 5,000 with 5 barley loaves and 2 fishes. When the crowd finds Jesus the next day, He tells them that He is the bread of life. As Jesus says, ". . . and the bread that I will give you is my flesh for the life of the world. . . . Whoever eats my flesh and drinks my blood has eternal life." So the Catholic Church has not, against the will of Jesus, made up its Sacrament of the Eucharist in which consecrated bread and wine become the real Body and Blood of Jesus. The Catholic Church gets the Sacrament of the Eucharist from Jesus Himself. As a result of this teaching of Jesus, many of those who had been followers of Jesus stop following Him. When Jesus asks the Twelve Apostles if they also want to leave, it is Peter who says, "Master, to whom shall we go? You have the words of eternal life."

Unlike the Synoptic Gospels, John's Gospel does not emphasize Jesus' parables. Skimming **Jn 3:4-8**, **4:4-38**, **11:20-27**, **18:33-38**, and **19:8-11** shows that in John's Gospel Jesus tends to teach by having dialogues and conversations with others.

WHAT DOES JESUS DO IN JOHN'S GOSPEL?

As in the Synoptic Gospels, John's Gospel give us examples of the miracles that Jesus performed. In the Synoptic Gospels Jesus uses miracles to reveal the Kingdom. In **Jn 2:1-11**, Jesus turns water into wine. Jesus did this to reveal His glory. Likewise, throughout John's Gospel Jesus uses miracles to reveal the glory He has because He is God. The purpose of Jesus' miracles in the Synoptic Gospels do not contradict but add to the purpose of Jesus' miracles in John's Gospel.

PERSONAL FAITH RESPONSE

Check any statements below that describe you.

In order to LIVE FULLY:

1. _____I agree with the objective truth in this chapter.

2. _____Although the world does not know the Word and His own people did not (all) accept Him, I will accept Jesus is the Word of God Who is God.

3. _____No matter how much darkness there is in the world and in my own life, I will follow Jesus Who is the Light that darkness cannot overcome.

4. _____I will eat the Flesh and drink the Blood of Jesus every Sunday, if I have been baptized in the Catholic Church and I am not in a state of mortal sin.

5. _____If I am not Catholic, I will seriously consider becoming Catholic so I can eat the Flesh and drink

   the Blood of Jesus.

6. _____I will have my own dialogue with Jesus throughout my life—asking him questions and giving my reactions while listening to His answers that come to me in Catholic Doctrine.

VOCABULARY

Prologue: Introduction.

Divinity: Being God/God-ness.

Part 5: What Does God Reveal through the New Testament?

Chapter V:

WHAT IS REVEALED ABOUT JESUS IN ALL FOUR GOSPELS?

SOURCES

- Pope Benedict XVI, *Jesus of Nazareth*, Volumes 1-3, (Doubleday).
- Scott Hahn, Gen. Ed., *Catholic Bible Dictionary* (Doubleday, 2009), "John the Baptist," "Passion of Christ," "Resurrection."

WHO IS JOHN THE BAPTIST?

The coming of Jesus had been prepared by God since the Fall of Adam and Eve had separated humanity from God. God had sent Patriarchs, Judges, Prophets, Priests, and Kings to the Chosen People in order to prepare the way of Jesus. Because John the Baptist speaks for God about Jesus, John the Baptist is the last and the greatest prophet before Jesus, as Jesus testifies in Mt 11:7-11.[166]

In **Mt (Matthew) 3**, we see that John the Baptist's gospel/basic message is the same as Jesus' gospel: "Repent, for the Kingdom of Heaven is at hand!" We also see that John helps people prepare for the coming of

---

[166] *CCC*, 522-523, 535-537, 717-720.

the Kingdom by baptizing them. But John thinks that it is not appropriate for him to baptize Jesus.[167]

In **Jn (John) 1:19-34**, John the Baptist makes it clear that he never considered himself to be the Messiah. The people and then the priest at Mass echo what John says in verse 29, "Behold, the Lamb of God, who takes away the sin of the world."[168] John the Baptist testifies not only that Jesus is the Messiah, but also that Jesus is God.

After Jesus is baptized by the John the Baptist, Jesus begins his public ministry/work. The long period of His private/hidden life (30 years?) is over.[169]

TO WHAT ELSE DO ALL FOUR GOSPELS WITNESS?

This section will help round out the life of Jesus.

All four Gospels agree on the following about Jesus' background. He is a legal descendant of David. Mary is His mother. God is His Father. Pontius Pilate is the Roman governor, the highest Roman authority on the scene. Caiaphas is the high priest.

All four Gospels agree on the following about Jesus' ministry. Jesus teaches that He has been sent by God, His Father. He forgives sin, which only God can do. He wants everyone to become His follower/disciple. He ministers in Galilee and Judea. He teaches in synagogues and in the Temple. He drives the money-changers out of the Temple. He gives commands. Jesus teaches that judgment is coming and damnation is possible. He debates the leaders of the Jews. He combats the Devil. He miraculously feeds 5,000 people. He heals the sick, the blind, and the paralyzed. He raises the dead. He predicts that He will be rejected and killed. He predicts that His disciples will be resisted and persecuted. The leaders of the Jews make plans against Him.

In all four Gospels, there is agreement about titles that Jesus lets others call Him or that He calls Himself because they accurately describe

---

[167] *CCC*, 535-537.
[168] *CCC*, 608.
[169] *CCC*, 531-534.

The Fullness of Life

Him: Lord, which the Jews had called God alone;[170] Son of God;[171] Christ/Messiah; Son of Man; Rabbi/Teacher; and Prophet.

All four Gospels agree on the following about Jesus' disciples. He has many disciples/followers. He chooses the Twelve Apostles to be the leaders of the rest of His disciples. He chooses Peter, one of the Twelve Apostles, to be the leader of the rest of the Twelve Apostles. Women ministered to Jesus' needs, the only one of whom mentioned by name in all four Gospels is Mary Magdalene. Peter, James, and John are fishermen.

All four Gospels agree on the following about the end of Jesus' physical presence on earth. Jesus makes a triumphant entry into Jerusalem. With the Twelve Apostles, He eats the Last Supper at which He predicts that Judas will betray Him and that Peter will deny Him. Jesus is betrayed by Judas and arrested. Peter does deny Jesus three times. Jesus is put on trial by the Sanhedrin, the council of Jewish leaders, which is led by Caiaphas. Then He is judged by Pilate, who has Him crucified on the day before the Sabbath. The Sabbath is on Saturday so Jesus is crucified on Friday. Jesus is buried in a tomb cut from a rocky hillside that is sealed with a great stone. Jesus rises from the dead on the day after the Sabbath, and so on Sunday. He is seen by, talks with, and eats with some of His disciples.

All four Gospels agree that Jesus taught that the world will end and that He will return in glory to judge humanity.

An episode or detail from the life of Jesus that is not in all four Gospels IS still important, e.g., only John's Gospel has Jesus' miracle at the wedding feast at Cana, Jesus raising Lazarus from the dead, and Jesus washing the feet of the Apostles at the Last Supper. Remember that the Four Gospels have different emphases that do not contradict each other, but complement/complete each other.

WHAT ARE IMPORTANT POINTS ABOUT THE PASSION OF JESUS?

In the context of Jesus' life, the word *Passion* means what it originally meant in Latin: Suffering. The same Latin root that gives us the English word *passion* also gives us the English noun *patient* that we use for

---

[170] *CCC*, 446-451.
[171] *CCC*, 441-445.

someone needing medical care because he or she is suffering. So "the Passion of Jesus" means "the Suffering of Jesus."

In **Mark 14:12-72**: The night before Jesus dies, He eats the Last Supper with the Twelve Apostles.[172] The meal that they eat at the Last Supper is the annual Passover meal that the Chosen People had been eating since the Exodus. At that meal, Jesus says that the bread they are eating is His Body and the wine they are drinking is His Blood.

After the Last Supper, Jesus and the Apostles go to the Garden of Gethsemane.[173] Jesus prays to His Father that He does not want to die, but He prays that His Father's will be done. Jesus freely choses to accept His death.[174] He is betrayed by Judas, arrested, and taken to the highest Jewish authority, which is a council called the Sanhedrin, led by the high priest.

The Sanhedrin finds Jesus guilty of blasphemy/disrespecting God because Jesus does not deny (to the leaders of the religion that believes in one God) that He is the Son of God, which would make Him divine; and so they sentence Him to death.[175] Jesus is only innocent of the Sanhedrin's charge if He really is the Son of God. Outside in the courtyard Peter denies that he knows Jesus three times.

In **Mt 27**: The leaders of the Jews take Jesus to the Roman governor named Pilate. Jesus does not deny that He is the King of the Jews, and so the Roman charge against Jesus is not blasphemy, which is a religious charge, but rebellion against the Roman emperor, which is a political charge. Jesus is only innocent of the Roman charge if His Kingdom really is not "of this world" (Jn 18:36).

---

[172] *CCC*, 610-611.
[173] *CCC*, 612.
[174] *CCC*, 609.
[175] *CCC*, 595-596.

The Fullness of Life

Jesus is tortured by getting scourged/whipped and having a crown of thorns put on his head in mockery of His claim to be a King with a Kingdom.

Jesus dies by being hanged on a cross, an event called the Crucifixion. Over Jesus' head, his executioners place the Roman charge against Him in an attempt to mock Him: "This is Jesus, the King of the Jews," which is abbreviated in Latin as "INRI."

Jesus' dead body is requested by Joseph of Arimathea, who buries it in his own new tomb.[176] The leaders of the Jews get Roman guards for Jesus' tomb so that His disciples cannot steal His body to pretend that Jesus rose from the dead as Jesus said He would.

WHAT IS *THE MOST IMPORTANT POINT* ABOUT THE DEATH OF JESUS?

The most important point about the death of Jesus is that it saves us from our sins.[177] All sinners throughout history are to blame for Jesus' Crucifixion and His entire Passion.[178]

Wrongs must be righted by returning things to the way they were before the wrong, e.g., if I steal your wallet, you won't be satisfied if I feel bad about it or even if I apologize to you, but only when I give your wallet back to you. So the wrong done to God by Original Sin and our own personal sins must be righted.

In order to right the wrong humanity commits when it rejects God's perfect love, it takes perfect love to repair our relationship with God and put things back the way they were before sin. Perfect love can only be given for humanity by someone who is both God and human and who takes upon Himself the guilt of all even though He Himself is innocent and pays the penalty that we need to pay.

---

[176] *CCC*, 624-637.
[177] *CCC*, 599-606, 613-618.
[178] *CCC*, 597-598.

That perfect love from humanity to God could only be given by Jesus' death on the cross. If Jesus is not God, then His death does NOT save us from our sins and is only a sad story.

Jesus' words over the bread and wine at the Last Supper anticipated His saving death. When Jesus said (and as the priest repeats at Mass when he consecrates the bread/host into the Body of Christ), "This is My Body, which will be given up for you," He meant that His body would be given up on the cross for us. When Jesus said (and as the priest repeats at Mass when he consecrates the wine into the Blood of Christ), "This is My Blood, which will be poured out for you and for many for the forgiveness of sins," He meant that His blood would be poured out on the cross for the forgiveness of sins.

Although Jesus died for our sins, we can NOT do whatever we want and still gain eternal salvation. Jesus' death "opens the gates" of the Kingdom which had been "closed" by the Fall, but each human being must choose (intentionally or unintentionally) to "go through" those gates and enter the Kingdom.

WHAT ARE IMPORTANT POINTS ABOUT THE RESURRECTION OF JESUS?

In **Lk 23:55-24:12**, Jesus rises from the dead, an event called the Resurrection, on the first day of the Jewish week, which in our calendar is Sunday. The first disciples to learn that Jesus rose were Mary Magdalene and other women. When they tell the Eleven Apostles that Jesus rose from the dead, the Eleven do not believe them. Peter goes to Jesus' tomb to see for himself.

In **Lk 24:13-49**: Jesus then appears to the Apostles. First, He appears to the two disciples walking to Emmaus. They do not recognize Him. Jesus explains to them how the Old Testament ("Moses and all the prophets") refers to Him. These two disciples finally know it is Jesus when He takes bread, blesses it, breaks it, and gives it to them.

The Fullness of Life

When Jesus suddenly appears in the midst of the Eleven Apostles, they think they are seeing a ghost so He shows them that He has flesh and bones and He eats fish. Again, Jesus explains how He fulfills the Old Testament.

Jesus' last instruction to them is that repentance in His name must be preached to all the nations, which keeps God's third promise to Abraham that all nations will find blessing in him because he began preparing the way for Jesus, and that they should await the Holy Spirit.

WHAT IS *THE MOST IMPORTANT POINT* ABOUT THE RESURRECTION OF JESUS?

The most important point about the Resurrection is that Jesus rises NOT to the same life He had before He was killed, BUT to the fullness of life that can ONLY be had by entering the Kingdom of God.[179] Jesus' own gospel had been that the Kingdom of God is coming. The Kingdom comes for Jesus when He rises from the dead. When Jesus rises from the dead, He rises into the Kingdom of God. Jesus' Resurrection fully reveals what the Kingdom is.

When Jesus rises from the dead, His immortal soul is reunited with a now-immortal body that will never get old, never need food and other necessities, never get sick and injured, and never die again. After Jesus rises from the dead, He has NOT only a natural existence with a physical body, NOT only a spiritual/supernatural existence like a ghost without a body, BUT both a physical and a supernatural existence at the same time. Even though there is something physical about Jesus' resurrected body, Jesus is no longer bound by space and time. Jesus has a ***glorified body***. He has perfect human existence and therefore perfect human happiness. This kind of rising from the dead is the first of its kind in human history.

---

[179] *CCC*, 645-646.

Jesus' Resurrection completes His Revelation of the Kingdom that began with His teaching and miracles.[180] Jesus reveals that the Kingdom of God is far more than a new era of greatness for the Chosen People that would be like what they had experienced during the reign of King David. Just as no one expected the Messiah to be God, no one expected the Kingdom to be perfect existence and happiness. There is no greater Revelation than the Resurrection which, more than anything else, shows who God is and what God wants for humanity. The Resurrection completes the Revelation that had begun with Abraham. The Resurrection is the most important event in human history.[181]

Jesus' Resurrection also completes His Revelation that He is God.[182] "In times past, God spoke in partial and various ways to our ancestors through the prophets; in these last days, He spoke to us through a Son, Whom He made heir of all things and through Whom He created the universe" (Hebrews 1:1-2).

All of this means:

- Jesus Christ is more alive now—2,000 years after His Crucifixion—than He was before He was murdered.

- Jesus Christ is the most important person in human history.

- Jesus Christ wants to be the most important person in your life, have a friendship with you, and lead you to the fullness of life in the Kingdom of God.

---

[180] *CCC*, 652, 654.
[181] *CCC*, 638-644, 647.
[182] *CCC*, 651, 653.

PERSONAL FAITH RESPONSE

Check any statements below that describe you.

In order to LIVE FULLY:

1. _____I agree with the objective truth in this chapter.

2. _____Like John the Baptist, I will "baptize," but what I will "baptize" are the non-religious things in my life so as to make them acceptable to God, e.g., I will make my studies, activities, and relationships acceptable to God.

3. _____Also like John the Baptist, I will give witness that Jesus is Lord and Savior.

4. _____I will try to imitate Jesus in the Garden of Gethsemane and do what the Father wants when it is not what I want.

5. _____I will live my life in thanksgiving to Jesus for dying for my sins so that I could have eternal life.

6. _____I will make sacrifices for others as Jesus made the ultimate sacrifice for me.

7. _____I will take responsibility for entering the Kingdom now that Jesus' death has opened its gates for me.

8. _____I will make my relationship with Jesus Christ the most important relationship in my life.

VOCABULARY

John the Baptist: The last and the greatest prophet before Jesus who helps people prepare for the coming of the Kingdom by baptizing them.

The Passion of Jesus: The suffering of Jesus.

The Last Supper: The meal Jesus eats with the Twelve Apostles the night before He dies, which is also the Passover meal.

The Garden of Gethsemane: Where Jesus is betrayed and arrested.

The Sanhedrin: The highest Jewish authority which is a council led by the high priest.

Blasphemy: Disrespecting God.

The Crucifixion: Jesus' death on the cross.

Pilate: The Roman governor, the highest Roman authority on the scene.

Scourging: Whipping.

Joseph of Arimathea: The one who requests Jesus' dead body and puts it in his own new tomb.

The Resurrection: Jesus' rising from the dead.

Glorified body: The immortal body that is both physical and supernatural that Jesus has after He rises from the dead.

Part 5: What Does God Reveal through the New Testament?

Chapter VI:

DOES REASON SUPPORT FAITH IN THE RESURRECTION?

SOURCES

- Peter Kreeft and Ronald Tacelli, SJ, *Handbook of Christian Apologetics* (InterVarsity Press, 1994), Chapter 8.
- http://www.catholic.com/magazine/articles/are-the-gospels-myth

HOW CAN WE USE REASON TO KNOW THE RESURRECTION IS REAL?

Recall that Faith is knowledge that comes from God by accepting Divine Revelation and Reason is knowledge that comes from the human ability to figure something out, examples of which are History, Math, Science, Economics, and Psychology.

Faith in the Resurrection is NOT irrational/unreasonable, BUT supra-rational/beyond-rational. Reason involves reasoning, which is having reasons/being logical/making sense/making an argument/proving/making a case. We cannot prove directly that the Resurrection is real. However, there is a process of reasoning known as the process of elimination, which proves something INDIRECTLY by ruling out/eliminating the alternatives, e.g., because the answer must be A, B, C, D, or E; and because it's not A, B, C, or D; therefore it must be E.

Professors Peter Kreeft and Ronald Tacelli, SJ, of Boston College have worked out how the process of elimination can be applied to proving indirectly that the Resurrection happened:

> Because there are only five possibilities about the Resurrection—one PRO-Resurrection (the Resurrection DID happen) possibility and four ANTI-Resurrection (the Resurrection did NOT happen) possibilities,
>
> and because only one of these five possibilities can be true,
>
> therefore if the four ANTI-Resurrection possibilities are FALSE,
>
> then the Resurrection DID happen   .

This chapter is heavily indebted to their work, cited above.[183] By using their process, we will find that there are reasons that the four anti-Resurrection theories are false. We will use Reason, NOT Faith. So we will find that Faith in the Resurrection is reasonable. Faith in the Resurrection makes sense. It is NOT stupid or irrational to believe Jesus rose from the dead.

One more note. Concluding that a particular anti-Resurrection theory is false does NOT require agreement with all of the reasons against it. It only requires agreeing that there are enough reasons against it.[184]

---

[183] Professors Kreeft and Tacelli's entire *Handbook of Christian Apologetics* is highly recommended for more in-depth treatment of other topics covered in this book.

[184] This is known in Logic as an inductive argument instead of a deductive argument. In a deductive argument, the conclusion necessarily follows from its premises/reasons. In a strong inductive argument, the conclusion probably follows from its premises; and in a weak inductive argument, the conclusion possibly follows from its premises. The word *only* in any process of elimination makes it a deductive argument, which is the case in our process of elimination above. Each of the following arguments against an anti-Resurrection theory is a strongly inductive argument.

The Fullness of Life

WHAT ARE THE FIVE POSSIBILITIES ABOUT THE RESURRECTION?

It might be easier to begin with a diagram and then it explain it below.

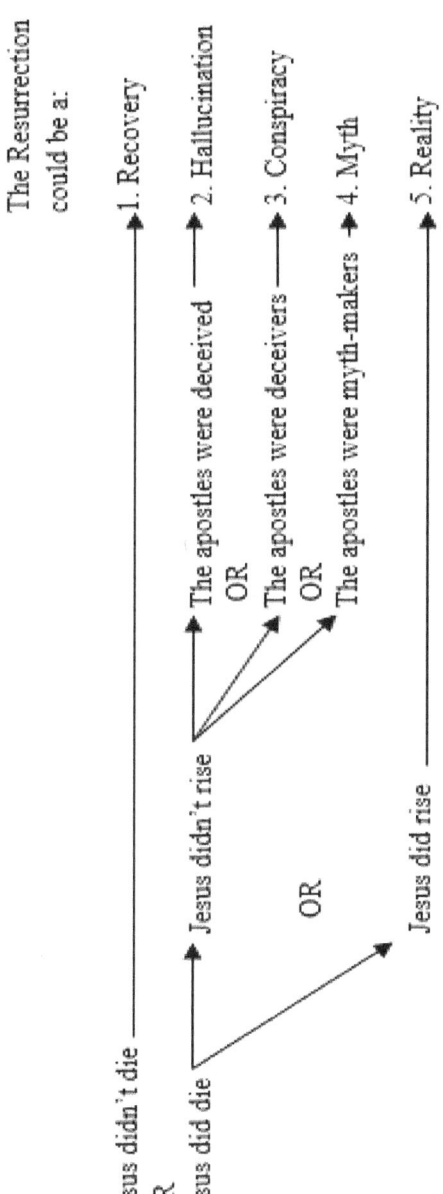

So one ANTI-Resurrection possibility is **Recovery**: Jesus did not die on the cross but only seemed to be dead. Since His apostles thought Jesus was dead, they buried Him in the tomb. While Jesus was in the tomb, He recovered from His injuries. The "Resurrection" is nothing more than Jesus surprising His apostles when He showed up after they thought He was dead—the recovery of a near-dead person, not a dead person rising to new life beyond space and time.

The second ANTI-Resurrection possibility is **Hallucination**: Jesus did die on the cross, but He did not rise from the dead. Instead, His apostles so wanted Him not to be dead that they imagined that He rose from the dead and believed their imagination. The "Resurrection" is a hallucination.

The third ANTI-Resurrection possibility is **Conspiracy**: Jesus did die on the cross, and His apostles knew He did not rise from the dead, but they agreed among themselves to lie to everyone else and say that He rose from the dead. The "Resurrection" is a conspiracy.

The fourth ANTI-Resurrection possibility is **Myth**: Jesus did die on the cross, and his apostles knew he did not rise from the dead. They created a myth that Jesus rose from the dead in order to express figuratively how much Jesus meant to them, which they never intended to be taken literally, but their myth became misinterpreted as literally true.

The fifth possibility, which is the only PRO-Resurrection possibility, is **Reality**: Jesus did die on the cross, and He did rise from the dead with a glorified body. The Resurrection is an objectively real event.

WHAT ARE THE REASONS AGAINST THE *RECOVERY* THEORY?

Here are the reasons for concluding that Jesus really did die on the cross.

Ancient anti-Christian sources (Tacitus, Seutonius, Pliny, Josephus, and the Talmud) support the fact that Jesus of Nazareth was crucified under Pontius Pilate and no expert in ancient history doubts it.

Jesus could not have survived his crucifixion since the procedure of being crucified made survival impossible. Furthermore, the Roman soldiers assigned to crucify someone would have been put to death for

The Fullness of Life

failing their job if the crucified person did not die, and we can assume that the Roman soldiers assigned to crucify Jesus did not want to be put to death. There is no record of anyone ever surviving crucifixion.

The Romans wanted to get the Crucifixion over with, and they broke the two thieves' legs since the two thieves were not dead yet and breaking their legs would quickly kill them; but the Romans did not break Jesus' legs since they were sure he was already dead (Jn 19:31-33).

When Jesus was stabbed, blood and water came from his side – a sure sign of death due to collapsed lungs (Jn 19:34-35).

Here are the reasons that Jesus, had He not died on the cross, could not possibly have recovered from being crucified.

After Jesus was brutally tortured as well as crucified, He could not have survived without medical treatment or water for the approximately 39 hours (3 PM Friday to 6 AM Sunday) that He was in His tomb.

A near-dead, severely wounded man would have had great difficulty getting out of the shroud in which he was wrapped (Mk 15:46; Jn 19:38-42). There is no way He could have moved the stone closing his tomb (Mt 27:60; Mk 15:46) or overpowered the Roman guards that Pilate had stationed there (Mt 27:62-66).

The New Testament writers portray the Risen Jesus as NOT having a merely recovered/revived/resuscitated body, but as having a supernatural/glorified/perfected body. If Jesus had merely recovered and not risen from the dead in His tomb, then He—a near-dead, severely wounded man who would have staggered out of his tomb—would not have been worshipped by the apostles as the Risen One who had entered the Kingdom, conquered death, and is God.

Jesus' Roman and Jewish enemies would have done everything they could to find Him once His apostles started preaching that He had risen, and yet there is no evidence that anyone except Jesus' apostles ever saw Him after His burial even though sooner or later someone besides His apostles would have seen Him if He were simply a person who recovered from near-death.

If Jesus only recovered from His crucifixion, then He would have really died sooner or later. Jesus' body has never been found even though Jesus' enemies would have resorted to any means to find it, including torturing His followers, once His apostles started preaching that He had risen.

WHAT ARE THE REASONS AGAINST THE *HALLUCINATION THEORY?*

An hallucination would explain only the post-resurrection appearances but not the empty tomb, the rolled-away stone, and the missing body. If the apostles were hallucinating, Jesus' corpse would have still been in His tomb and the stone would still be closing His tomb, yet the tomb was empty, the stone was rolled away, and the body was missing (Mt 28:1-8; Lk 24:36-43; Jn 20:1-10).

If the apostles were hallucinating, Jesus' corpse would have still been in his tomb and the Roman guard would have still been posted, and yet after sunrise on Easter there was no more Roman guard at his tomb (Mt 28:11-15) because there was no body to guard.

The apostles were aware that they might be hallucinating, they did not want to hallucinate (Mk 16:9-13; Lk 24:36-43), and so they proved to themselves they were not hallucinating by looking in the tomb (Lk 24:11-12; Jn 20:1-10).

No two people have the same hallucination and yet over 500 people saw Jesus at the same time after His burial (1 Corinthians 15:3-8).

Hallucinations usually last minutes, not 40 days (Acts 1:3), which was the length of time Jesus' apostles saw Him after He rose (until the Ascension).

Hallucinations cannot take food, eat it, and make it disappear, but Jesus took food, ate it, and made it disappear (Lk 24:42-43; Jn 21:1-14).

Hallucinations cannot be touched, but Jesus was touched (Mt 28:9; Lk 24:39; Jn 20:27).

If the apostles were hallucinating, they would not have gotten Jesus' body and hidden it but would have left it in the tomb, and yet Jesus' body was not found in the tomb by His enemies.

WHAT ARE THE REASONS AGAINST THE *CONSPIRACY* THEORY?

Those who said they saw Jesus risen from the dead were not known to be liars or have bad character but to be loving, virtuous people.

The apostles would not have been loyal to Jesus by doing something (lying/conspiring) that He would not have approved, just like George Washington's admirers have not been loyal to him by trying to get America to become a colony of Great Britain or Abraham Lincoln's admirers have not been loyal to him by trying to bring back slavery and trying to get the South to secede from the Union.

There was no motive/advantage for the apostles to lie that Jesus rose from the dead. Preaching the Resurrection got the apostles scorned, hated, persecuted, imprisoned, tortured, exiled, or executed in horrible ways (stoned, crucified, stabbed, beheaded).

Not one of the over 500 apostles who said they saw Jesus after he had risen, even when tortured and facing horrible execution, ever "cracked" and confessed to a conspiracy.

Jesus' enemies never produced His body, which would have been there somewhere if it had not been glorified and ascended.

In order for the apostles to have gotten away with the conspiracy that Jesus "rose from the dead," they would have had to get rid of Jesus' body, but the apostles could not have gotten away with stealing his body since they could not have overpowered the Roman guard.

The apostles could not have gotten away with the "lie" that Jesus rose by proclaiming it a mere seven weeks after the Crucifixion (on Pentecost) at the very scene of the "crime" (Jerusalem) since there would have been too many "eyewitnesses" to the "truth" that Jesus did not rise to disprove the "lie."

WHAT ARE THE REASONS AGAINST THE *MYTH* THEORY?

This is the theory that is currently most popular with those college professors who do not believe in the Resurrection and worship the cleverness of their own minds instead of worshipping the Truth.

There was no good reason the New Testament writers would have written a myth glorifying Jesus if He did not rise from the dead because Jesus would have severely disappointed them since He led them to believe He was God yet ended up crucified.

First Century people (both Christians and non-Christians) knew the difference between myth and fact; and Luke (Lk 1:1-4), John (Jn 21:24-25), Peter (2 Pt 1:16), and Paul (Galatians 1:11-12; 1 Timothy 1:3-7; 2 Timothy 4:3-4) explicitly affirm that the Resurrection is a fact and not a myth.

There was not enough time for the New Testament writers to be misinterpreted since their writings were being read and quoted by others while they were still alive.

The first witnesses of the Resurrection were women (Mt 28:1-10; Mk 16:1-8; Lk 24:1-11; Jn 20:1-2) in a society which did not accept women as legal witnesses, and myth-makers would not have based their myth on "unreliable" sources, whereas those committed to the truth hold to the truth no matter how socially or legally unaccepted it is.

There was no motive/advantage for the apostles to spread their "myth"—preaching the Resurrection got the apostles scorned, hated, persecuted, imprisoned, tortured, exiled, or executed in horrible ways (stoned, crucified, stabbed, beheaded).

WHAT IS REASONABLE TO CONCLUDE?

Because these five possibilities—one pro-Resurrection and four anti-Resurrection—are the only possibilities about the Resurrection,

And because only one of them can be true (due to the Law of Non-contradiction),

Therefore it is reasonable to conclude that the Resurrection is real since the four anti-Resurrection possibilities are false.

Although Faith in the Resurrection is still needed for us to know that it is real, we now see that there are good reasons to believe in the Resurrection and that believers are not Neanderthals trying to live in a pre-scientific era. The truth of Jesus' Resurrection can be discovered by developing a personal relationship with Him in which He becomes the most real and important person in one's life, as He has for countless people over the last two thousand years.

Alleluia! Alleluia! He is risen, as He said! Love and truth have conquered evil! Jesus Christ is Lord and God! Alleluia!

PERSONAL FAITH RESPONSE

Check any statements below that describe you.

In order to LIVE FULLY:

1. _____I agree with the objective truth in this chapter.

2. _____I will be confident that Jesus rose from the dead in a glorified body.

3. _____I will continually grow in my relationship with Jesus.

4. _____I will be confident that love and truth ultimately conquer evil.

5. _____I will be able to give reasons for accepting the Resurrection when my faith is questioned.

VOCABULARY

The Recovery Theory: The false theory that Jesus did not die on the cross but only seemed to be dead. The "Resurrection" is nothing more than Jesus surprising His apostles when He showed up after He recovered from the attempt to kill Him.

The Hallucination Theory: The false theory that the apostles hallucinated that Jesus rose from the dead.

The Conspiracy Theory: The false theory that the apostles conspired to deceive people that Jesus rose from the dead.

The **Myth Theory**: The false theory that the apostles created a myth that Jesus rose from the dead in order to express figuratively how much Jesus meant to them, which they never intended to be taken literally, but their myth became misinterpreted as literally true.

Part 5: What Does God Reveal through the New Testament?

Chapter VII:

WHAT IS THE NEW COVENANT?

SOURCES

- Pope Benedict XVI, *Jesus of Nazareth*, Volumes 1-3, (Doubleday).
- Scott Hahn, Gen. Ed., *Catholic Bible Dictionary* (Doubleday, 2009), "Covenant," "Freedom," "Judgment," "Kingdom," "Law," "Love," "Parousia," "Resurrection."

HOW DID JESUS' PHYSICAL PRESENCE ON EARTH END?

In **Acts 1:1-12**, after Jesus rises from the dead, He appears to the Apostles for 40 days speaking to them about what else? The Kingdom. The Apostles ask Jesus if He will now establish the Kingdom, and Jesus replies that it is not for them to know.

Jesus' physical presence on earth ends when He is then taken up into Heaven, an event called the Ascension.[185] Two men dressed in white (angels) tell the Apostles that Jesus will return in the same way. After the Ascension, Jesus continues to have and will always have a glorified body.

In **Jn 13:31-14:7**, Jesus explains that He must leave His followers in order to prepare a place for them.

---

[185] *CCC*, 659-667.

WHAT WILL HAPPEN WHEN JESUS RETURNS?

In **Mt 24:30-31**, Jesus teaches that He will return to Earth after His Ascension.[186] Two names for this event are the Second Coming (after Jesus' First Coming to earth as an infant) and the Last Day (since it will be the last day of human history).[187]

In **1 Cor 15:12-26, 33-56**, it is revealed that when Jesus returns, everyone else will have the opportunity to enter the Kingdom of God.[188] At the Second Coming, both those who are living and those who are dead will be transformed to have supernatural bodies, like the body Jesus has had since His Resurrection. Those who are dead will have their souls reunited with their dead bodies which will be transformed into supernatural bodies. Those who are living will have their natural bodies transformed into supernatural bodies without dying first. As we say in the Nicene Creed, Jesus will "come again in glory to judge the living and the dead and His kingdom will have no end" and at the end of the Creed "I look forward to the resurrection of the dead (those who have already died)."

In **Rev 21:1-8**, it is revealed that when Jesus returns, what will happen to individual human bodies will also happen to the whole universe—it will be transformed into a physical yet supernatural reality.[189] In the Kingdom all that is true and good in this life will be magnified and perfected as anything in this life that is false and bad will be transformed or eliminated. The Second Coming will not so much be the end of the world—it is NOT that the world will no longer exist at all after the Second Coming—as much as the Second Coming will be the end of the world as we now know it with imperfections and evil. The Kingdom will be a combination of a new Heaven and a new earth, in which God will dwell with His people. In the Kingdom, there will be no more death or mourning, wailing or pain. As we also say at the end of the Nicene Creed, "I look forward to . . . the life of the world to come (in the Kingdom)."

---

[186] As He did in all of Mt 24-25 (and Mk 13 and Lk 21); Mt 16:27 (and Mk 8:38 and Lk 9:26); Mt 26:64 (and Mk 14:62); Jn 5:28-29; Jn 6:40, 44, 54. This is echoed many times in the rest of the New Testament.

[187] Other names are: the Parousia, the Eschaton, the Apocalypse, the End of Time, the Day of the Lord, Judgment Day, and Doomsday.

[188] *CCC*, 655, 678-679, 988-1001, 1038-1041.

[189] *CCC*, 1042-1050.

The Fullness of Life

This passage, along with so many others in the New Testament, adds to what Jesus had consistently warned about in His teaching: Hell.[190] After the Second Coming there will be the second death, which is Hell, the destination of the "cowards, unfaithful, depraved, murderers, unchaste, sorcerers, idol-worshipers, and deceivers of every sort." There will be something physical about Hell. Both those in the Kingdom and those in Hell will have transformed, supernatural bodies—not only souls—for all eternity.

In **1 Cor 13:9-12**, "When the perfect comes" and "then" refer to the Second Coming. It was Original Sin, and NOT God, that pulled the curtain/veil between us humans and God and that gave us a fallen/weakened human nature which is not able/not "equipped" to see God face-to-face/to know God directly/to experience God fully. At the Second Coming (and at the time of death before then), the curtain/veil between us humans and God will be completely pulled back.

In effect, the Garden of Eden will be restored in the Kingdom, where there will be perfect human existence and perfect human happiness that include:

- A perfect relationship between every human and God.

- A perfect relationship within every human between the mind, the will, the emotions, and the body.

- A perfect relationships between every human and every other human.

- A perfect relationship between humans and nature.

Jesus came that we might have the fullness of life (Jn 10:10)—life in superabundance, life overflowing, bounteous life. This is the will of God—what God wanted for the first humans, what God has always wanted and still wants for all human beings, and what was lost by the Fall. This fullness of life can only be had in the Kingdom of God. All of this is what Jesus taught us to pray for in the "Our Father"/"Lord's Prayer" when we pray "Thy Kingdom come, Thy will be done on earth as it is in Heaven." The Kingdom of God will completely come when God's will is done on earth as

---

[190] *CCC*, 1033-1038.

it is already being done in Heaven.

WHAT IS GOD'S PLAN FOR THE TIME BETWEEN THE FIRST COMING OF CHRIST AND THE SECOND COMING OF CHRIST?

In **Mt 13:31-32**, God's plan is for the Kingdom to start small like a mustard seed and grow until it is full-grown at the Second Coming, and the seed that grows into the Kingdom is the Church that Jesus founded.[191]

In **Jn 14:25-27**, God's plan is to send the Holy Spirit to teach the Church and to remind its members of Jesus' teaching until the Second Coming.

Understanding that we live in the time between the First Coming and the Second Coming also helps us understand why there is evil.[192] In **Mt 13:24-30, 36-43**, the sower/planter of the good seed is Jesus; the good seed is the Church; the weeds are those who cooperate with the Devil, who is the sower of the weeds; the harvest is the Second Coming; being burned in the fiery furnace is Hell; and the sower's barn is the Kingdom. There is evil because the Second Coming has not taken place.

In **Mt 24:1-28**, Jesus warns that there will be a final unleashing of evil before His Second Coming. This evil will include the deception of an Antichrist, many losing the Faith, and persecution of those who keep the Faith.[193]

In **Mt 24:36-44**, Jesus tells us that it is not for us to know when the Second Coming will take place.[194] As St. Paul says, it will come "like a thief at night" (1 Thessalonians 5:2).

WHAT IS THE GOSPEL?

Gospel literally means "good news." Jesus' gospel during His public ministry, as we see in **Mk 1:15**, was that the Kingdom of God is coming. And, of course, a Gospel is a genre of New Testament literature in which

---

[191] *CCC*, 668-670.
[192] *CCC*, 671-672.
[193] *CCC*, 675-677.
[194] *CCC*, 673, 997-1001, 1040.

we find Jesus' gospel as well as His actions, Passion, and Resurrection.

There is a third meaning of *Gospel*: "the essence of Christian Faith." In light of everything we covered in this book, we can now summarize the Gospel/the essence of the Christian Faith as:

- Christ has died and Christ is risen to begin the Kingdom of God, and

- Christ will come again to complete/finalize the Kingdom of God.

This IS good news, great news, the best possible news! It is such good news that some, sadly, find it too good to believe, even as they seek, knowingly or unknowingly, the fullness of life.

WHAT IS THE NEW COVENANT?

The Old Covenant was the covenant God made, especially through Abraham, Moses, and David, with the Chosen People before Christ. God's part was to choose Abraham's people to be His Chosen People and thus to make them a nation great in number, with their own land, with an everlasting royal house, and a blessing to the other nations. The Chosen People's part was to be faithful to God by obeying His Law, especially the Ten Commandments.

The New Covenant is the covenant God makes to fulfill the Old Covenant through Jesus Christ with the new People of God.[195] God's part is to bring His Kingdom to all the nations who can now become the People of God. The People of God's part is to follow Jesus Christ to the Kingdom of God.

HOW DOES THE PARABLE OF THE VINEYARD TENANTS SUMMARIZE THE NEW COVENANT?

The prophet Isaiah had told the "Vineyard Song" (**Is 5:1-7**) in order to summarize God's relationship to the Chosen People in the Old Covenant. In **Mk 12:1-9**, Jesus tells the rest of the story. As in Is 5:1-7, the vineyard owner in the parable symbolizes God and the work of the owner (planting,

---

[195] *CCC*, 577, 611, 762, 781.

etc.) symbolizes God's faithfulness to the covenant. In Mk 12:1-9, it is better to see that the vineyard is the Old Covenant and the tenant farmers symbolize members of the Chosen People of the Old Covenant. In the parable, the badly treated representatives of the vineyard owner symbolize the prophets God sent before Jesus. The beloved son of the vineyard owner who is killed by the tenants symbolizes Jesus. The others to whom the owner will give the vineyard symbolize the new People of God, the Christians, to whom God will give a New Covenant.

The tenants more accurately symbolize those members of the Chosen People who rejected Jesus unlike those members of the Chosen People who became followers of Jesus like Peter, the other Apostles, Mary Magdalen, Paul, and thousands of others (e.g., Acts 2:41).

WHAT ARE SOME KEY EXAMPLES OF HOW THE NEW TESTAMENT FUFILLS THE OLD TESTAMENT?

1. Instead of being a purely human Messiah,	1. Jesus is a Messiah who is both God and man.
2. Instead of being a king like David and Solomon who brings an era of greatness to the Promised Land,	2. Jesus brings the Kingdom of God.
3. Instead of inspiring the Chosen People to have new enthusiasm for the old covenant,	3. Jesus establishes a new covenant, as He said at the Last Supper.
4. Instead of saving only the Chosen People who are the biological children of Abraham with Twelve Tribes as their foundation,	4. Jesus establishes a new People of God, which is the Catholic Church that has Twelve Apostles as its foundation and that is open to all people who, through Baptism, become the spiritual children of Abraham.
5. Instead of continuing the old Passover Meal that had unleavened bread and that was first eaten before their	5. Jesus establishes a new Passover Meal, which is the Eucharist that has unleavened

freedom from slavery by people who were saved from death by the blood of a sacrificed lamb on their door frames,	bread which becomes the Body of Jesus and wine which becomes the Blood of Jesus and that is eaten before their freedom in the Kingdom by people for whom the Lamb of God/Jesus was sacrificed to save them from sin, evil, and death itself.

PERSONAL FAITH RESPONSE

Check any statements below that describe you.

In order to LIVE FULLY:

1. _____I agree with the objective truth in this chapter.

2. _____I will live every day as though it is the day I will meet God face-to-face.

3. _____I will pray the "Our Father" thoughtfully.

4. _____I will follow Christ in the Church He founded.

5. _____I will celebrate the Eucharist at least once a week on the day He rose from the dead.

6. _____I will help as many people as possible enter the Kingdom.

VOCABULARY

Ascension: The event when Jesus is taken up into Heaven and His physical presence on earth ends.

Second Coming: The event when Christ returns in glory to judge and the living and the dead and complete the Kingdom of God.

Last Day: Another name for the Second Coming because it is the last day of human history.

New Covenant: The covenant God makes to fulfill the Old Covenant through Jesus Christ with the new People of God.

The Gospel: (1) The good news that Jesus Himself preached that the Kingdom of God is coming, (2) a kind of book in the New Testament, and (3) the essence of Christian Faith that Christ has died and is risen to begin the Kingdom of God and Christ will come again to finalize the Kingdom.

Unit 5: What Does God Reveal through the New Testament?

Chapter VIII:

WHAT ARE OTHER KEY PASSAGES IN THE NEW TESTAMENT?

WHAT ARE OTHER KEY PASSAGES FROM THE GOSPELS ON JESUS' TEACHINGS?

- Mt 5-7: The Sermon on the Mount.

- Mt 10:26-32: Courage during persecution.

- Mt 18:21-22: Forgiving.

- Mt 22:34-40: The Two Great Commandments.

- Mt 24:4-44: The end of this world.

- Mt 25:31-46: The Last Judgment.

- Lk 9:23-24: Jesus' followers must take up the cross.

- Lk 12:2-9: Giving witness.

- Lk 12:51-53: Not peace, but a sword.

- Lk 20:20-26: Render to Caesar.

- Jn 3:16-21: God so loved the world.

- Jn 4:1-42: The Samaritan Woman.

WHAT ARE OTHER KEY PASSAGES FROM THE GOSPELS ON JESUS' PARABLES?

- Mt 13:44-46: The Hidden Treasure and the Pearl of Great Price.

- Mt 24:42-44: The Thief in the Night.

- Mk 4:1-20: The Sower.

- Lk 10:25-37: The Good Samaritan.

- Lk 10:25-37: The Rich Fool.

- Lk 15:11-32: The Prodigal Son.

- Lk 18:9-14: The Pharisee and the Publican.

WHAT ARE OTHER KEY PASSAGES FROM THE GOSPELS ON EVENTS IN JESUS' LIFE?

- Mt 16:13-23: Jesus makes Peter the rock on which He will build His church.

- Mk 3:13-19: Jesus gives authority to twelve of His disciples.

- Lk 4:1-13: The Temptation of Jesus.

- Lk 4:31-37: Jesus casts out a demon.

- Jn 2:13-17: Jesus drives out the money-changers from the Temple.

WHAT ARE OTHER KEY PASSAGES FROM THE GOSPELS ON JESUS' MIRACLES?

- Jn 2:1-12: The Wedding at Cana.

- Lk 5:17-26: The paralytic.

- Mt 8:5-13: The centurion's servant.

- Mt 14:22-33: Walking on water.

- Mk 9:2-8: The Transfiguration.

- Jn 9:1-41: The man born blind.

- Jn 11:1-57: The raising of Lazarus.

WHAT ARE OTHER KEY PASSAGES FROM THE ACTS OF THE APOSTLES?

- 2:1-41: Pentecost.

- 2:42-47; 4:32-37: Life in the early Church.

- 5:17-42: The Twelve on trial.

- 6:1-7: The Twelve need assistants.

- 6:8-7:60: The martyrdom of Stephen.

- 9:1-22: The conversion of Saul.

- 10: The mission to the Gentiles begins.

- 13: Paul's missionary ministry begins.

- 15:1-34: The Council of Jerusalem.

- 17:22-34: Paul in Athens.

WHAT ARE OTHER KEY PASSAGES FROM THE EPISTLES/LETTERS?

- Rom (Romans) 8:14-39: We conquer through Christ, through Whom we are adopted by the Father and receive the Spirit.

- Rom 9:30-11:2: God has not rejected Israel.

- 1 Cor (Corinthians) 6:9-20: Your body is a temple of the Holy Spirit.

- 1 Cor 11:23-32: Origin and meaning of the Eucharist.

- 1 Cor 13: Love.

- 1 Cor 15: The Resurrection of Christ and the resurrection of the dead at the Second Coming.

- 2 Cor 4-5: A model of ministry.

- 2 Cor 8:1-15: Guidance on giving.

- Gal (Galatians) 1:11-2:21: Paul's defense of his criticism of Peter.

- Gal 5:13-6:10: True freedom.

- Ephesians 4:1-23: One body, many gifts.

- Philippians 2:6-11: A beautiful hymn about Christ.

- Colossians 3:5-4:6: How to live.

- 1 Thes (Thessalonians) 4:13-5:11: The Second Coming.

- 2 Thes 1:3-10: God's judgment.

- 1 Tm (Timothy) 1:1-11; 4:1-16, 6:3-16: Against false doctrine.

- 2 Tm 3-4: Paul's reflections on the last days, his own end, and his experience as an apostle.

- Titus 1:5-9: The qualities of a bishop.

- Philemon 8-18: Treat your slave as a brother.

- Heb (Hebrews) 1:1-4: Summary of Divine Revelation.

- Heb 4:12: The word of God.

- Heb 4:14-5:10: Jesus is the great high priest.

- Heb 8:7-9:28: The difference between the Old Covenant and the New Covenant.

- Jas (James) 2:14-26: Faith without works is dead.

- Jas 5:13-18: The sick should be anointed.

- 1 Pt (Peter) 2:4-10: The followers of Christ are God's people.

- 1 Pt 3:13-4:2: On suffering.

- 2 Pt 3:1-16: On those who doubt the Second Coming.

- 1 Jn (John) 2:18-23: Antichrists.

- 1 Jn 4:7-21: Love.

WHAT ARE OTHER KEY PASSAGES FROM THE BOOK OF REVELATION?

- 1:1-11: The context of the book.

- 4:1-11: Worship in Heaven.

- 7:9-17: The triumph of the faithful.

- 12: The woman and the dragon.

- 13: The beasts.

- 19:11-20:10: The triumph of the King.

- 20:11-15: The final judgment.

- 21:1-11: The Kingdom of God completed.

"Behold, I am coming soon.

I bring with me the recompense I will give to each according to his deeds.

I am the Alpha and the Omega, the first and the last, the beginning and the end."

Amen! Come, Lord Jesus!

—Rev 22:12, 20

PART 6:

What Is the Fullness of Revelation?

Chapter I: WHAT IS THE FULLNESS OF WHO IS JESUS?

Chapter II: WHAT IS THE FULLNESS OF WHO GOD IS?

Chapter III: WHAT IS THE FULLNESS OF FOLLOWING JESUS CHRIST?

Chapter IV: WHAT IS THE ROLE OF THE MAGISTERIUM IN THE CHURCH?

Chapter V: WHAT IS THE ROLE OF ST. MARY IN SALVATION HISTORY?

Part 6: What Is the Fullness of Revelation?

Chapter I:
WHAT IS THE FULLNESS OF WHO JESUS IS?

HOW DOES JESUS' CLAIM TO BE GOD FIT IN HISTORY?

Because Jesus claims to be God in the Gospels, and because the Gospel writers knew Jesus better than anyone since then (even someone with a PhD in Theology), therefore Jesus really did claim to be God. In the history of the world, Jesus is the only great religious figure in world history who has ever claimed to be the one true God. Neither Muhammad, nor Confucius, nor Lao Tzu, nor any founder of one of the world's great religions claimed to be divine—not even Buddha, although some Buddhists consider him divine anyway while other Buddhists do not.

Alone among the ancient peoples, the Jews were consistently and significantly monotheists. As we have seen, the Jews living in 30 AD when Jesus was preaching and performing miracles were not expecting that the Messiah would be God. To the good/pious/faithful Jews living in 30 AD, Jesus' claim to be God was very hard to accept.[196]

---

[196] *CCC*, 587-591.

Martin Dybicz

WHAT ARE THE THREE POSSIBILITIES ABOUT WHO JESUS IS?

Are you who you are regardless of what others feel/believe/think about you? Yes, others could be mistaken about you. Does the same hold true for every person you have ever encountered? Yes, you could be mistaken about someone else. In fact, it is true about every person who has ever existed that the reality of one's identity is essentially objective. Just as someone can be mistaken about another, someone can be mistaken about who Jesus is.

"Jesus is God to you, but He is not God to me" is NOT an accurate description of Jesus, BUT an accurate description of what is in two different minds. Jesus cannot both be God and not be God at the same time and in the same way. Jesus either is right about Himself or He is mistaken about Himself.

As C. S. Lewis spelled out in his great classic *Mere Christianity*, there are three logical possibilities about who Jesus is because of His claim to be God—both for those who encountered Jesus in 30 AD and for everyone ever since, including us:

1) When Jesus says He is God, He is wrong about who He is, and He KNOWS He is wrong but wants others to think He is right, and so Jesus is a **Liar; OR**

2) When Jesus says He is God, He is wrong about who He is, but He does NOT know it because He sincerely believes He is right/He is severely out of touch with reality but does NOT know it, and so Jesus is a **Lunatic**[197]**; OR**

3) When Jesus says He is God, He is right about who He says He is, and so Jesus is **Lord**, which the Old Testament title reserved only for God.[198]

---

[197] It is more polite to call someone who is wrong about something "mistaken" and to call someone who is severely out of touch with reality "mentally ill" or "emotionally disturbed." C. S. Lewis uses *lunatic* (1) to emphasize how shocking Jesus' claim was and (2) to use alliteration.

[198] *CCC*, 446-451.

The Fullness of Life

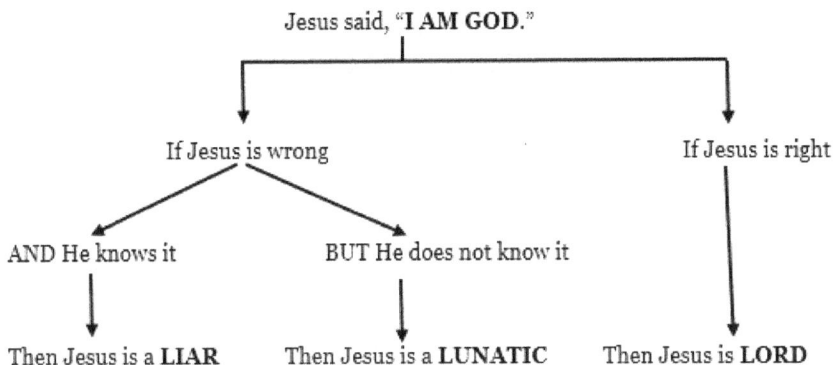

One of these three possibilities must be objectively true and the other two possibilities must be objectively false. If Jesus is God, then Jesus is the most important person in history and the most important person to get to know. No one who has read the Gospels can honestly claim that Jesus talks and acts like a liar or a lunatic. No one who has read the New Testament can honestly claim that Jesus' followers and friends seem like liars or lunatics.

We can be confident that the man who rose from the dead with a glorified body transcending space and time is God.

WHAT DOES JESUS' DIVINITY MEAN <u>ABOUT HIM</u>?

The term for God becoming man and taking on human flesh in Jesus Christ is the *Incarnation*, which literally means (from the Latin) the in-flesh-ment.[199] Because Jesus is God, and because God always existed and had no beginning, therefore Jesus, as God, always existed and had no beginning.[200]

From the moment of His conception, and forever after His conception, Jesus is 100 percent Divine and 100 percent human—fully/completely God and fully/completely human.[201] Jesus is one person with two

---

[199] *CCC*, 461-463, 484-486, 515.
[200] *CCC*, 257, 456, 479.
[201] *CCC*, 464-478.

natures: divine nature and human nature.[202] A term for the unity of Jesus' two natures in His one Person is the *hypostatic union*, which literally means (from the Greek) under-that-which-is standing, and so it is the foundation underlying what we see. Yes, Jesus worked with human hands, had emotions, and experienced pain. But it is clear from the Gospels that Jesus knew he was God.

One way to understand something is to understand what it is NOT. E.g., it easier to learn what a stock is by learning what a bond is. Let's identify some common MIS-understandings of Jesus. When God became human in Jesus, Jesus did NOT stop being God at the same time that He was human. It is NOT that some parts of Jesus were God (e.g., His mind), and some parts of Jesus were human (e.g., His body).[203] It is NOT true that God did not actually take on human flesh so Jesus only appeared to be human, to suffer, and to die.[204] Jesus' humanity was NOT completely absorbed into His divine nature—He did NOT start His existence as completely human but then become God so that when He became God, He stopped being human.[205] Jesus is NOT simply the greatest being created by God, but not equal to God.[206]

Jesus is the one and only perfect Mediator (which means "go-between") to bring together God and humanity, separated by the Fall, because He is both God and human.[207] In Jesus, the offices of prophet, priest, and king are re-united, and they are re-united perfectly.[208] Jesus is the perfect prophet—He not only speaks the Word of God, He is the Word of God, the perfect revelation and communication of God. Jesus is the perfect priest—He not only offers sacrifice to God, He is the sacrifice offered to God, the Lamb of God Who takes away the sin of the world. Jesus is the perfect king—He not only rules the Kingdom, He is the Resurrection and the Life (Jn 11:25).

---

[202] To believe that Jesus is two persons is the heresy of Nestorianism; to believe that Jesus has one nature is the heresy of Monophysitism.

[203] This is the heresy/false belief of Apollinarism.

[204] This is the heresy of Gnosticism and of Docetism.

[205] This is the heresy of Adoptionism.

[206] This is the heresy of Arianism.

[207] *CCC*, 618, 1544-1545.

[208] *CCC*, 436.

WHAT DOES JESUS' DIVINITY MEAN **FOR US**?

Jesus invites everyone to follow Him and do God's will. By becoming human, and by his Death and Resurrection, Jesus Christ unites us to God.[209]

Jesus reveals the best way to leave sin behind and to live the best possible life. Jesus gives us the grace/spiritual power to overcome sin and evil and to do God's will.[210]

As human, Jesus shows us the profundity of what it means to be human. Jesus Christ reveals who we humans most essentially are. We were created to know, love, and serve God in this life and to be happy with Him in His Kingdom. We can become the brothers and sisters of Jesus, and so we can become the freely adopted sons and daughters of His Father.[211]

Jesus is the Way, the Truth, and the Life (Jn 14:6).

---

[209] *CCC*, 517, 519.
[210] *CCC*, 521.
[211] *CCC*, 518, 520.

PERSONAL FAITH RESPONSE

Check any statements below that describe you.

In order to LIVE FULLY:

1. _____I agree with the objective truth in this chapter.

2. _____I will be realize that Jesus is Lord and God, not a lunatic or a liar.

3. _____I will relate to Jesus as Someone who is fully God and fully human.

4. _____I will know, love, and serve God in this life in the hope of being happy with Him in His Kingdom.

VOCABULARY

Liar: Someone who is wrong, knows it, but wants others to think he is right.

Lunatic: Someone who is seriously wrong, but he does not know it.

Lord: The Old Testament title reserved only for God.

Incarnation: God becoming man and taking on human flesh in Jesus Christ.

Hypostatic Union: The unity of Jesus' two natures in His one Person.

Mediator: Jesus as the perfect go-between Who brings together God and humanity.

Part 6: What Is the Fullness of Revelation?

Chapter II:

WHAT IS THE FULLNESS OF WHO GOD IS?

WHAT IS THE MOST IMPORTANT DOCTRINE OF THE CATHOLIC FAITH?

The doctrine of the Trinity—that there is one God in three Divine Persons—is the most important doctrine of the Catholic Faith.[212] It expresses the ultimate Revelation about the most important reality, which is God. The English word *Trinity* come from the Latin *trinus* which means "triple."

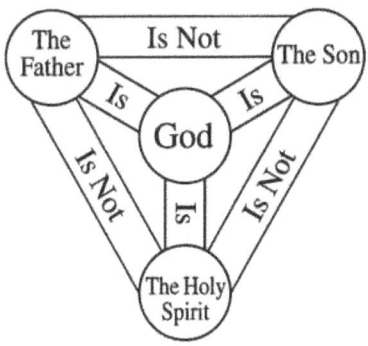

---

[212] *CCC*, 234, 261.

As in the "Shield of the Trinity" above, the Father is God, the Son is God, and the Holy Spirit is God, but the Father is not the Son or the Holy Spirit, the Son is not the Father or the Holy Spirit, and the Holy Spirit is not the Father or the Son.[213] The Trinity is NOT three Beings, BUT three Persons in one Being.[214] The Father is the First Person of the Trinity; the Son is the Second Person of the Trinity; and the Holy Spirit is called the Third Person of the Trinity. St. John Damascene taught that the Trinity is like a tree where the Father is the root, the Son is the branches, and the Holy Spirit is the fruit.

Each Divine Person is God whole and entire, e.g., the Holy Spirit is God whole and entire.[215] Each Divine Person has the same attributes/characteristics as the other Two, e.g., all-loving.[216] Although each Person is distinct from the Others, whatever One Person does involves the Other Two Persons,[217] e.g., Jesus both rose from the dead and was raised from the dead.[218]

Christians would be polytheists—which is what Jews and Muslims consider Christians to be—IF the Trinity were three Beings. Jews and Muslims believe, in effect, that there is one Person in one God.

WHAT IS IMPORTANT TO UNDERSTAND ABOUT THE NICENE CREED?

The Creed usually said at Mass is usually called the *Nicene Creed*. Its more accurate name is the *Niceno-Constantinopolitan Creed*, which is why just about everyone calls it the *Nicene Creed*. It was a result of the first

---

[213] *CCC*, 254.
[214] *CCC*, 253, 689.
[215] *CCC*, 253.
[216] *CCC*, 257.
[217] *CCC*, 255.
[218] *CCC*, 648-655. For another example of how no Person of the Trinity acts without the Other Persons, see *CCC* 290-292 on how Creation is the work of the Trinity and not just the Father.

two ecumenical[219] councils, the Council of Nicaea in 325 and the Council of Constantinople in 381, which dealt with heresies that had arisen about Jesus and the Holy Spirit.

The Nicene Creed reveals that the Father is the "maker of heaven and earth, of all things visible and invisible." The Father created the universe—all that exists besides God—from nothing.[220] Only God has always existed with no beginning. The complete meaning of "maker of heaven and earth" is that the Father also preserves the universe, which means that the only reason the universe exists right now is because the Father keeps it existing, and He does so moment by moment, instant by instant, nanosecond by nanosecond.[221]

However, the Father made/created neither the Son nor the Holy Spirit. Each Person of the Trinity has no beginning and has always existed.[222]

We know from the Nicene Creed that God the Son is "begotten" of the Father, which means He is eternally begotten of the Father. There is no beginning and no end to the Son's being begotten.[223]

God the Son is "consubstantial with the Father," which means that the Father and the Son share one and the same substance/nature/being. Although the Creed does not say so, the Holy Spirit is also consubstantial with the Father and the Son.[224]

It was by the Holy Spirit that God the Son "was incarnate of the Virgin

---

[219] An ecumenical council makes decisions for the whole Church and not just one region. Vatican II (1962-65) was the most recent of the twenty one ecumenical councils in the history of the Catholic Church.

[220] *CCC*, 295-300.

[221] *CCC*, 301.

[222] *CCC*, 246.

[223] *CCC*, 240.

[224] *CCC*, 253.

Mary" and became the man Jesus. As we have seen, Jesus is fully God and fully human. Once incarnate, God the Son has never stopped being human.[225]

The Holy Spirit is the "giver of life," which means He is the giver of supernatural life.[226] The Holy Spirit is the Sanctifier, the Divine Person Who makes (*fier*) someone holy (*sancti*), which means being a great son or daughter of the Father and a great follower, friend, and brother or sister of the Son.[227] We grow in our relationship with God when we grow in wisdom, understanding, counsel, fortitude, knowledge, piety, and fear of the Lord, which are the gifts of the Holy Spirit.[228] We grow in our relationship with God when we grow in charity, joy, peace, patience, kindness, goodness, generosity, gentleness, faithfulness, modesty, self-control, and chastity, which are the fruits of the Holy Spirit.[229]

The Holy Spirit proceeds from both "the Father and the Son." The Spirit is eternally proceeding from the Father and the Son, with no beginning and no end to the proceeding.[230]

The Holy Spirit "has spoken through the prophets," which means that He inspired (a word from the Latin that means "breathed into") the prophets. All of Sacred Scripture and Sacred Tradition were inspired by the Holy Spirit.[231]

HOW DO WE KNOW GOD IS THE TRINITY?

We know God is the Trinity from Revelation, not Reason.[232] Knowing God is a Holy Trinity is not like knowing that God is the Uncaused Cause. Before Jesus, no one could have known that God is a

---

[225] *CCC*, 659-667.
[226] *CCC*, 683-686.
[227] *CCC*, 688, 731-741.
[228] *CCC*, 1831.
[229] *CCC*, 1832.
[230] *CCC*, 245-248, 254-255.
[231] *CCC*, 76, 78-79, 81, 83, 109-11
[232] *CCC*, 237, 249-251.

The Fullness of Life

Trinity because the Trinity is not a reality that can be reasoned to without first being revealed.

It is easier to understand and believe in the Trinity if we start with Jesus.[233] Once we accept that Jesus is Lord and God—and NOT a lunatic or a liar—then we realize that there are at least two Persons in one God, e.g., God the Father was not crucified. Once we accept that there are two Persons in one God, it is relatively easy to accept that there are three Persons in one God.

It is especially easier to accept the reality of the Trinity when it is revealed by Jesus Himself, the God-Man. In **Mt 28:19**, Jesus tells His apostles, "Go therefore and make disciples of all nations, baptizing them in the name of the Father and of the Son and of the Holy Spirit."[234] And in **Jn 14:16-17**, Jesus says, "And I (the Son) will ask the Father, and He will give you another Advocate to be with you always, the Spirit of truth . . . The Advocate, the Holy Spirit that the Father will send in My name—He will teach you everything and remind you of all that I told you." These are two examples of how we know from Jesus that God is a Trinity of Three Divine Persons: the Father, the Son, and the Holy Spirit.

We also have the witness of the first Catholics.[235] The Holy Spirit[236] most fully revealed Himself to them on the Jewish feast of Pentecost, which means "fiftieth" because it was celebrated fifty days after Passover, and so this Revelation of the Holy Spirit occurred fifty days after the Last Supper. In order to approximate that, Pentecost is celebrated by the Church every year on the seventh Sunday (forty nine days) after Easter.

The Revelation that God is the Trinity is reinforced by reflecting on love. Christianity is the only religion that says: "God is love." If God were alone and solitary, He could not love from all eternity. If God were only One Person in One God instead of Three Persons in One God, then He would have been alone and solitary before He created anything. Because

---

[233] *CCC*, 238-242.

[234] *CCC*, 233.

[235] *CCC*, 244.

[236] Key Scripture passages about the Holy Spirit: Jgs 3:7-11; Nm 11:16-17, 25; Dt 34:9; 1 Sm 11:5-6, 16:13; Ps 104:27-30; Is 11:1-3, 42:1-4, 44:2-3, 61:1-3; Ez 11:17-21; Jl 3; Mt 1:18-20, 12:28; Mk 1:12; Lk 12:10-12; Acts 6:1-7, 8:14-25, 8:26-40, 10:44-11:18; 1 Cor 3:16-17, 6:19-20.

God is love always, and because there was a time when God existed and nothing else existed, and so there was nothing outside of God for God to love, therefore there was "something inside" God for God to love. God must be a Communion of Persons so that God always had "something" to love. Each Divine Person had the other Divine Persons to love before Creation. If God is not a Trinity, [237] then God is not love.

Once we have the eyes of Faith, we can also know God is the Trinity by experiencing each Person. We experience the Father, e.g., in His gift of existence, in His Creation, and in His love. We experience the Son, e.g., in the Church He founded. We experience the Holy Spirit, e.g., when we are inspired to greater truth and when we grow in His gifts and fruits.

Since Faith is a relationship with God, we now know that mature Faith is a relationship with the Father, the Son, and the Holy Spirit. It is appropriate to address our prayer to God, to the Father, to Jesus, to the Holy Spirit, or to the Trinity. Even though God is a Trinity, God should be referred to as "He" and "Him" instead of "They" and "Them" because "He" and "Him" express that there is ultimately one God whereas "They" and "Them" makes it sound like there are three Gods.

HOW DOES KNOWING THAT GOD IS THE TRINITY HELP US UNDERSTAND WHY WE EXIST?

No one has a right to exist. No one did anything to deserve to exist. (Which is different than the right of someone to life once conception has taken place.)

Every person exists because God created each of us out of free and unselfish love. The essence of love is to give and to share. Knowing that God is an eternal community of perfect and absolute love between Father, Son, and Spirit helps us realize that we have been given the gift of existence so that we can share/participate in the Trinity's perfect and absolute love.[238]

---

[237] Key Scripture passages about the Trinity: Mt 28:16-20; Mk 1:9-11; Jn 14:16-17, 16:4-15; Acts 2:1-41; Rom 5:1-11, 8:1-39; 1 Cor 2:6-16, 6:9-11, 12:1-31; 2 Cor 5:1-10, 13:13; Gal 4:1-7; Eph 1:3-14.

[238] *CCC*, 221, 260, 265, 293-294.

The Fullness of Life

You are God: we praise You.
You are the Lord: we acclaim you,
Father of majesty unbounded,
Your true and only Son, worthy of all worship,
Your Holy Spirit, Advocate and Guide.
—The *Te Deum*

PERSONAL FAITH RESPONSE

Check any statements below that describe you.

In order to LIVE FULLY:

1. _____I agree with the objective truth in this chapter.

2. _____I will be realize that God is three Divine Persons in one Divine Being.

3. _____I will be grateful that God did not have to create me but that He freely did it so I could share in the perfect love of the Trinity by growing in relationship with each Divine Person.

VOCABULARY

The Trinity: God is three Persons in one Being.

The First Person of the Trinity: God the Father.

The Second Person of the Trinity: God the Son, Jesus Christ.

The Third Person of the Trinity: God the Holy Spirit.

Consubstantial: Sharing one and the same substance/nature/being.

Part 6: What Is the Fullness of Revelation?

Chapter III:

WHAT IS THE FULLNESS OF FOLLOWING JESUS CHRIST?

WHY DOES THE CHURCH EXIST?

Jesus called everyone He met to follow Him to the Kingdom of God.[239] Jesus still wants every human being to be His disciple. Christians are those who are disciples of Jesus Christ by being baptized with water in the name of the Father, the Son, and the Holy Spirit. The Church is all people who are Christians.[240] Jesus began founding the Church when He called the first person to follow Him.[241]

The Church is more than an institution because she is a mystery that, like Jesus Himself, is both human and divine at the same time.[242] The

---

[239] *CCC*, 542-543.
[240] Jesus' followers were first called Christians about 40 AD in the city of Antioch (Acts 11:26).
[241] *CCC*, 541, 764. The founding of the Church should be understood as a process rather than as a distinct, isolated moment. Other steps in the founding of the Church were the Crucifixion (*CCC*, 766) and Pentecost (*CCC*, 767-768) and even Creation, the call of Abraham, and the call of Israel to be the Chosen People (*CCC*, 760-762).
[242] *CCC*, 771.

Church is the Mystical Body of Christ.[243] As Jesus said of His relationship with His disciples, "I am the vine, you are the branches" (Jn 15:5). After the Ascension, when Saul (who later became St. Paul) was on the road from Jerusalem to Damascus to persecute the Church, he heard the Resurrected Jesus say to him, "Why do you persecute me?" (Acts 9:4).

The way Jesus is still present on Earth between the Ascension and the Second Coming is the Church, His Mystical Body. The Church exists so that people can answer Jesus' call to follow Him. The Church's mission is to be the Kingdom of God and spread the Kingdom of God in all nations as much as possible between the Ascension and the Second Coming.[244]

God does NOT agree with people who say that they do not need to belong to the Church because they are following Christ "in their own way" or that they "are spiritual" or "have a spirituality" without the Church.[245]

WHO BELONGS TO THE CHURCH?

Jesus founded one Church.[246] Yet Christians are divided. The three biggest divisions of Christians today are:

1) Catholic Christians.

2) Eastern Orthodox Christians, who are usually subdivided by nationality such as Greek Orthodox, Russian Orthodox, Serbian Orthodox, etc.

3) Protestant Christians, who are subdivided (1) by denomination such as Lutheran, Baptist, Anglican/Episcopalian, Presbyterian, Methodist, etc. and (2) by movement such as evangelical, fundamentalist, Pentecostal, etc.

---

[243] *CCC*, 787-801.
[244] *CCC*, 768, 865.
[245] *CCC*, 759-760, 772-776, 846-848.
[246] *CCC*, 813-822, 874.

The Fullness of Life

The most important difference between Catholics and the Eastern Orthodox is that the Eastern Orthodox do not recognize the leadership of the pope (Papal Primacy). However, Eastern Orthodox leaders (bishops) can trace their authority back to the Twelve Apostles, and so Eastern Orthodox Christianity has Apostolic Succession in common with Catholic Christianity. Eastern Orthodox bishops and priests can consecrate bread and wine into the Body and Blood of Christ (the Eucharist) because it takes Apostolic Succession for the sacred power to consecrate bread and wine into the Eucharist.

There are several important differences between Catholic Christianity and Protestant Christianity. Like the Eastern Orthodox, Protestants do not recognize Papal Primacy. More than that, Protestant leaders cannot trace their authority back to the Twelve Apostles, and so there is no Apostolic Succession in Protestant Christianity. Therefore Protestants ministers cannot consecrate bread and wine into the Body and Blood of Christ.

Catholic Christians, Eastern Orthodox Christians, and Protestant Christians all belong to the one Church of Jesus Christ since they all have been baptized. This is why the Catholic Church does NOT re-baptize an Eastern Orthodox or Protestant who converts to the Catholic Church. Catholics should consider those who are Eastern Orthodox and Protestant as their brothers and sisters in Christ.

Yet by the time of Jesus' Ascension, the first Christians had both the leadership of St. Peter (Papal Primacy) and the Eucharist. So the first Christians were Catholics, who accept the leadership of St. Peter and have the Eucharist—NOT Eastern Orthodox, who reject Papal Primacy but have Apostolic Succession the Eucharist and NOT Protestants, who reject Papal Primacy and do not have Apostolic Succession or the Eucharist.

The Church that Jesus founded subsists in the Catholic Church.[247] Since the word *subsists* means "extends beyond but most completely exists in," the Church that Jesus founded extends beyond the Catholic Church to include Eastern Orthodox and Protestant Christians, but most completely exists in the Catholic Church. Catholic Christians, Eastern Orthodox Christians, and Protestant Christians do NOT belong to the Church of Jesus Christ to an equal degree.

---

[247] *CCC*, 816, 830.

Jesus is most present on Earth between the Ascension and the Second Coming in the *Catholic* Church. The best way to make the Kingdom of God planted and grow in all nations is expanding the *Catholic* Church. While all Christians belong to the one Church of Jesus Christ, the more one is truly Catholic, the more one belongs to the one Church of Jesus.[248]

In order to be fully Catholic, one must be in union with the pope and the bishops, profess the entire Catholic Faith, and receive the Sacraments.[249] Someone is NOT fully Catholic just because he was baptized Catholic. It follows that a baptized Catholic who believes whatever doctrines he wants and sees these doctrines as subjectively true is NOT as good a Christian as a baptized Eastern Orthodox or Protestant who believes in doctrines shared with the Catholic Church and sees these doctrines as objectively true.

One of Jesus' most important concerns was the unity of His followers, for which all Christians should work.

WHAT IS THE RELATIONSHIP OF THE CATHOLIC CHURCH TO ALL NON-CATHOLIC RELIGIONS?

Our English word *Catholic* comes from the ancient Greek words *kat'* ("according to") and *holon* ("the whole"), so *Catholic* most basically means "according to the whole" or "complete." In order to emphasize that point, *Catholic* will be hyphenated as *Cat-holic* in this section.

Of all the religions in the world—Christian and non-Christian—it is through the Cat-holic Church that God wholly/most completely/most fully REVEALS Himself. Of all the religions of the world, it is through the Cat-holic Faith that one wholly/most completely/most fully RESPONDS to Revelation.

God's primary way to save the human race is the Cat-holic Church.[250] Because Christ sent the Cat-holic Church to all nations, real Cat-holics are constantly trying to evangelize (spread the Good News) by inviting non-

---

[248] *CCC*, 838.
[249] *CCC*, 836-837.
[250] *CCC*, 845.

The Fullness of Life

Cat-holics to convert to the Cat-holic Faith.[251]

The Cat-holic Church respects and promotes freedom of religion as a human right.[252] The Cat-holic Church proposes the Faith to others. It does NOT imposes the Faith on others.

All who, by no fault of their own, do not know Christ or his Church but sincerely seek God can attain eternal salvation.[253] Even atheists can attain eternal salvation. Non-Cat-holics can be eternally saved, and Cat-holics can be damned.[254]

But salvation and damnation are objectively best described by Cat-holic doctrine.[255] Non-Cat-holics will NOT end up in whatever eternity they believe in. It is NOT true that Muslims will end up in Paradise with Allah, Buddhists will attain Nirvana, Hindus will attain Moksha, atheists will cease to exist, agnostics won't know where they are, etc. All non-Cat-holics, as well as all Cat-holics, will end up either in the Kingdom of God, which will be the perfected Cat-holic Church;[256] or they will end up in Hell.

While there is one true God, there is NOT one true religion with every other religion being completely false. There is one truEST religion.[257] All non-Cat-holic religions and philosophies have some truth, but Cat-holic Faith has the most truth.

---

[251] *CCC*, 849-856, 1533, 1816.
[252] *CCC*, 856, 2104-2109.
[253] *CCC*, 847.
[254] *CCC*, 837.
[255] *CCC*, 1051-1060.
[256] *CCC*, 769, 865.
[257] *CCC*, 817-819, 839-845.

All non-Cat-holic religions and philosophies are reductionisms—they reduce the whole truth about God and/or reality to part of the truth about God and/or reality and so leave out other parts of the truth about God and/or reality. A good analogy comes from the great Cat-holic thinker and writer, G. K. Chesterton. It is from him that we get the now-common saying that the optimist sees the glass half-full and the pessimist sees the glass half-empty. However, Chesterton's point in saying so is all but forgotten. Chesterton's point was that both the optimist and  the pessimist are wrong because both are reductionists. Both see only part of the glass and neither sees the whole glass. Both reduce the whole truth of the glass to part of the truth about the glass.

Non-Cat-holic religions and philosophies are true when they agree with/intersect with Cat-holic doctrine; but even then they only have incomplete doctrine. Non-Cat-holic religions and philosophies are false when they disagree with/contradict Cat-holic doctrine.

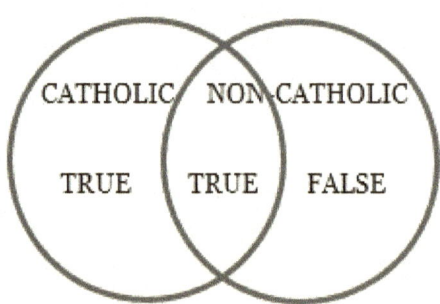

Religion, as we have seen, is not only a matter of beliefs, but also a matter of action. God is not only Someone to know, but also Someone to interact with. Just as the Cat-holic Church has Four Pillars of Creed, Morality, Worship, and Prayer, so too do non-Cat-holic religions have creeds, moralities, ways of worshipping, and ways of praying. It is by these means/ways that religious people try to have a good eternity/to have a good afterlife/to be saved.

The Cat-holic Church has the fullness of the means of salvation.[258] Just as there are varying degrees of truth in the creeds of non-Cat-holic religions, there are varying degrees of good in the moralities, worship, and prayer of non-Cat-holic religion. The Cat-holic Church has the whole/most complete/fullest Creed, Morality, Worship, and Prayer.

WHY BE CATHOLIC?

The answer to the subtitle amounts to a summary of everything we have covered so far.

The reason God created everyone is to have a relationship with Him, and so He reveals Himself and invites Faith, which is acceptance of that Revelation.

It is NOT true that God ONLY reveals Himself in the Sacred Scripture and Sacred Tradition of the Catholic Church. It is NOT true that religion is a purely subjective choice because there is no way of knowing where God reveals Himself. It is NOT true that religion is a purely subjective choice because God reveals Himself equally in all the different religions and spiritualities even though they contradict each other. It IS true that God MOST DIRECTLY reveals Himself in the Sacred Scripture and Sacred Tradition of the Catholic Church founded by Jesus Christ.

It is NOT true that the Catholic Faith is the ONLY good response to Divine Revelation for all people to make. It is NOT true that the Catholic Faith is only ONE good response to Divine Revelation for one person to make, but another religion might be just as good of a response to Revelation for another person to make. It IS true that the Catholic Faith is the BEST response to Divine Revelation for all people to make.

It is NOT true that being Catholic is the ONLY good way to have a relationship with God. It is NOT true that being Catholic is only ONE good way to have a relationship with God, but another way of having a relationship with God might be just as good for another person. It IS true that being Catholic is the BEST way to have a relationship with God.

It is NOT true that being Catholic is the ONLY good way to be a

---

[258] *CCC*, 824.

follower and friend of Jesus. It is NOT true that being Catholic is only ONE good way to be a follower and friend of Jesus, but another way of following Jesus might be just as good for another person. It IS true that being Catholic is the BEST way to be a follower and friend of Jesus.

The ONLY way to find the fullness of life is in the Kingdom of God.

It is NOT true that being Catholic is the ONLY good way to find the fullness of life in the Kingdom of God. It is NOT true that being Catholic is only ONE good way to enter the Kingdom, but another way of entering the Kingdom might be just as good for another person. It IS true that being Catholic is the BEST way to enter the Kingdom.

ONLY the Catholic Church has the fullness of the means of salvation.

God wants everyone to know the truth. Being Catholic is the best way to harmonize Reason and Faith—the best way to avoid both Rationalism (valuing Reason without valuing Faith) and Fideism (valuing Faith without valuing Reason).

PERSONAL FAITH RESPONSE

Check any statements below that describe you.

In order to LIVE FULLY:

1. _____I agree with the objective truth in this chapter.

2. _____I will follow Jesus in the Catholic Church.

3. _____I will invite non-Catholics to join the Catholic Church.

4. _____I will find what is both true and false in non-Catholic religions and philosophies.

VOCABULARY

Christian: A disciple of Jesus Christ who was baptized in water in the name of the Father, the Son, and the Holy Spirit.

The Church: The people who are Christians.

Catholics: (1) Christians who recognize Papal Primacy and Apostolic Succession and whose bishops and priests can consecrate bread and wine into the Body and Blood of Christ; and (2) the Church in which subsists the one Church that Jesus founded.

Eastern Orthodox: Christians who do not recognize Papal Primacy, but whose bishops have Apostolic Succession and whose bishops and priests can consecrate bread and wine into the Body and Blood of Christ.

Protestant: Christians who do not recognize Papal Primacy, whose leaders do not have Apostolic Succession, and whose ministers cannot consecrate bread and wine into the Body and Blood of Christ.

Subsist: Extends beyond but most completely exists in.

Reductionism: The reduction of the whole truth about God and/or reality to part of the truth about God and/or reality which therefore leaves out other parts of the truth about God and/or reality; every non-Catholic philosophy and religion.

Part 6: What Is the Fullness of Revelation?

Chapter IV:
WHAT IS THE ROLE OF THE MAGISTERIUM IN THE CHURCH?

SOURCES

- Pope John Paul II, *Apostolos Suos*, 1998.
- Congregation for the Doctrine of the Faith, "Doctrinal Commentary on the Concluding Formula of the *Professio Fidei*," 1998.
- Avery Dulles, SJ, *The Craft of Theology* (Crossroad, 1992, 1995).
- Avery Cardinal Dulles, SJ, *Magisterium: Teacher and Guardian of the Faith* (Sapientia Press, 2007).

WHAT MAKES CATHOLICISM DIFFERENT FROM EVERY OTHER RELIGION?

There is a range of similarities shared by Catholicism and all the other religions. As we have seen, Catholicism shares the most in common with Eastern Orthodoxy, and it shares much in common with traditional Protestantism which considers the Nicene Creed to be objectively true. All who are religious or spiritual agree that there is something spiritual about reality, that there is more to reality than meets the eye and stimulates the five senses, that human beings are not mere collections of biological and chemical processes. In a world where militant and aggressive secularism increasingly combats religion and denies religious freedom, it is important for all who are religious to find common ground and work together to discover the truth about God and morality, while being honest with each other about where we disagree.

The differences, both in belief and in practice, between Catholicism and other religions can be very obvious. Unlike Hinduism, for example, Catholicism worships one God. Unlike Theravada Buddhism, Catholicism seeks an eternity in which individual personality remains. Unlike Islam and Judaism, Catholicism asserts that Jesus is God.

It is the Magisterium, especially Papal Primacy, which makes Catholicism different from every other religion. There is no religion that has the equivalent of Papal Primacy. There is no other head of a religion who has the power in that religion which the pope has in the Catholic Church.

Recall that the Magisterium is made up of the bishops under the leadership of the Bishop of Rome, the pope. The word *Magisterium* can be used either for the office held by all the bishops or for the bishops holding the office. Although bishops cannot act and teach without the approval of the Pope, the Pope has the power to act and teach without the approval of the bishops.[259]

WHAT IS THE POWER OF THE MAGISTERIUM?

In the Church, all power comes from Christ, which is why the Church is not a democracy.[260] Christ has given St. Peter and the popes succeeding him the power to be the final authority in:[261]

- Doctrine, which is a specific Magisterial teaching that makes Revelation and Faith clearer and that is true for all times and places, and so defines the Catholic Faith. (The Catholic Faith includes both Revelation and the Catholic response to it.)

---

[259] *CCC*, 881-883.
[260] *CCC*, 864, 874.
[261] *CCC*, 553.

- Discipline, which is the laws and rules of the Catholic Church that must be followed in order for one to be a *disciple* of Christ. In the context of the Church, *discipline* is NOT a synonym for *punishment*, as it tends to be in everyday language. An important source of discipline is the *Code of Canon Law*, although discipline is set forth in many other documents, too, e.g., the *General Instruction of the Roman Missal*.

An important difference between doctrine and discipline is that doctrines CANNOT change because they define the Catholic Faith, but disciplines CAN change because they do NOT define the Faith but are applications of the Faith to specific situations of the Church. E.g., it is a doctrine that the consecrated bread and wine are really the Body and Blood of Christ, whereas the language used at Mass, e.g., Latin or English, is a discipline. It is a doctrine that only men can be ordained a deacon, priest, or bishop, whereas it is a discipline that priests cannot get married (in the Latin Rite of the Catholic Church, as opposed to its Eastern Rite). The date on which Easter is celebrated is a discipline, bit the Resurrection is a doctrine.

WHAT IS INFALLIBILITY?

Infallibility is the ability to be free from error. Under certain conditions, both the pope and bishops—all those in the Magisterium—are infallible.[262] Both the pope and bishops can be infallible when they exercise their ordinary and universal Magisterium, which means when they teach any doctrine that is definitive and necessary for keeping the Deposit of Faith. The pope can be infallible when he teaches *ex cathedra*, which requires certain conditions. Only a very few doctrines have been declared infallible by the pope *ex cathedra*. The bishops can also teach infallibly in an ecumenical council under the leadership of the pope.

No other gathering of bishops is infallible. Since Vatican II (1962-1965), bishops have regularly met in two ways: (1) national conferences in their own countries and (2) synods in Rome led by the pope and attended by representatives of the bishops conferences. The decision of a bishops conference has no authority over an individual bishop unless the pope adds his authority to it. Synods are purely advisory to the pope.

---

[262] *CCC*, 889-892.

Infallibility only applies to doctrine. The Magisterium is infallible ONLY when it makes authoritative decisions about doctrine. Even then doctrine falls into three categories: (1) infallible doctrine that is NOT reformable, which is also known as dogma, and which is the most authoritative doctrine; (2) infallible doctrine that IS reformable; and (3) doctrine that is NOT infallible. Neither the pope nor a bishop has the authority to contradict doctrine, even non-infallible doctrine. [263] The Magisterium can further develop reformable infallible doctrine and non-infallible doctrine without contradicting them.

The pope and bishops are NOT infallible in any other way. They are NOT infallible when they make decisions about discipline. The power of infallibility does NOT make the pope and bishops more intelligent or knowledgeable than they were before they became the pope and bishops. The power of infallibility does NOT make the pope and bishops unable to commit personal sins. The process for selecting bishops is NOT infallible, and the conclave that elects the pope is NOT infallible, which is why there have been bad bishops and bad popes in the long history of the Catholic Church. We should have absolute faith only in God, NOT in men. We should respect the offices of bishop and pope while realizing that the men holding those offices have fallen within the entire spectrum of virtue and vice. Sin confirms the truth of Catholic moral doctrine—when Catholic moral doctrine is obeyed, there is no sin.

How well do you know the Catholic Faith? Which of the following doctrines is infallible? Some we have covered already, and some we have not.

- Original Sin—humans are born into an evil and sinful condition from which only God can save them.

- The Incarnation—Jesus Christ is both God and man.

---

[263] Vatican I: "[T]he Holy Spirit was promised to the successors of Peter *not so that they might, by his revelation, make known some new doctrine*, but that, by his assistance, they might religiously guard and faithfully expound the revelation or deposit of faith transmitted by the apostles (emphasis added)."
Vatican II: "[T]he task of authentically interpreting the word of God, whether written or handed on, has been entrusted exclusively to the living teaching office of the Church [the Magisterium] . . . *This teaching office is not above the word of God, but serves it, teaching only what has been handed on* (emphasis added)."

- The Redemption—Christ's death on the cross saves humanity from its sins.

- The Resurrection—Christ rose from the dead into the Kingdom of God.

- The Ascension—Christ's glorified body became no longer visible.

- The Second Coming—Christ will come again in glory to judge the living and the dead and finish the establishment of the Kingdom.

- Apostolic Succession—the bishops are the successors of the Twelve Apostles.

- Papal Primacy—the pope, as the successor of Peter, is the leader of the bishops.

- The Seven Sacraments were instituted/established/begun by Jesus Christ.

- Abortion is murder.

- Sexual intercourse between a married person and someone other than his or her spouse (adultery) is a sin.

- Sexual intercourse between two unmarried people (fornication) is a sin.

- Marriage is only between one man and one woman.

All of the above are infallible doctrines. Catholic doctrine is challenging for EVERYONE. With God's grace, we CAN meet the challenge. And for those times we fail to meet the challenge, God has given us the Sacrament of Confession (to be explained in a later chapter).

DOES THE MAGISTERIUM TEACH ANYTHING BESIDES DOCTRINE AND DISCIPLINE?

The Magisterium teaches more than doctrine and discipline. The Magisterium frequently gives its social analysis and makes prudential judgments when teaching. Social analysis is the Magisterium's own opinion about the condition of society, e.g., whether or not human pollution is causing climate change. Prudential judgments are the Magisterium's own opinions about how a doctrine should be applied to a particular situation, e.g., whether legislation about climate change should be supported. The Magisterium's social analysis and prudential judgments are never infallible.

Here is one example of the difference between doctrine and prudential judgment. That every country has the right to defend itself and that military force should be used as a last resort are doctrines. They are true for all times and places. When a pope or bishop advises against using military force, he is making a prudential judgment that is his opinion about one time and place that might be very different from another time and place.

Complicating things even more is that there can be spirituality and theological opinion in a Magisterial teaching. E.g., a pope might end his teaching with a beautiful prayer to the Blessed Mother, but every Catholic is not required to pray that prayer.

The pope and bishops do NOT always make clear what part of their teaching is infallible doctrine, what part is doctrine that is not infallible, what part is discipline, what part is social analysis, what part is prudential judgment, what part is spirituality, and what part is theological opinion.

Only those who know these distinctions actually understand the Magisterium well. When someone says, "But the Church teaches . . .," the real question is, "What exactly is the nature of that Church teaching?" Is it infallible doctrine or something else?

MUST A GOOD CATHOLIC ALWAYS AGREE WITH THE MAGISTERIUM?

Recall that only doctrine is infallible and that not all doctrine is infallible. Disciplinary decisions are NOT infallible. The social analysis, prudential judgment, spirituality, or theological opinion of a pope, an individual bishop, or bishops conference is NOT infallible.

The Apostles inherited the offices of Prophet, Priest, and King from Jesus, and the Magisterium has inherited these offices from the

The Fullness of Life

Apostles.[264] Doctrine and discipline directly come from these offices.

In order to be a good Catholic, one must agree with ALL doctrine given by the Magisterium. To be Catholic is NOT to believe whatever one wants. Doctrine is a great gift from God through the Magisterium to help us know Him more clearly, love Him more dearly, and follow Him more nearly, as St. Richard of Chichester would say. Only those with the proper theological qualifications may dissent from/disagree with non-infallible doctrine. And there are proper ways and improper ways for such dissent to be expressed.

In order to be a good Catholic, one must agree with ALL discipline given by the Magisterium. Just like any purely human organization, the Church has rules and rule-makers. Without rules, there is no organization. Discipline, at its best, is a great gift from God through the Magisterium to help us love Him more dearly and follow Him more nearly. Even when the Magisterium makes a mistake about discipline, e.g., a mistake could be made in a how a bishop reorganizes parishes, good Catholics do their best to cooperate as constructively as possible.

Although one must take the Magisterium's social analysis seriously, one does NOT have to agree with the Magisterium's social analysis in order to be a good Catholic. Social analysis is NOT part of the Magisterium's expertise. Good social analysis results from good information and knowledge of the social sciences, e.g., economics, finance, history, sociology, etc. While every bishop has a graduate degree in Theology, the great majority of bishops do not have a graduate degree in a social science and have only taken a few social science courses on the college level. When it comes to social analysis, a bishop is like the rest of us. His social analysis will only be as good as the sources to which he turns.

Although one must take the Magisterium's prudential judgments seriously, one does NOT have to agree with the Magisterium's prudential judgments in order to be a good Catholic. Prudential judgments result from not only doctrine, but also social analysis. Reasonable people can reasonably disagree about social analysis and, thus, about prudential judgments.

In order to be a good Catholic, one also does not have to agree with a pope or bishop's spirituality or theological opinion. E.g., the Catechism

---

[264] *CCC*, 873.

suggests that every Catholic household have a "prayer corner" dedicated to prayer with spiritual items like a Bible, religious art, etc.[265] While this is a helpful suggestion, it is just that—a suggestion and neither a doctrine nor a discipline. Every Catholic household is not required to have a prayer corner.

---

[265] *CCC*, 2691.

PERSONAL FAITH RESPONSE

Check any statements below that describe you.

In order to LIVE FULLY:

1. _____I agree with the objective truth in this chapter.

2. _____I will agree with all doctrine and discipline taught by the Magisterium.

3. _____I will seriously consider the social analysis and prudential judgments taught by the Magisterium.

4. _____When I disagree with the Magisterium's social analysis and prudential judgments, I will do so respectfully.

VOCABULARY

The Magisterium: The pope and bishops together as the leaders of the Church.

Doctrine: A Magisterial teaching that makes Revelation and Faith clearer and that is true for all times and places.

Discipline: The laws and rules of the Catholic Church that must be followed in order to be a *disciple* of Christ.

Infallible: Free from error.

Social Analysis: An opinion about the condition of society.

Prudential Judgment: An opinion about how a doctrine should be applied to a particular situation.

Part 6: What Is the Fullness of Revelation?

Chapter V:

WHAT IS THE ROLE OF ST. MARY IN SALVATION HISTORY?

WHY IS ST. MARY THE "BLESSED VIRGIN"?

As we have seen, Jesus' real father is God. St. Mary, the mother of Jesus, is a virgin[266] because she never had sexual intercourse with Joseph, which is why Joseph is Jesus' legal father but not His biological father.

Mary did NOT have other children besides Jesus. When the Gospels speak about Jesus' "brothers and sisters," they mean His cousins since the words for *brother* and *sister* also were used for cousins in the language Jesus spoke (Aramaic). Since Mary was also a virgin after Jesus was born, she is also

---

[266] *CCC*, 496-498.

called "ever-virgin."[267]

Mary has been revered as the Blessed Virgin both before and after Jesus' birth since the earliest days of the Church. The reason St. Mary was always a virgin was because of her complete gift of herself to God's will.[268] The reason St. Mary is blessed is because she is the mother of the Savior of the world.

WHY IS ST. MARY THE "BLESSED MOTHER"?

St. Mary is the "Blessed Mother," the "Mother of God," because Jesus, her Son, is God.[269] Mary is NOT the mother of the Father or the Holy Spirit.

The doctrine of the Immaculate Conception is that Mary was conceived immaculately, i.e., without Original Sin.[270] It is NOT about Jesus being conceived immaculately. Mary is the only person who is only human who was conceived without Original Sin. This is so Mary would be worthy to be the Mother of God.

Mary also never committed a personal sin. Because Mary was always without sin ("full of grace, as we quote the angel Gabriel in the "Hail Mary"), she is also "the new Eve." She shows us what Eve would have been like if Eve had never sinned, just as Jesus is the "new Adam."

The Feast of the Immaculate Conception is December 8, which is celebrated nine months before the Feast of the Nativity of the Blessed Virgin Mary on September 8. The feast of the Immaculate Conception is a holy day of obligation, a day when Catholics are obligated to go to Mass.

---

[267] *CCC*, 499-501.
[268] *CCC*, 502-507.
[269] *CCC*, 495.
[270] *CCC*, 490-493.

The Fullness of Life

Mary is the patron of the United States under the title of the Immaculate Conception.

Mary freely chose to be the Mother of God. She could have declined.[271]

When Jesus was on the cross, He made St. Mary the mother of St. John the Apostle (Jn 19:27). This is another sign that Mary had no other children. Mary would not have needed someone to take care of her if she had other children. By making Mary the mother of John, Jesus made Mary the mother of all His disciples, including those who follow Jesus today.[272]

It is NOT appropriate to call God "Our Mother" instead of "Our Father." To call God "our mother" goes against Jesus Who gave us Mary as our mother. Jesus always referred to God as "My Father," "the Father," or "Our Father." Jesus told His disciples to call God "Our Father." To call God "mother," in effect, claims to know God better than Jesus knows God. If calling God "Father" is sexist, then Jesus is sexist. But Jesus is NOT sexist, and so it is NOT sexist to call God "Father."

Mary is also the Mother of the Church.[273] She was the first disciple.[274] She is the perfect disciple.[275]

HOW HAS GOD REVEALED HIMSELF THROUGH ST. MARY?

St. Mary has appeared at different times and places. Here are three important appearances of Mary, confirmed by the Magisterium.

In 1531 at Guadalupe, Mexico, St. Mary was seen by a man, Juan Diego (who is now recognized by the Magisterium as a saint). When, at Mary's direction, Juan Diego picked roses (which were out of season and growing in rocky ground where flowers never grew), put them in his cloak, and then spilled them from his cloak in front of the bishop, an image of St. Mary was on the cloak. That image is still on that cloak. Science cannot explain how

---

[271] *CCC*, 488, 494.
[272] *CCC*, 964.
[273] *CCC*, 967-970.
[274] *CCC*, 773.
[275] *CCC*, 144, 507, 972.

the image got there and how the cloak, made of a fabric that should not have lasted more than 60 years, has lasted almost 500 years.

In 1858 at Lourdes, France, St. Mary was seen in a grotto/shallow cave by a girl, Bernadette Soubirous (who is now recognized by the Magisterium as a saint). Bernadette at first did not know who the mysterious beautiful woman in the grotto was. When Bernadette asked Mary her identity, Mary replied, "I am the Immaculate Conception." A spring of water appeared where there had been none before. It still flows today, and many miracles have been connected to it. St. Bernadette, who died over 130 years ago, now has an incorruptible body.[276]

In 1917 at Fatima, Portugal, St. Mary was seen by two girls and a boy, Lucia Santos, Jacinta Martos, and Francisco Martos. Mary gave a vision of Hell to the children. She made several predictions. Mary predicted that a mysterious light would appear at night to signal a worse war than the then-occurring World War I if people continued to offend God; on the night of January 25, 1938, a mysterious light was seen across Europe for 5 hours, and 47 days later Hitler invaded Austria. She predicted, before the Communist Revolution in Russia when it was a religious but backward society, that Russia would become a powerful source of evil in the world if the world did not turn away from sin. And she also predicted that there would be an assassination attempt on a pope, John Paul II. Because Mary had promised a miracle, 70,000 people came in a drenching rain to the place where St. Mary had appeared and saw the sun zig in the sky, come closer to the earth so that the ground immediately dried up, and then move back to its normal position.

God has used St. Mary at these times, and many other times

---

[276] The Church uses the term *incorruptible* to describe dead bodies that have not decayed in whole or in part in the natural way of other dead bodies. There are over 150 dead bodies of saints that fit this description.

throughout history, to show that He is real and that all human beings need to do His will. These appearances of Mary are examples of *Private Revelation*, which Catholics are NOT required to accept, even when they are recognized by the Magisterium.[277] Private Revelations do NOT improve or complete the Public Revelation that most fully and definitively is in the life, teachings, Passion, Resurrection, and Ascension of Jesus Christ and that is then found in Sacred Scripture and Sacred Tradition as they are interpreted by the Magisterium.

WHY SHOULD WE PRAY TO ST. MARY?

Catholic Faith does NOT include the worship of St. Mary. Only God should be worshipped. Catholics venerate/revere/honor Mary. We turn to Mary because she leads us to Jesus.[278]

Mary does NOT have the power to answer prayers on her own. Only God has the power to answer prayers. Just as we ask people to pray for us and our intentions, we should even more so ask Mary to pray for us and our intentions.[279] Since Mary is already in Heaven, she knows better than we how to pray to God. When Mary was on earth, she cooperated with God to do good for others, so now in Heaven she continues to cooperate with God by doing good for others.

All of this about Mary applies to all the saints.

The most well-known and beloved prayer to Mary is the "Hail Mary":

Hail Mary, Full of Grace, the Lord is with thee.

Blessed art thou amongst women, and blessed is the fruit of thy womb, Jesus.

Holy Mary, Mother of God,

Pray for us sinners now and at the hour of our death. Amen.

---

[277] *CCC*, 67.
[278] *CCC*, 487, 971.
[279] *CCC*, 2683.

The "Hail Mary" developed over time, and its history is not completely clear. The first line quotes the Angel Gabriel (Luke 1:28), except that "Mary" was added later. The second line quotes Elizabeth, the mother of John Baptist (Lk 1:42), except that "Jesus" was added later. Elizabeth said this in response to Mary's greeting when Mary, who was pregnant with Jesus, visited Elizabeth, who was pregnant with John (Lk 1:39-56). These two lines were joined to form one prayer in the sixth or seventh century. The last two lines were added by the fifteenth century. The prayer in its entirety was made official by Pope Pius V in 1568.

PERSONAL FAITH RESPONSE

Check any statements below that describe you.

In order to LIVE FULLY:

1. _____I agree with the objective truth in this chapter.

2. _____I will regularly pray to the Blessed Mother.

3. _____I will celebrate the Feast of the Immaculate Conception.

VOCABULARY

The Immaculate Conception: (1) Mary's conception without Original Sin and (2) the feast celebrated.

Venerate: Revere/hold in great respect.

Private Revelation: A Revelation that Catholics are NOT required to accept, even when it is recognized by the Magisterium.

PART 7:
WHAT IS LIVING FULLY?

Chapter I: WHAT IS HUMAN NATURE?

Chapter II: WHAT IS THE PURPOSE OF LIFE?

Chapter III: WHAT DO FEELINGS HAVE TO DO WITH HAPPINESS?

Chapter IV: WHAT IS THE ROLE OF SEXUALITY IN HAPPINESS?

Part 7: What Is Being Fully Alive?

Chapter I:
WHAT IS HUMAN NATURE?

SOURCES

- Stefan Swiezawski, *St. Thomas Revisited* (Peter Lang Publishing, 1995), trans. Theresa Sandok, OSM.

HOW DO WE KNOW WHAT HUMAN NATURE IS?

In order to live fully, we need to know what human nature is. The way we know what human nature is—who we are—is the same way we know Who God is. As we have seen, there are two ways:

1) Faith, which is knowledge that comes accepting from Revelation.

2) Reason, which is all other true knowledge that comes from human beings figuring things out on their own by using natural evidence and logic, e.g., Science.

Remember that we humans can mistake false Faith for true Faith, unreal Revelation for real Revelation, and wrong Reason for right Reason. Throughout this chapter and this entire book, *Revelation* means real Revelation, *Faith* means true Faith, and *Reason* means right Reason.

Remember, too, that Reason and the human mind are gifts from God and are part of His plan for humanity. Faith and Reason never contradict each other, but Faith gives knowledge that is beyond Reason's ability to give.

WHAT DOES REASON TEACH US ABOUT HUMAN NATURE?

It might be easier to begin by comparing and contrasting human beings with other beings.

At first we will use a chart. The different kinds of beings are listed horizontally. The different kinds of attributes/characteristics/traits/qualities/features/properties of beings are listed vertically. The definition of each attribute appears in italics below it. A ✓ indicates which being has which attribute.

The Fullness of Life

Being: ⟶ Mineral Plant Animal Human
Attribute: ↓

Attribute	Mineral	Plant	Animal	Human
Existence — *Having objective reality*	✓	✓	✓	✓
Substantiality — *Having an objective identity/essence/nature that endures through all changes*	✓	✓	✓	✓
Corporeity — *Having a physical body*	✓	✓	✓	✓
Nutrition — *The ability and need to be fed*		✓	✓	✓
Growth		✓	✓	✓
Reproduction		✓	✓	✓
5 Senses — *Sight, Hearing, Tasting, Smelling, Touching*			✓	✓
Instinct — *Having wants/desires that are NOT freely chosen*			✓	✓
Emotions			✓	✓
Memory — *Retaining images and associations/mental connections*			✓	✓
Will — *Having wants/desires that are freely chosen*				✓
Intellect — *Actively thinking about things by forming concepts/definitions, combining concepts to make statements, and combining statements to reason/be logical; asking questions; telling a joke; conducting scientific experiments; designing cathedrals and video games*				✓

Reason teaches us that all the attributes checked in the "Human" column make up human nature, which is that which makes a human a human and not another being. What especially make a human a human are intellect and will.

So what attributes do we humans have in common with ALL beings? Existence and substantiality.

What attributes do we human beings have in common ONLY with PLANTS and ANIMALS? Nutrition, growth, and reproduction.

What attributes DO we humans have in common with ANIMALS that we do NOT have in common with PLANTS? The Five Senses, instinct, emotions, and memory. Mental activity begins with the formation of images inside the mind. Images do form inside the minds of the higher animals and so animals are capable of having memories, which in them are passive and contribute to their response to stimulus.

What attributes do we humans NOT have in common with ANIMALS? Will and intellect. If animals have free will, then they can sin and commit crimes. Should we accuse carnivores of murder? No animal can do anything in the definition given for intellect. No animal can actively think about things by forming concepts/definitions, combining concepts to make statements, and combining statements to reason/be logical. No animal can ask questions, e.g., about what gender he is or would like to be; or tell a joke; or conduct scientific experiments; or design cathedrals or video games. Humans are NOT the same beings/species as animals.

What attributes make up the human soul, besides existence? Intellect, will, memory, and emotions. There is more to a human being than his material body with its biological and chemical processes. If we only have material bodies without immaterial intellects, wills, memories, and emotions, then our "intellects" (e.g., insights) and "wills" (e.g., decisions) are nothing more than automatic biological and chemical processes for which we can take no credit. Is there anyone who says to their friends, "You know, you are just a biological and chemical process, and so is our friendship"? Of course not, because the reality of friendship proves that there is more to a human being and to human relationships than material processes, namely, intellect, will, memory, and emotions (again, the soul). And since the soul is immaterial, the soul can exist without the body and survive death.

WHAT DOES FAITH TEACH US ABOUT HUMAN NATURE?

Faith agrees with Reason. The human nature we just learned from Reason was created by God. Each of us human beings has been created by

God in His image and likeness,[280] which is especially reflected in our intellect and will. The things that are closest in resemblance to God are the human intellect and the human will. Animals are NOT created in the image and likeness of God. Only a human being is a person because only a human being has an intellect and a free will.

God gives each person a soul at the moment of his conception.[281] This means that every person has an intellect, will, memory, and emotions at conception, but in potential. These spiritual attributes become actualized over time just as the physical attributes start in potential and become actualized over time.

The part of a human that survives death is the soul.[282] After human beings die, they do NOT become angels.[283] It is not natural to angels—it is not angelic nature—to have a physical body. Human beings are not complete without their bodies,[284] which is why eternal human existence in the Kingdom of God will include having bodies.[285]

Human beings are superior to every other material creation of God.[286] Every person has human dignity from being made in the image and likeness of God.[287] We must respect the human dignity of every person, even when someone does not respect his own dignity. To hate sin but love sinners means that there is more to us than our actions, even our mental actions, and our personality. What is more to us than our actions is our human dignity, the image of God that is inside each of us.

Faith also teaches us that human nature is fallen/weakened due to Original Sin.[288] Our bodies, emotions, memories, wills, and intellects are fallen/weakened. Another way in which human nature is fallen is that our

---

[280] *CCC*, 356-360.
[281] *CCC*, 366.
[282] *CCC*, 366, 997, 1021.
[283] *CCC*, 328-336.
[284] *CCC*, 364-365.
[285] *CCC*, 988-1004.
[286] *CCC*, 342-344.
[287] *CCC*, 356-368, 1929-1933.
[288] *CCC*, 386-409.

attributes are often out of harmony with each other. Our bodies, emotions, memories, wills, and intellects are often in tension or in conflict with each other. E.g., what I know is good for me (my intellect) I do not always want (my will), what feels good to me emotionally is not always good for me physically, etc.

To be fully human and fully alive is to become the person God created us to be, which is revealed in the Resurrected Jesus,[289] which will only happen in the Kingdom of God. We come closest in this life to actualizing our human potential the more we become Catholic in our thinking, actions, worship, and prayer. To try to free ourselves from human nature will only ending up dehumanizing us. The solution to our human problems is to not to become other-than-human, but to let ourselves be saved by God.

WHO AM I?

Let's put all this in more personal terms.

It is NOT true that I am only my body and that I have no soul. It is NOT true that my soul is trapped in my body during life and is only perfected after it escapes from my dead body. It IS true that my soul is not complete without my body. In order to be fully human, my perfected soul must be united with my perfected body in eternity.

It is NOT true that I am a completely and absolutely unique and individual, that I am completely different from any other human being. It is NOT true that I am exactly the same as every other human being. It IS true that I am an individual human being. I share a common human nature with other human beings <u>and</u> there are things about me that are unique to me.

It is NOT true that animals and humans are the same species. It is NOT true that I am inferior to animals, that I am to the planet Earth what cancer is to an organism. It IS true that I am superior to animals, that I am made in the image of God and animals are NOT. I have rights, and animals do not. It IS also true that God has entrusted the rest of His creation to human care.

---

[289] *CCC*, 504, 520-521.

Some of the key things that make me who I am are:

- My free will, and so my choices.
- My emotions/feelings.
- My intellect/ability to think.
- My body.
- My desires/wants.
- My soul.
- My personality.
- My age.
- My family background.
- My friendships.
- My talent.
- My race.
- My culture.
- My gender.
- My sexual orientation.
- My economic class.
- My relationship with God.

What MOST makes me who I am is my relationship with God, good or bad.

Everything in this section that is written in the first person applies to all human beings.

WHAT IS REAL SELF-ESTEEM?

We all need to have self-esteem/have self-confidence/love ourselves.[290] We do NOT love ourselves/have real self-esteem/have real self-confidence by loving everything about ourselves. Real self-esteem is being able to look at myself objectively and admit both my objective strengths and objective weaknesses. Real self-esteem is being able to admit that I need the salvation that God alone can give, which means that I cannot save myself by myself, although as St. Augustine advised, "Pray as though everything depended on God. Work as though everything depended on you."

---

[290] *CCC*, 2264.

The surest way to have real self-esteem is to know that the Lord God, the Most High, the All-Holy Supreme Being, loves us while He hates our sins. We do not deserve God's love, which is His free gift. We should neither love ourselves so much that we love our sins and defects nor hate our sins and defects so much that we hate ourselves.

Does God *love you* just the way you are? God *cares for you and wants what is best for you* just the way you are. God does NOT *like everything about you* just the way you are—you would have to be perfect and sinless. God loves us in spite of some of the ways we are. "But God proves His love for us in that while we were still sinners Christ died for us" (Romans 5:8). Someone who thinks God loves him just the way he is does NOT have real self-esteem.

Who has real self-esteem? Who is fully alive? He who says with conviction, "Lord, I am not worthy that You should enter under my roof, but only say the word and my soul shall be healed."

When Jesus preached the Good News that the Kingdom of God is near, He also preached the "bad news" that we need to repent—we need to change, all is not well with us, we freely choose to do what is wrong, we sin, we make mistakes, we have defects, we are not perfect, we are not God, we are in need of salvation.[291] Real self-esteem is being able to hear the bad news as well as the Good News.

---

[291] *CCC*, 545, 588, 1439.

PERSONAL FAITH RESPONSE

Check any statements below that describe you.

In order to LIVE FULLY:

1. _____I agree with the objective truth in this chapter.

2. _____I will thank God for being made in His image and likeness and for saving me from Original Sin.

3. _____I will recognize the common human nature of every person.

4. _____I will recognize the individuality of every other person.

5. _____I will have real self-esteem.

6. _____I will thank God for being made in His image and likeness and for saving me from Original Sin.

VOCABULARY

Will: The attribute of having wants/desires that are freely chosen.

Intellect: The attribute of actively thinking about things.

Human Nature: That which makes a human a human and not another being.

Person: A being with an intellect and a free will.

Fallen Human Nature: Human nature that has each attribute weakened and out of harmony with the other attributes.

Part 7: What Is Being Fully Alive?

Chapter II:
WHAT IS THE PURPOSE OF LIFE?

WHAT HAS GOD REVEALED IS THE PURPOSE OF LIFE?

As we have seen, God created the first humans with everything they needed. They were in harmony with God. They were in harmony with each other. They were in harmony with the rest of Creation in a perfectly good world. Their attributes of mind, will, emotions, and body were in harmony with each other. All of this means that the first humans were happy. God created them happy. God created them to stay happy.

Their happiness was far different from what our Subjectivist culture promotes as happiness. Our Subjectivist culture tends to equate happiness with feeling good. It tells us that we are happy when we feel good either physically (as from comfort or pleasure) or emotionally (as from enjoyment or "feeling good about myself"). Nowadays about the only use of the word *happiness* is for a temporary state of feeling good emotionally or physically. Someone is "happy" who is cheerful, glad, satisfied, comfortable, joyful, ecstatic, etc.

God creates us human beings in order for us to be far happier than that.[292] God creates human beings not just to <u>feel</u> good, but to <u>be</u> good—

---

[292] *CCC*, 1716-1729.

to have a good ***existence***, a great existence.[293] God creates us not just to feel good physically, but to have good bodies. God creates us not just to feel good about ourselves, but to have good selves. God creates us not just to feel fully alive, but to be fully alive.

Jesus says (e.g., Jn 3:16, 10:10, 15:11) that His mission is to bring the fullness of life. Jesus' mission is to make human beings happy—to make their existence better. Jesus made people happy—made their existence better—when He performed miracles. Jesus will bring perfect happiness when He comes again in glory at the end of time to complete the establishment of the Kingdom of God because there will be perfect human existence in the Kingdom.[294]

Knowing that God is an eternal community of perfect and absolute love between Father, Son, and Spirit helps us realize that God freely created us so that we can actually share/participate in—not just "feel"—that perfect and absolute love. "God the Son became human so that humans could become like God," to paraphrase St. Athanasius.

Everything we humans seek (e.g., food, clothing, shelter, friendship), we seek in order to be happy—in order to have a better existence. God designed human nature to need and seek happiness.

Therefore God has revealed that the purpose of life is happiness, rightly understood. God created us so that we will be happy. To be fully alive—to have the best possible existence—is to be happy. God is good!

WHAT IS THE BEST FORMULA FOR HAPPINESS?

St. Augustine has given us what might be the best formula for happiness. To paraphrase him, happiness is getting NOT simply what we want, BUT what we should want. St. Augustine was not a Subjectivist. He meant that we should want that which will give us a good existence.

Upon reflection, we realize that we ourselves have learned this from any achievement or success. When we got good grades, played well in a sport, performed well in an art, got the promotion at work, etc., we did not

---

[293] *CCC*, 295, 374-378.
[294] *CCC*, 655.

The Fullness of Life

do simply what we wanted since there were times we did not want to study or practice or work, but we did what should have wanted (to study, to practice, to work).

So everything we want is NOT always what we should want. We have bad wants that we should NOT want. We have good wants that we should want.

How do we know what we should want? By using Faith (Catholic doctrine) and Reason (e.g., true biology, true psychology, good advice, common sense).

WHAT GOAL OF LIFE SHOULD WE WANT?

What we should want is unlimited/absolute/eternal happiness. What we should want is perfect existence. So far in your life whatever you have gotten what you thought would make you happy has not made you completely happy but has left you wanting more happiness. The rest of your life will be like your life has been so far: whatever you get will not make you completely happy but will leave you wanting more happiness.

The goal of life—what we should want more than anything else—is the perfect happiness that can only be found in the Kingdom of God. That will come after Jesus' Second Coming when He judges the living and the dead in the Last Judgment or General Judgment of all humanity together at one time.

There is another judgment: Immediately after death, there is the Particular Judgment when God judges each person.[295] Death ends the ability of each person to accept or reject God. After death we no longer are able to choose whether to accept or reject God. God gives us for all eternity the choice we made before death whether to accept Him or reject Him.

God is willing to forgive any sin.[296] God's forgiveness/mercy can only be accepted by repenting, which means being sorry and doing penance.[297] God does NOT force anyone to have a relationship with Him. God does

---

[295] *CCC*, 1021-1022.
[296] *CCC*, 545, 604-605, 1439, 1443, 1846-1848.
[297] *CCC*, 1430-1439.

NOT force anyone to accept His mercy. God does not force anyone to accept His love.

Hell is someone's choice to have nothing to do with God for all eternity.[298] Jesus said that Hell is real and often warned people that they could end up there. No one gives us more freedom than God. God gives us a terrifying amount of freedom.

After the Particular Judgment, one of three things happens to a soul:

1) If the soul IS in friendship with God and is without any sin, it enters Heaven,[299] which is living in the direct presence of God, OR

2) If the soul IS in friendship with God but is in the state of minor/venial sin, it enters Purgatory,[300] which is the purification/cleansing from sin that ultimately leads ONLY to Heaven, OR

3) If the soul is NOT in friendship with God and so is in the state of major/mortal sin, it enters Hell,[301] which is the eternal rejection of God.

Every choice we make is significant and meaningful. Every choice turns us closer to God or farther away from God. Every choice makes us more fully alive or less fully alive. Every choice takes us closer to eternal life or eternal death.

The separation of a person's soul and body at death BEFORE the Second Coming is temporary, NOT permanent. AFTER the Second Coming, there will only be the Kingdom and Hell, and in both places everyone will have a soul reunited with a transformed, supernatural body.

---

[298] Satan famously expresses the attitude of those who reject God in John Milton's *Paradise Lost*, "Better to reign in Hell than serve in Heaven." Or as C. S. Lewis writes in *The Great Divorce*, "There are only two kinds of people in the end: those who say to God, 'Thy will be done,' and those to whom God says, in the end, '*Thy* will be done.'"

[299] *CCC*, 1023-1029.

[300] *CCC*, 1030-1032.

[301] *CCC*, 1033-1037.

The General Judgment will confirm/ratify the Particular Judgment. Eternal salvation is in Heaven after the Particular Judgment and then the Kingdom after the General Judgment.

Both the living who are in the Church and the dead who are saved belong to the Communion of Saints.[302] So we can ask those who died, the saints and dead relatives and friends we believe are in Heaven or on their way to Heaven in Purgatory, to pray for us. And we can pray for dead relatives and friends in case they are in Purgatory and not yet in Heaven, as well as for all the souls in Purgatory.

There is one other person besides Jesus who no longer lives on this Earth but already has body and soul reunited in a glorified body in eternity, and that is St. Mary. The event of her having a glorified body immediately after leaving this earth before the Second Coming is called the Assumption,[303] which is celebrated by the Catholic Church on August 15. It remains a mystery whether she died before she was assumed into Heaven. Unlike the other saints, there has never been a tomb or relic for St. Mary because there has never been a dead body of hers on earth.

IF GOD WANTS US TO BE HAPPY, WHY IS THERE SUFFERING?

God does NOT cause suffering.[304] Because God is goodness itself, God only brings about what is good. When there is evil and suffering, God allows it as part of the freedom He has given His Creation.

God freely created us out of love so we could love Him in return.[305] A relationship of love can only exist when it is freely chosen. God gives us the freedom to choose whether to love Him.[306] The choice we make, like all choices, has consequences.

Original Sin and personal sin have resulted in a fallen universe with

---

[302] *CCC*, 954-959.
[303] *CCC*, 966, 974.
[304] *CCC*, 309-315, 1500-1501.
[305] *CCC*, 374-379.
[306] *CCC*, 396.

fallen creatures that originally were all good. Evil and suffering are sometimes the work of the Devil,[307] e.g., temptation and, in extreme cases, demonic possession. Sometimes evil and suffering are caused by humans mistreating other humans.[308] God does NOT make humans hurt themselves or others. Sometimes the cause is fallen Creation/Nature.[309] Nature is a threat to us, e.g., natural disasters, cancer cells, etc., which are NOT signs of God's punishment.

In spite of humanity's rebellion against God, God reveals in many ways His love for us and so His desire for us to be happy.

God shows us His love for us in Creation. Although Nature is a threat, it also can be good and beautiful.

God created human beings in His image and likeness with the ability to give and receive love. God began the salvation of humanity from Original Sin, and thus from all suffering, by making the Old Covenant with the Chosen People. God continued the salvation of humanity by sending His Son, Jesus Christ, to make the New Covenant that invites all human beings who ever lived to enter His Kingdom and then share perfect happiness eternally with Him.[310] God the Son freely lowered Himself to human existence. God the Son shared our suffering in His suffering and death, which alone made it possible for us to enter the Kingdom. God spared Abraham's beloved son from being sacrificed; God did not spare His Own Beloved Son from being sacrificed.

God reveals His love for us through the Catholic Church, which Jesus founded not only to provide eternal happiness, but also to provide the greatest amount of happiness in our life on earth.[311] He reveals His love for us in Sacred Scripture.[312] In the Old Testament, the Psalms, the Book of Job and the other Wisdom Books, and the prophets especially offer insights and consolation when we are suffering. God reveals His love for

---

[307] *CCC*, 395.
[308] *CCC*, 1849, 1852-1853.
[309] *CCC*, 310, 400.
[310] *CCC*, 599-605.
[311] *CCC*, 688.
[312] *CCC*, 80-82.

us through worship (the Sacraments and other rituals), especially the Eucharist, through which He deepens His relationship with us.[313] God gives us saints to provide examples of how to make life meaningful.[314] He gives us the Magisterium, which provides doctrine to help us understand both His Revelation and how to best respond in Faith. Growing in faithfulness to Catholic doctrine is the best way to handle suffering and maintain an underlying sense of joy in spite of the evil in our lives.

God helps us know and experience His love through the people and events of our lives—all the good people we meet and all the good experiences we have. And God allows our own personal suffering, when we unite it to Jesus' suffering, to be redemptive for ourselves and others, and so our suffering can help ourselves and others be free from sin and suffering.[315]

---

[313] *CCC*, 1067, 1084-1090, 1324-1327.
[314] *CCC*, 2683-2684.
[315] *CCC*, 1851.

PERSONAL FAITH RESPONSE

Check any statements below that describe you.

In order to LIVE FULLY:

1. _____I agree with the objective truth in this chapter.

2. _____I will try to get what I should want and not simply what I want.

3. _____I will use Faith and Reason to know what I should want.

4. _____I will not expect to be perfectly happy until, and if, I enter the Kingdom of God.

5. _____I will make eternal salvation the goal of my life.

6. _____I will celebrate the Feast of the Assumption.

7. _____I will not blame God for the suffering in the world and in my life.

8. _____I will unite my suffering to the suffering of Jesus in order to make it redemptive for me and others.

9. _____I will thank God for the many ways He loves me and everyone else.

VOCABULARY

Happiness: Getting not simply what we want, but getting what we should want.

The General Judgment: God's judgment of all humanity together at the Second Coming.

The Particular Judgment: God's judgment of each person immediately after death.

Heaven: The soul living in the direct presence of God.

Purgatory: The soul being cleansed from sin in preparation for Heaven.

Hell: The eternal rejection of God.

Eternal salvation: To be in Heaven or the Kingdom.

The Communion of Saints: The community of both the living who are in the Church and the dead who are saved.

The Assumption: (1) The event of St. Mary having a glorified body immediately after leaving this earth before the Second Coming and (2) its celebration by the Catholic Church on August 15.

Part 7: What Is Being Fully Alive?

Chapter III:
WHAT DO FEELINGS HAVE TO DO WITH HAPPINESS?

IS IT WRONG TO FEEL GOOD?

Upon reflection, we know that what feels good to someone at the time can turn out to be bad for him and others. An alcoholic/addict feels good while getting drunk/high, but drinking/using is bad for him. Eating too much junk food feels good but is bad for our health. Cutting corners in practice, in studying, or on the job feels good but is bad for our own success and the success of those depending on us.

To re-word St. Augustine's definition of happiness ***in terms of feelings***: Happiness is getting NOT simply what feels good, BUT what is objectively good.

Success in life sooner or later involves making sacrifices, which feel bad at the time; and so happiness—a good existence—can sometimes feel bad. Someone who is high or drunk feels better than someone who at the same time is doing a good job at work, in school, or in sports or working out. Someone who is high or drunk feels better than someone who at the same time is making a sacrifice for and being generous to someone else. But who has a more meaningful life, and so who is more deeply happy?

The underlined parts of the Beatitudes are where Jesus points out that feeling bad can lead to happiness:

Blessed are the poor in spirit, for theirs is the Kingdom of Heaven.

Blessed are they who <u>mourn</u>, for they will be comforted.

Blessed are the meek, for they will inherit the land.

Blessed are they who <u>hunger and thirst for righteousness</u>, for they will be satisfied.

Blessed are the merciful, for they will be shown mercy.

Blessed are the clean of heart, for they will see God.

Blessed are the peacemakers, for they will be called children of God.

Blessed are they who <u>are persecuted</u> for the sake of righteousness, for theirs is the Kingdom of Heaven.

Blessed are you when they <u>insult you and persecute you and utter every kind of evil against you [falsely]</u> because of Me. Rejoice and be glad, for your reward will be great in heaven. Thus they persecuted the prophets who were before you.

Blessed in this passage is also accurately translated as *happy* in some Bibles. The blessedness/happiness that Jesus is talking about here is a state of existence. Jesus is not saying, "It feels good to mourn, to hunger and thirst for righteousness, to be persecuted, to be insulted and have evil uttered against you. He is saying, "That which feels bad because of Me will lead you to the Kingdom of Heaven, the deepest kind of comfort and satisfaction, the blessed state of existence."

To answer our subtitle question, feeling good is wrong or right depending on its relation to our state of existence:

- Feeling ***good*** is a GOOD thing when what-feels-good is objectively good for us and/or others.

- Feeling ***good*** is a BAD thing when what-feels-good is objectively bad for us and/or others.

- Feeling **bad** is a GOOD thing when what-feels-bad is objectively good for us and/or others.

- Feeling **bad** is a BAD thing when what-feels-bad is objectively bad for us and/or others.

The best happiness is experienced when what-is-good also feels good and when what-we-should-want also is what we do want. There are rightfully subjective feelings—what feels good (or bad) to two different people can be bad for one and good for the other.

Someone can mindlessly live life by going from one thing that feels good to another thing that feels good without ever understanding happiness. The great danger is that feeling good itself can become addictive—which explains the power of alcohol, drugs, sex, music, video games, playing or watching sports, gambling, getting attention, etc.

God bless you! You are living at a time in history when it has never been easier to feel good, and so it is easier than ever to equate happiness with feeling good and to get addicted to something. Especially given where we are in history, we especially need to learn what we should want and what is objectively good.

WHAT SHOULD WE DO WITH OUR FEELINGS?

We human beings cannot avoid having physical feelings—such as pleasure and pain, comfort and discomfort. And we cannot avoid having emotional feelings—such as joy, gladness, love, hope, daring, sadness, hate, despair, fear, worry, anger, disgust. We should be in touch with/not deny our feelings and know what we are feeling no matter what our feelings are.

But, in order to be happy, we human beings should NOT base our lives on our feelings. To be happy, we human beings need to use our will to control our feelings, and we need to know how to use our will by using our intellect. In terms of St. Augustine's definition of happiness, in order to be happy, we human beings need to control our feelings by what we should want (using our will), and we need to know the difference between what we should want and what we shouldn't want by using our intellect.

Feelings do NOT tell us what we should want. As we have seen, feeling good is not always a good thing, and feeling bad is not always a bad thing. Feelings can be very deceptive. When you felt afraid of the monster in your bedroom, was there really a monster in your bedroom? More seriously, victims of abuse first <u>felt</u> safe to be alone with their abusers, but they <u>were not</u> actually safe.

Only Faith and Reason tell us what we should want. We need Catholic doctrine to tell us what we should want. We need Reason to tell us what we should want. We need Reason from as many different sources as we can get it—either by our own learning or by getting advice. In order to know what we should want, we need the truth, we need knowledge, about everything in our lives—careers, finances, plumbing, sports, sex, medicine, clothes cleaning, education, parenting, beer, and on and on.

Feelings are so powerful that either we will control our feelings or our feelings will control us. We already control our feelings whenever we achieve success. If we have wisdom, we will control our feelings in all areas of our lives—sex, socializing, spending money, etc. We should NOT imitate the many people who have tremendous self-control in one area of their lives, such as sports, studies, or work, and then lack self-control in other areas of their lives, such as sex or whatever makes them feel good.

ARE FEELINGS EVER SINFUL?

In and of themselves, spontaneous feelings are NOT sinful. It is NOT a sin simply to feel pleasure.[316] It is NOT a sin simply to spontaneously have strong emotions, e.g., hate, anger, disgust, sexual feelings.

We are guilty of sinning when we freely choose not to control our feelings so that our feelings cause us to act badly.[317] We are guilty of sinning when we freely choose to cultivate or dwell on negative feelings. The key word here is *freely*. Someone who is psychologically incapable of controlling their feelings, no matter how negative they are, is NOT guilty of sinning. Someone in that condition needs to get professional help,

---

[316] *CCC*, 1767.
[317] *CCC*, 1762, 1767-1770.

preferably from an expert who is also a person of Faith.

WHAT ARE GOOD WORDS TO LIVE BY?

Which of the following are good words to live by or good advice to give? "Be yourself"? "Do whatever makes you feel good about yourself"? "Follow your heart/dreams/passion"? None! All of them presume that what a person wants is what he should want, and that what feels good to a person is what is good for him and others.

None of these expressions passes the "Adolf Hitler Test" because no one in their right mind would say those things to Hitler, who is a dramatic example of how what a person wants (in his case, dehumanizing and murdering people in concentration camps and invading countries) can be what he should not want and what feels good to a person (Hitler's "successes" felt good to him) can be bad for him or others.

Better—but not nearly as catchy—words to live by are:

- Be yourself when "yourself" is good—otherwise change yourself to be the person God wants you to be.
- Do whatever makes you feel good about yourself when it is good for you and others.
- Follow your heart/dreams/passion when your heart/dreams/passion is good—otherwise change your heart/dreams/passion.

Life would be a lot simpler if what we want is always what we should want and if what feels good is always good and what feels bad is always bad. But life just is not that simple. And there is no better explanation than Original Sin.

HOW DO WE FIND HAPPINESS IN RELATIONSHIPS?

In order to make others happy, we should give others NOT what simply makes them feel good, BUT what is objectively good for them regardless of how it feels to them at the time. We know we are dealing with a mature person when he respects us for giving him what is good for him regardless of how it feels to him at the time. We need to be prepared for the fact that others will NOT always appreciate it when we are making them happy the right way.

When we need to give others what is good for them but feels bad to them, we must be very careful to do it in a way that is in harmony with Reason and Catholic doctrine, which might require the advice of someone wiser than us.

We need to realize that others make us happy when they give us what is good for us regardless of how it feels to us at the time. When we first fail to appreciate others making us happy the right way, we need to admit it. When others are trying to give us what is good for us but feels bad to us, we must make sure that they are doing it in a way that is appropriate because it is in harmony with Reason and Catholic Doctrine.

PERSONAL FAITH RESPONSE

Check any statements below that describe you.

In order to LIVE FULLY:

1. _____I agree with the objective truth in this chapter.

2. _____I will seek a good existence, fulfillment, a meaningful life, a life worth more than what feels good physically or emotionally at the time.

3. _____I will recognize when feeling good is good or bad and when feeling bad is good or bad.

4. _____I will stay aware of becoming addicted to whatever makes me feel good—alcohol, drugs, sex, music, video games, playing or watching sports, gambling, getting attention, whatever stimulates my hormonal system and central nervous system.

5. _____I will be in touch with my feelings and know what I am feeling no matter what my feelings are.

6. _____I will use my will to control my feelings, and I will use my intellect (Faith and Reason) to control my will.

7. _____I will stop taking literally or using literally expressions like "Be yourself," "Do whatever makes you feel good about yourself," and "Follow your heart/dreams/passion."

8. _____I will find happiness in relationships by giving and receiving what is good and not simply what feels good.

9. _____I will be careful about what feels bad in relationships by making sure that the goal and the method of what feels bad is in harmony with Reason and Catholic Doctrine.

Part 7: What Is Being Fully Alive?

Chapter IV:
WHAT IS THE ROLE OF SEXUALITY IN HAPPINESS?

SOURCES

- Pope John II, Familiaris Consortio, 1981.

- Pope John Paul II, On the Dignity and Vocation of Women, 1988.

- Pontifical Council on the Family, The Truth and Meaning of Human Sexuality, 1995.

- Congregation for the Doctrine of the Faith, Letter to the Bishops of the Catholic Church on the Collaboration of Men and Women in the Church and in the World, 2004.

- United States Conference of Catholic Bishops, Marriage: Love and Life in the Divine Plan, 2009.

- United States Conference of Catholic Bishops, Made for Each Other: Sexual Difference and Complementarity, 2010.

- Pope Francis' General Audiences on the Family, Gender and Marriage, April 8-May 13, 2015.

- Pope Francis, Amoris Laetitia, 2016.

- Christopher West, Good News about Sex and Marriage (Servant Books, 2004).

WHAT IS SEXUALITY?

Sexuality is the meaning that sex has/the role sex plays in being human. As with so many other things, there are different views of sexuality. Contradictory views of sexuality are NOT equally true—views of sexuality are better or worse depending on how close or far they are to the reality of sexuality.

This chapter studies the objective essence/nature of sexuality. We will NOT focus on psychology, which is the study of a person's motivations and personality, or sociology, which is the study of how groups act. People's thoughts, feelings, and actions can be out of touch with the reality of sexuality.

Only theology and philosophy study the essence/nature of things. Catholic doctrine has given us the objectively truest view of sexuality.

Again, the Catholic way of judging those who disagree with Catholic Faith and Reason is to judge that their thoughts and/or actions are objectively mistaken. Such judgments are NOT being prejudiced, intolerant, uncompassionate, insensitive, hateful, mean, etc. It is NOT to judge that their souls are automatically going to Hell. It is NOT to judge that they have no human dignity or human rights. To one degree or another, we all fall short of having the sexuality we should have, but universal falling short does NOT mean that a mistake is no longer a mistake and a sin is no longer a sin.

Because the Catholic view of sexuality is objectively true, to a great extent it can be shared and is shared by anyone who uses Reason and common sense.

At the center of sexuality is gender, which is the division of humanity into male and female. It might be helpful to understand the Catholic view of gender, masculinity, and femininity by first looking at its RIVALS.

- Male Chauvinism: There is a real difference between males and females, and the difference is that MALES ARE SUPERIOR to females.

- Radical Feminism: There is a real difference between males and females, and the difference is that FEMALES ARE SUPERIOR to males.

- Unisexism: Males and females are essentially the SAME; they are only different in unimportant/minor/superficial ways.

- Jungian Psychology (the psychological theory of Carl Jung): Masculinity and femininity are DIFFERENT SIDES WITHIN each human being, and so a male should get in touch with his feminine side and a female should get in touch with her masculine side.

- Gender Theory: Masculinity, and femininity, are created/constructed either by society (which is "bad") or by an individual (which is "good"), and so gender is completely SUBJECTIVE and there is an almost unlimited number of genders.

We will compare and contrast these sexualities with Catholic sexuality.

ARE MALES AND FEMALES EQUAL?

Catholic doctrine teaches that males and females ARE equal in important ways. Both males and females are made in the image and likeness of God so they are equal in human dignity and human rights. Both males and females have human minds, human wills, human emotions, and human bodies and therefore have the same human nature. Both males and females are affected by Original Sin, and so they are equally in need of salvation, which can only come from Jesus Christ.

From Catholic doctrine, we now know that both Male Chauvinism and Radical Feminism are mistaken because they do not believe in the equal humanity of males and females. We still need to explore whether males and females are different.

IS THERE EVIDENCE FROM REASON THAT MALES AND FEMALES ARE DIFFERENT?

There is actually overwhelming evidence from Reason that males and females are different.

The biology is obvious:

- From the moment of conception, a male has an x chromosome and a y chromosome; a female has two x chromosomes.

- The male body is different from the female body—different skeletal and muscular structures, differences in facial hair, different sexual organs, different hormonal systems.

- Females can get pregnant; males cannot get pregnant.

Here are more controversial examples that research and common experience seem to confirm. They are descriptions and NOT value judgments. God has NOT revealed the following examples. Someone can be a good Catholic, or a good person, and disagree with the following if he has better research and analysis. Everyone should be committed to the objective truth about sexuality and let the truth correct any biases we might have.

- Males tend to be stronger, faster, and more athletic than females. The strongest man will always be stronger than the strongest woman. The fastest man will always be faster than the fastest woman. Although the most athletic females will be more athletic than many males, the most athletic man will always be more athletic than the most athletic woman.

- Males have different temperaments than females—males tend to be more aggressive, competitive, volatile, exploratory, impulsive, visual, and abstract than females.

- Females tend to be more sensitive to others than males tend to be.

- Females tend to be more talkative and more expressive of their emotions than males.

- Without adult influence, little boys play differently than little girls. Boys tend to play rougher than girls, especially in a group of only boys, e.g., a group of boys will wrestle each other and a group of girls will not. The play of boys tends to be more thing-oriented, e.g., boys tend to choose to play with a toy truck instead of a doll; and the play of girls tends to be more person-oriented, e.g., little girls tend to play with a doll instead of a toy truck.

- Females tend to mature physically and psychologically faster than males.

- When talking about a problem, males tend to want to get to the solution more quickly than females do, and females tend to want to talk about their feelings about the problem before they get to solving it more than males do.

- Females tend to worry more than males.

- Males tend to have more anger-management challenges than females.

- Males tend to like videogames much more than females do.

- The great majority of violent crime is committed by males in their teens and twenties.

- There is an old saying: "Girls use sex to get love, and boys use love to get sex." It is better stated in our Subjectivist culture: "Girls are more naturally tempted to use sex in order to get the feeling (not the reality) of being loved, and boys are more naturally tempted to use the feeling (not the reality) of being loved in order to get sex."

- Males tend to want to have sex more frequently than females tend to want to have sex. Females are more satisfied with simply cuddling or other signs of affection than males are. Foreplay is more important for a female to have an orgasm than it is for a male.

- Males are more attracted to visual pornography whereas females are more attracted to romantic stories. Females tend to need the build-up of drama in a romantic story whereas males tend to settle for images.

- Girls tend to get better grades than boys, but boys tend to get higher standardized test scores than girls.

- While there are some females who excel in STEM (science, technology, engineering, and math), males tend to have more interest in STEM than females do.

Males and females have the same human nature but with different forms—just as different church buildings have different architectural forms, but a church is still a church and not an apartment building. The major differences between males and females are mainly the result of "Nature," NOT "Nurture." The differences are innate; human beings are born with the differences. All differences are NOT merely a result of culture/society/upbringing/"assignment." Gender has a physical basis—chromosomes, DNA, organs, and other biological, chemical, and psychological factors distinguish males from females.

And yet a male can rebel against his masculinity, and a female can rebel against her femininity. A boy or girl can be confused about gender, especially when getting contradictory messages about gender from adults. Gender is also something that must be freely accepted and cultivated.

From Reason, we now know that Unisexism and Gender Theory are mistaken because they do not realize the objective natural differences between males and females.

WHAT DO WE KNOW FROM <u>FAITH</u> ABOUT THE DIFFERENCE BETWEEN MALES AND FEMALES?

Again, Faith does not contradict Reason; but Faith gives knowledge that is beyond Reason's ability to give. From Faith in Divine Revelation we know several things.

"In the image of God He created them; male and female He created them" (Gn 1:27). God created males and females as equally human.[318] God created gender and the difference between males and females.[319] God wants males to be masculine and females to be feminine. It is possible for every male to be masculine and every female to be feminine.

"The LORD God said, 'It is not good for the man to be alone. I will make a helper suited to him.' So the LORD God formed out of the ground all the wild animals and all the birds of the air . . . but none proved to be a helper suited to him. So the LORD God cast a deep sleep on the man, and while he was asleep . . . He built the rib that He had taken from the man into a woman . . . That is why a man leaves his father and mother and clings

---

[318] *CCC*, 369.
[319] *CCC*, 369.

to his wife, and the two of them become one flesh" (Gn 2:18-24). God created the difference between male and female to be complementary, which means that God designed males and females to complete/need each other.[320] A male needs females and femininity in his life in order to be fulfilled and completed. A female needs males and masculinity in her life in order to be fulfilled and completed.

Catholic Sexuality, based on Reason and Faith, is the objectively true view that males and females are equal in humanity but are significantly different from each other while needing each other. From Divine Revelation, we now know that Male Chauvinism, Radical Feminism, Unisexism, Jungian Psychology, and Gender Theory are mistaken. Neither a new law or Supreme Court decision, nor public opinion polls and referenda, nor surgery and hormone therapy can change Divine Revelation, can change God's mind,

We can see why people are tempted to believe these false sexualities. Like any false ideology or heresy, there is a germ of truth. Male Chauvinism, Radical Feminism, and Jungian Psychology recognize that there is an essential difference between masculinity and femininity, although without understanding the nature of the difference. Unisexism recognizes that there is an equality involved in the relationship between masculinity and femininity, although without understanding the nature the equality. Gender Theory recognizes that there is a freedom involved in gender, without understanding the nature of that freedom. As we are about to see, Jungian Psychology recognizes the complementarity between males and females, without understanding the nature of that complementarity.

HOW ARE MALES AND FEMALES COMPLEMENTARY?

Males and females are complimentary in real relationships and situations. The femininity that males need and the masculinity that females need is NOT found <u>within</u> themselves, BUT <u>outside</u> of themselves in good, healthy relationships with each other along the entire range/spectrum of possibilities: they need to be good sons and daughters, brothers and sisters, husbands and wives, fathers and mothers, cousins, nephews and nieces, grandsons and granddaughters, friends, boyfriends and girlfriends, co-workers, students, etc. The great majority of comple-

---

[320] *CCC*, 371-372, 1604-1605.

mentary relationships with the opposite sex are NOT romantic or erotic.

Yes, differences between males and females were exaggerated before the 1960s when, for example, males were discouraged from expressing emotions and females were excluded from vigorous physical activities. On the other hand, the traditional stereotypes—that the male is the warrior and defender of the family and the mother is the homemaker and nurturer—are somewhat true. There are roles and responsibilities that men and women can share, and there are roles and responsibilities that more naturally belong to males and roles and responsibilities that more naturally belong to females.

Masculinity is primarily defined by fatherhood, and femininity is primarily defined by motherhood. Persons who are not actually husbands/fathers or wives/mothers can grow in good masculinity and femininity by developing the habits and character of good husbands/fathers or wives/mothers.

Still, while a boy can learn to be a good <u>human being/person</u> from both good men and good women, and a girl can learn to be a good <u>human being/person</u> from both good men and good women; nevertheless a girl better learns to be a good <u>woman</u> from good women and a boy better learns to be a good <u>man</u> from good men. Those males in their teens and twenties who commit violent crime usually do not have in their lives fathers or adult males with good masculinity to show them how to have good masculinity. The solution to the problem of bad masculinity is good masculinity, not feminized masculinity.

The Magisterium does NOT explain in great detail the roles and responsibilities of males and females because God expects us to use Reason as well as Faith/Revelation to know sex roles, and because we are still learning about sex roles as women are given more opportunities and as more research is done. Reasonable people can reasonably disagree (and so Catholics are free to disagree) on several related topics: when males and females should be treated the same, whether there is some kind of conspiratorial "patriarchy" or "glass ceiling" in place today, whether sex roles changed as quickly as they should have, and whether changing sex roles have always been good, especially for children.

It cannot be stated strongly enough that the differences between men and women do NOT excuse either men or women from becoming moral and virtuous human beings.

WHAT IS THE PURPOSE OF SEX?

God has given two purposes for sex/genital activity, which can also be known by Reason alone:[321]

1) Love, which means union/commitment to what is good for the husband or wife, as expressed in the wedding vow, "I promise to be true to you in good times and in bad, in sickness and in health. I will love you and honor you all the days of my life."

2) Life, which means procreation/reproduction/baby-making.

God has made genital activity body language. The body language of genital activity objectively "says"—regardless of whether those involved want it to—"I give myself, including my fertility, to you—I share not just my body but my whole life with you." Genital activity without the purposes of love and life is dishonest/false/mistaken body language. The total gift of one's entire self (NOT just one's genitals) in love to the husband or wife, the giving and receiving of entire lives (NOT just feelings) in marriage is a sharing in and reflection of the total giving and receiving of (non-sexual) love by each Divine Person in the life of the Trinity.

God wants sex/genital activity to take place only in a marriage between one man and one woman.[322] Even though Jesus was perfectly aware of the Greco-Roman world in which He lived and which valued same-sex relationships, Jesus made the marriage of one man to one woman a Sacrament.[323] God disagrees with those who want to re-define marriage as something other than a life-long, faithful union between one man and one woman who are open to having children. It is infallible doctrine that marriage is only a life-long, faithful union between one man and one woman. The Magisterium will NOT one day approve of same-sex "marriage," polygamy or polyamorous "marriage," or incestuous "marriage." To approve of one false form of "marriage" is to open the door to the other false forms of marriage. To make consent between adults the moral standard for genital activity is to open the door to all false forms of

---

[321] *CCC*, 1601-1603, 1643-1654.
[322] *CCC*, 1612-1613, 1638-1640.
[323] *CCC*, 1601, 1638-1640, 1660

marriage and reject God's plan for the family.[324]

These two God-given purposes of sex (love and life) were generally supported in American society until two historical developments increasingly made feeling good, physically or emotionally, the purpose of sex for much of Western society. Artificial methods of birth control, especially since 1960 when the birth control pill[325] was put on the market, have separated sexuality from life/procreation. The "hook-up culture" that has been growing since the 1980s separates sexuality not only from procreation, but also from love/union.

WHY ISN'T FEELING GOOD THE PURPOSE OF SEX?

Feeling good is NOT the purpose for sex because it is a side effect/indirect result of sex, although a powerful one. Orgasm always involves baby-making organs that are naturally complementary to the other gender.

Feeling good is to sex what feeling good is to food. Although we are all tempted to eat only for feeling good, it is NOT healthy to eat only for feeling good. It is NOT healthy (physically, psychologically, socially, and spiritually) to have sex only for feeling good. Our society needs to wake up to having sex for the right reasons just like it has woken up to eating for the right reasons. As society has increasingly valued food that is natural, it has increasingly valued sex that is artificial (denying human biology, artificial contraception, in vitro fertilization, procedures to try to change gender, etc.). The virtue of temperance applies to sex as much as it applies to eating.[326]

Sex only for feeling good leads to—among other things—the following,

---

[324] *CCC*, 2201-2233.

[325] Historical note on which reasonable people can reasonably disagree: Two major reasons that women before the 1960s needed to stay home after marriage instead of getting jobs outside of the home are (1) there was no effective natural family planning (approved by the Magisterium) or artificial birth control (disapproved by the Magisterium) and so women tended to have many children who then needed care and (2) much work outside the home needed physical strength. The people who invented effective birth control and developed the technology needing only the physical ability to push a button or click a mouse, which "liberated" women, were males.

[326] *CCC*, 1809.

all of which were far less common before 1960: abortions; epidemic sexually transmitted diseases and infections; addiction to sex; young adults not getting married; spouses being unfaithful, and divorce; children born to unmarried parents; and children growing up without being raised by two parents, especially fathers. In general, there has been a breakdown of the family, which is the foundation of society.[327] The weaker families are, the weaker society is.

Our sex drive is not simply a drive/urge to have orgasm; but, much more than that, our sex drive is really a drive/urge to unite ourselves with the opposite sex and so find completion/wholeness along the entire spectrum of non-romantic male-female relationships, especially in a good marriage.

Without the purposes of love and life, sex is beneath human dignity, sinful, and will not help us be fully alive.

---

[327] *CCC*, 2207-2213.

PERSONAL FAITH RESPONSE

Check any statements below that describe you.

In order to LIVE FULLY:

1. _____I agree with the objective truth in this chapter.

2. _____I will use my sexuality to bring me closer to God, not farther from God.

3. _____I will control my hormones and not let my hormones control me.

4. _____I will be the best possible husband and father or a wife and mother, or develop those virtues and characteristics.

5. _____I will have good relationships with the opposite sex across the entire spectrum of relationships.

6. _____I will respect the common humanity of the opposite sex.

7. _____I will not need a member of the opposite sex to be my trophy.

8. _____I will work to make abortion illegal.

9. _____I will stay away from pornography and romantic fantasies that make it more difficult for me to develop relationships with real, flesh-and-blood members of the opposite sex who will always be imperfect, and I will remember that a fantasy cannot care for me.

10. _____I will be as good as I can at being romantic, but I will never use romance to manipulate a member of the opposite sex.

11. _____I will defend the traditional definitions of marriage and gender rooted in Reason and Revelation.

12. _____I will recognize the common humanity of those with same-sex attraction and gender dysphoria and stand against unjust discrimination.

13. _____I will not equate loving those with same-sex attraction and gender dysphoria with approving beliefs and actions that contradict Catholic Sexuality.

14. _____I will make a good Confession to receive God's mercy and turn my life around whenever I have not been the person that God wants me to be.

15. _____I will turn to Catholic resources, such as the excellent websites www.chastity.com and couragerc.org.

16. _____If I am unmarried, I will meet as many members of the opposite sex as possible in order to understand the opposite sex better, but especially to get to know the right members of the opposite sex (that are mature, moral, etc.).

17. _____If I am unmarried, I will save any and all genital activity for marriage to a member of the opposite sex whose happiness is more important to me than my own happiness.

- I will never risk bringing into the world a child whose happiness is less important to me than my own happiness, and so I will never have intercourse before marriage.
- As a female, I will never abort my child; as a male, I will never risk conceiving a child who could be aborted without my approval or even without my knowing it.
- I will realize that once I conceive a child, I am that child's parent forever—I cannot undo becoming a parent even though my child can be killed before it is born.
- I will never spread an STD/STI so I will never risk getting an STD/STI.

18. _____If I am unmarried, I will ask myself, with every member of the opposite sex I meet, if he or she would be a good husband/wife by (1) being a good father/mother to our children and (2) being my best friend so that we can have a happy marriage.

VOCABULARY

Sexuality: The meaning that sex has in being human.

Gender: The division of humanity into male and female.

Male Chauvinism: The view that there is a real difference between males and females, and the difference is that MALES ARE SUPERIOR to females.

Radical Feminism: The view that there is a real difference between males and females, and the difference is that FEMALES ARE SUPERIOR to males.

Jungian Psychology: The view that masculinity and femininity are DIFFERENT SIDES WITHIN each human being.

Unisexism: The view that males and females are essentially the SAME; they are only different in unimportant/minor/superficial ways.

Gender Theory: The view that masculinity, and femininity, are constructed either by society (which is "bad") or by an individual (which is "good), and so gender is completely SUBJECTIVE.

The Complementarity of the Sexes: The design by God for males and females to complete each other.

Catholic Sexuality: The view that realizes that males and females are equal in humanity but are significantly different from each other while needing each other and that the purposes of genital activity are love and life.

Procreation: Reproduction/baby-making.

PART 8:

WHAT IS THE FULLNESS OF RESPONDING TO REVELATION?

Chapter I: Why End with This Part?

Chapter II: What Is the Fullness of Responding to God in Morality?

Chapter III: What Is the Fullness of Responding to God in Worship?

Chapter IV: What Makes the Eucharist Especially Important?

Chapter V: What Else Is Important to Know about the Sacraments?

Chapter VI: What Is the Fullness of Responding to God in Prayer?

Chapter VII: What Is the Fullness of Sharing the Faith?

Chapter VIII: What Is the Fullness of Faith?

Part 8: What Is the Fullness of Responding to Revelation?

Chapter I:
WHY END WITH THIS PART?

We have learned that in order to live fully—to have the best possible existence and NOT just feel good at the moment—and in order ultimately to find eternal salvation, we should get NOT what we want, BUT what we should want.

What we should want more than anything else is to have a relationship with God—to know Him and interact with Him. What we should want more than anything else is to enter the Kingdom of God, which is the only place where the fullness of a relationship with God can take place and, therefore, the only place where we can be most fully alive. What we should want is to make the most of the gift of life God has given us.

Between the Fall of the first humans and one's own death or the Second Coming, God reveals Himself most directly through Jesus Christ, and so the best way to have a relationship with God is by having a relationship with Jesus Christ. The best way to enter the Kingdom is to follow Jesus to it.

The best way to accept Jesus' invitation to be His follower and friend is found in the Four Pillars of the Catholic Faith. The best way to be as happy and as fully alive as we can be (which will not always feel good) until we enter the Kingdom is found in the Four Pillars. What we should want is a life based on the Four Pillars, which are:

- Creed;

- Morality;

- Worship; and

- Prayer.

Because up until now we have concentrated on the pillar of Creed, we will end by studying the pillars of Morality, Worship, and Prayer.

Part 8: What Is the Fullness of Responding to Revelation?

Chapter II:

WHAT IS THE FULLNESS OF RESPONDING TO GOD IN MORALITY?

WHAT IS MORALITY?

Morality is how we should act and how we should want to act, outside the purely technical sphere. Moral acts are good acts, and immoral acts are bad acts, which are also known as sins.[328] E.g., the wrong technique in gardening is not a sin. This chapter is about the Catholic doctrines we need to know in order to be as moral as possible. It is NOT claiming that Catholics actually act morally more than non-Catholics.

Morality has to do with actions that are freely chosen, actions that are the result of a decision.[329] Human beings and angels can act morally or immorally because only human beings and angels have the two attributes that it takes to make a free choice: free will and intellect. Animals can NOT act morally or immorally.

There is a difference between the deed and the doer of the deed; there is a difference between the action and the person committing the act. This explains why God hates the sin, which is a bad deed, but loves the sinner,

---

[328] *CCC*, 1849-1850.
[329] *CCC*, 1749.

who is the doer of the bad deed. We, also, should hate/disapprove of the bad deed, including our own bad deeds, but love the doer, including ourselves. One wrong extreme is to so love sinners that we love sins; and another wrong extreme is to so hate sin that we hate sinners.

When a deed is immoral, what about the doer?[330] The doer of a bad deed may or may not be at fault depending on the reasons for the deed. For example, two drivers commit the same deed of hitting a child. One driver hits a child because he, the driver, is texting but would have been free to stop in time if he had not been texting. The second driver hits a child even though he was driving responsibly because the child ran out in front of his car at the last second. Although they have committed the same deed, the first driver is at fault whereas the second driver is not at fault. Fault/guilt for a bad deed depends on how free the doer was. The first driver freely chose to drive irresponsibly and could have been free to stop in time. The second driver was not free to stop in time.

SHOULD EVERYONE BE MORAL?

Morality is NOT just for Catholics. All human beings should be moral.[331] All human beings can be moral to the extent that they have adequate intellect and free will. Children, people with developmental disabilities, and people who are psychologically troubled are examples of people who do not always have the adequate intellect and free will to know and do the moral thing.

With adequate intellect, all people can use Reason alone (without Revelation) to know that they should do good and avoid evil by applying principles that transcend individual and cultural differences. These transcendent principles are called the *Natural Law* in Catholic doctrine because they are "laws" or principles that are rooted in the human nature that is common to all human beings. The reality of Natural Law explains why so many religions and societies have common moral principles, e.g., "tell the truth," "do not steal," "do not kill an innocent person." It is Natural Law that determines the basis for each person's fundamental rights and duties. Civil law should be rooted in Natural Law.

---

[330] *CCC*, 1730-1761.
[331] *CCC*, 1954-1960.

The Fullness of Life

Every human being with adequate intellect and will can be virtuous (have good moral habits).[332] There are virtues that can be known by Reason alone, as we see in pagan philosophers such as Aristotle and Cicero. Every virtue is a "golden mean/middle" between an excess and a defect. There are four virtues traditionally known as the Cardinal Virtues[333] because they are the most basic virtues on which all the other virtues hinge (and *cardinal* comes from the Latin *cardo*, meaning "hinge"):

1) Prudence, which makes good applications of moral principles to particular cases; its excesses are craftiness and deceit, and its defects are negligence and recklessness; related virtues are foresight, teachability, care, and circumspection. Prudence is a virtue of the intellect.

2) Justice, which renders to others their rights/what is due to them/what belongs to them; its excess is severity, and its defect is lenience. Justice is a virtue of action.

3) Temperance, which moderates the attraction of pleasures, provides balance in the use of created goods, and keeps desires within limits; its excesses are austerity, impassiveness, and sullenness, and its defects are gluttony, drunkenness, lust, pride, vanity; related virtues are self-control, humility, modesty. Temperance is a virtue of the will/having the right willpower.

4) Fortitude, which is bravery, firmness in difficulties, constancy in the pursuit of the good, strength in face fear and obstacles; its excesses are boldness, presumption, stubbornness, and ruthlessness, and its defects are cowardice, weakness, impatience, and irresoluteness; its related virtues are perseverance, patience, and magnanimity. Fortitude is a virtue moderating emotions, not eliminating emotions. The brave person still experiences fear, but controls that fear rather than letting that fear control him.

Everyone should strive to be prudent, just, temperate, and courageous. Having the virtues is what gives us moral character. We need the fullness of virtue—one virtue needs the other. Without the other virtues,

---

[332] *CCC*, 1804.
[333] *CCC*, 1805-1809.

what starts as a virtue ends as a vice/bad habit. In order to be fully alive, we need to have the Cardinal Virtues.

WHAT IS CONSCIENCE?

Another reason that every human being should be expected to be moral is that every human being has a conscience.[334] Conscience is not an emotion or an intuition/hunch or a little voice. Conscience is a reasoning process that applies a moral principle to a make a specific moral choice.[335] Prudence is the habit of making good moral choices. The reasoning of conscience goes like this:

Because of a moral principle (e.g., because lying is wrong),

And because of the application of the principle to a particular case (e.g., telling my teacher the dog ate my homework is a lie),

Therefore a moral choice (e.g., telling my teacher the dog ate my homework is wrong).

Conscience can be correct or mistaken.[336] It can make a right choice or an erroneous choice. Therefore conscience must be formed/educated, which is a lifelong task.[337] Conscience must be formed by Reason, e.g., accurate information, the advice of competent people, etc. It is more fully formed by Faith, (e.g., Catholic doctrine, spiritual direction that never contradicts Catholic doctrine, etc.).

Someone who is not aware that his conscience is error and that his choice is bad is not guilty/blameworthy/at fault for his wrong judgment and the sin he commits.[338] However, when an action is bad, it is bad. Lack of awareness of an act's badness does change the nature of the act.

---

[334] *CCC*, 1776.
[335] *CCC*, 1777-1782.
[336] *CCC*, 1790-1794.
[337] *CCC*, 1783-1788.
[338] *CCC*, 1793.

WHAT IS SOCIAL JUSTICE?

Every human being should be held to practicing justice, which is the rendering of rights. There are two kinds of rights. Contract rights are what is owed in a one-on-one relationship based on an agreement. Human rights are what are owed to every human being (ultimately because of the human dignity that comes from being created in the image of God). Besides the many one-on-one relationships in our lives, we human beings are members of society. Social justice is the rendering of human rights to every member of society and sustaining the common good.[339]

There are two sides of social justice. Contributive justice is what the individual owes society, what the individual should contribute to society's common good.[340] Distributive justice is what society owes the individual, what each individual should receive as his fair share of the common good.[341] Both contributive justice and distributive justice require democratic methods in harmony with natural Law.

Social justice is actually well summarized in the motto of the Three Musketeers, "One for all, and all for one," in the Pledge of Allegiance's "liberty and justice for all" and in the dictum, "In essential things, unity; in non-essential things, liberty; in all things, charity." So what is immoral is rugged individualism which ignores the common good;[342] collectivism which ignores individuality, liberty, and subsidiarity;[343] and utilitarianism which seeks only the greatest good for the greatest number of people.[344] Social justice requires a wealth of free associations of citizens and only that amount of government which is necessary with legislative, executive, and judicial branches that are independent of each other while adhering to a constitution based on Natural Law.

---

[339] *CCC*, 1928, 1930, 1905-1912. In the history of modern Catholic social teaching by the popes, which began with Pope Leo XIII's *Rerum Novarum* in 1891, the rights in the U. S. Bill of Rights and the United Nations' *Universal Declaration of Human Rights* provide a good list of rights that the Magisterium has taught are human rights.

[340] *CCC*, 1913-1917.

[341] *CCC*, 1934-1938.

[342] *CCC*, 1939-1942.

[343] *CCC*, 1882-1885.

[344] *CCC*, 1881, 1929-1933.

Social justice is practiced by applying Natural Law (and, even better, Catholic doctrine) to social issues. This involves social analysis of current conditions and then making a prudential judgment as to how to best apply doctrine to current conditions. Right Reason allows everyone to agree on the principles of Natural Law. Reasonable people can reasonably disagree on social analysis and prudential judgment. Making accurate social analysis is crucial to practicing social justice. People often disagree about prudential judgments because they have different views of human nature, often subconsciously.

WHAT IS THE ESSENCE OF REVEALED MORALITY?

Faith adds to our Reason's understanding of morality, e.g., Catholic doctrine provides the most complete understanding of social justice. God has revealed the essence of morality in two stages.[345] The first stage is the Old Covenant/Testament, summed up in the Ten Commandments. The second stage is the New Covenant/Testament, given by Jesus Christ and summed up in the Two Great Commandments, which are (paraphrased):

- The First Great Commandment: Love God more than anything else .

- The Second Great Commandment: Love your neighbor, who is everyone.

WHY IS LOVE A COMMANDMENT?

One common way that Jesus is misinterpreted and misused is for someone to incorrectly define love, intentionally or unintentionally, and then claim Jesus supports/agrees with him. Let's again make sure we know what love is.

Our Subjectivist culture defines love as no more and no less than a feeling/emotion—to equate loving with liking and feeling good. If I am a Subjectivist (knowingly or unknowingly), and if my action makes someone feel good, physically or emotionally, I will call that "love." If my action or

---

[345] *CCC*, 1961-1974, 1980-1986.

the actions of others toward me make me feel good, I will call that "love." Those are really false forms of love.

Real love involves feelings; but it is much more than feelings. Real love is a commitment to value/prize/treasure/cherish by giving what is good and what should be wanted. The First Great Commandment is to make the commitment to value God more than anything else. The Second Great Commandment is to make the commitment to value others by making them happy.

When Jesus commanded us to love everyone, He meant that we should NOT simply give others what they want and what makes them feel good, BUT give others what they should want and what is good for them regardless of how it feels to them at the time. We know others love us when they give us what we should want and what is good for us regardless of how it feels to us at the time, and NOT simply what we want and what makes us feel good.

These commitments often involve sacrifices that do not always feel good to us and that we will not always like making. Love is a commandment from Jesus because we need Him to command us due to our fallen human nature. Commandments are needed because God knows what is good for us infinitely more than we do.

Let us also remind ourselves that Jesus was always perfectly loving to everyone. Yet, although Jesus' love was returned by some, His love was not returned by others; Jesus was crucified. If we love others, if we do what is good for others, then will they always do good to us in return? No, they still might treat us badly. Just as Jesus chose to die for everyone, including those who treated Him badly and not only those who treated Him well, we also need to stay committed to doing what is good for those who treat us badly. Christ commands us to love our enemies (Mt 5:43-47; Lk 6:27-36). That does mean liking them or liking the way they treat us or giving up our right to self-defense.[346]

---

[346] *CCC*, 2263-2267.

WHAT ARE THE TEN COMMANDMENTS?

The Ten Commandments were given by God out of His love for us.[347] They are how we should want to act, NOT how we will always want to act due to our fallen human nature. They will NOT always feel good to us due to our fallen human nature. BUT obeying them is good for us as well as for others. To be fully alive is to obey the Ten Commandments.

The 1st Commandment is: You shall not have strange gods before me. Sins against the 1st Commandment include idolatry (making anything else more important than God), heresy (presenting as Christian that which is not really Christian), apostasy (leaving the Faith), schism (refusing the authority of the Magisterium), Satanism, superstition, divination, and spiritism.

The 2nd Commandment is: You shall not take the name of the Lord your God in vain. Sins against the 2nd Commandment include cursing (calling down evil on another), perjury (lying under oath), and blasphemy (disrespect of God).

The 3rd Commandment is: You shall keep holy the Lord's Day. Sins against the 3rd Commandment include not going to Mass Sunday (or the Sunday vigil on Saturday evening) or on a holy day of obligation, and not getting rest and relaxation.

The 4th Commandment is: Honor your father and your mother. Sins against the 4th Commandment include disrespecting (and thus not cooperating with) all proper authorities who are being reasonable.

The 5th Commandment is: You shall not kill. Sins against the 5th Commandment include abortion, euthanasia, terrorism, unjust war or violence, disrespecting one's own body, and suicide.

The 6th Commandment is: You shall not commit adultery. Sins against the 6th Commandment include any genital act that is not done to express both life-long commitment to love and openness to bring new life into the world, such as adultery (sex between a married person and a non-spouse), fornication (sex between two people who are not married at all), pornography, rape, prostitution, masturbation, homosexual acts, and

---

[347] *CCC*, 2052-2063, 2083-2557.

uncontrolled sexual desire.

The 7th Commandment is: You shall not steal. Sins against the 7th Commandment include cheating, lack of care for the environment, greed, unfairness/injustice, failure to share reasonably, and uncontrolled desire for others' things.

The 8th Commandment is: You shall not bear false witness against your neighbor. Sins against the 8th Commandment include lying, dishonesty, gossip, and bragging.

The 9th Commandment is: You shall not covet your neighbor's wife. Sins against the 9th Commandment include those against the 6th Commandment.

The 10th Commandment is: You shall not covet your neighbor's goods. Sins against the 10th Commandment include those against the 7th Commandment.

The 4th through 10th Commandments are expressions of Natural Law confirmed by Revelation. Every human being, deep down, knows that he should do or not do the things those Commandments tell him. Even the 1st through 3rd Commandments express what every human being knows deep down: there is a Higher Power which he must respect.

WHAT IS THE CONNECTION BETWEEN THE GREAT COMMANDMENTS AND THE TEN COMMANDMENTS?

The relationship between the Ten Commandments and the Two Great Commandments is that the Ten Commandments express/spell out the Two Great Commandments.[348] Jesus gave the Two Great Commandments about 1,200 years after God, through Moses, gave the Ten Commandments. Jesus knew the Ten Commandments and the entire Law of the Old Covenant backwards and forwards. The Two Great Commandments are His brilliant summary and synthesis of the Law.

Jesus shows how The Ten Commandments form a unity, not a random list.[349] Each commandment refers to the others because they all spell out

---

[348] *CCC*, 2064-2068.
[349] *CCC*, 2069.

ways of loving God and our neighbor. The Ten Commandments are concrete/specific ways of loving God and our neighbor. The 1st, 2nd, and 3rd of the Ten Commandments are about our relationship with God and spell out how to practice the First Great Commandment. The 4th-10th Commandments are about our relationship with others and spell out how to practice the Second Great Commandment.

WHAT IS THE DIFFERENCE BETWEEN MORTAL SIN AND VENIAL SIN?

Sin is an offense against God, turning away from God, refusing to love. Sin can be either mortal or venial.[350]

Mortal sin is serious sin, sin so serious that if one dies in a state of mortal sin, one cannot enter the Kingdom of God. That means Hell. For someone to be guilty of mortal sin, there must be three conditions: (1) the action must be seriously wrong and (2) the person committing the action must have full knowledge of how serious it is and (3) must have complete freedom to commit it. Disobeying the Ten Commandments is what makes a sin serious, although not every sin against the Ten Commandments is equally serious. Murder is more serious than theft.

Venial sin is less serious sin. For someone to guilty of venial sin EITHER the action is less serious than mortal sin but it is committed with full knowledge of its sinfulness and complete freedom to do it OR the action is serious but it is committed with less than full knowledge of its sinfulness or less than complete freedom.

---

[350] *CCC*, 1854-1864.

PERSONAL FAITH RESPONSE

Check any statements below that describe you.

In order to LIVE FULLY:

1. _____I agree with the objective truth in this chapter.

2. _____I will love God more than anything else by doing my best to obey the 1st-3rd Commandments.

3. _____I will admit that God knows what is good for me and everyone else infinitely more than we do.

4. _____I will love others by doing my best to obey the 4th-10th Commandments.

5. _____I will grow in virtue—I will become more prudent, just, temperate, and brave.

VOCABULARY

Morality: How we should want to act.

Natural Law: Moral principles rooted in the human nature that is common to all human beings that transcend individual and cultural differences and can be known by Reason alone.

Virtue: A good moral habit.

The Cardinal Virtues: The most basic virtues on which all the other virtues hinge: Prudence, Justice, Temperance, and Fortitude.

Prudence: The virtue of making good applications of moral principles to particular cases.

Justice: The virtue of rendering to others their rights/what is due to them/what belongs to them.

Temperance: The virtue of moderating the attraction of pleasures, provides balance in the use of created goods, and keeps desires within limits.

Fortitude: The virtue of being brave, firm in difficulties, constant in the pursuit of the good, strong in facing fear and obstacles.

Conscience: The reasoning process that applies a moral principle to a make a specific moral choice.

Justice: The rendering of rights.

> **Contract justice** is rendering contract rights, which are what is owed in a one-on-one relationship based on an agreement.
>
> **Social justice** is the rendering of human rights, which are rights owed to every member of society, and the sustaining the common good.
>
> **Contributive justice** is what the individual owes society and the common good.
>
> **Distributive justice** is what society owes the individual, what each individual should receive as his fair share of the common good.

The Ten Commandments: The 1st Stage of God's Revelation of the essence of morality.

The Two Great Commandments: The 2nd Stage of God's Revelation of the essence of morality.

The First Great Commandment: Love God more than anything else.

The Second Great Commandment: Love your neighbor.

Love: A commitment to value/prize/treasure/cherish by giving what is good and what should be wanted.

Sin: An offense against God.

Mortal sin: Serious sin.

Venial sin: Less serious sin.

Part 8: What Is the Fullness of Responding to Revelation?

Chapter III:

WHAT IS THE FULLNESS OF RESPONDING TO GOD IN WORSHIP?

WHAT IS WORSHIP?

Worship is public, not personal, prayer done by a congregation/group/assembly of people in order to pay homage to/acknowledge/adore and to get closer to what is most important in reality.[351] *Liturgy* and *worship* are synonyms.

There is more to Catholic worship than the Mass. Examples of other ways to worship God in the Catholic Church are:

- Funeral rites in church and at the cemetery.
- Adoration of the Blessed Sacrament.
- The Stations of the Cross.
- Praying the Rosary.
- The Liturgy of Ash Wednesday.
- The blessing of throats on the Feast of St. Blaise.
- A May Crowning.
- The Rite of Christian Initiation for Adults.
- The Liturgy of the Hours/Divine Office.

---

[351] *CCC*, 1066-1067.

Worship becomes meaningful and interesting not when there are great music, excellent reading style by the lectors, and inspiring homilies but when one is aware that God is present. As was noted about the inability of some people to see Revelation, if someone attends Catholic worship and does not see what is there, it is because he does not know what to look for, he is distracted, his self is not clean enough, or he is ignoring God. The good news is that anyone who wants to can learn what to look for, to overcome distraction, to make himself cleaner, and to pay attention to God.

WHY DOES THE CATHOLIC CHURCH WORSHIP?

In one sense, the Catholic Church worships because its members are human beings. Human beings cannot not worship. To not worship is to not be true to human nature. God made us to worship. Worship is the natural response to what is perceived to be divine, as the entire history of all human religion shows.

Each one of us must have a highest priority. Each one of us must have a "sun" around which we orbit in the "solar system" of our lives. Each one of us must value something more than everything else. Each one of us must adore and be in awe of something or somebody. If we do not worship the one true God, we will worship someone or something else (even ourselves) and treat that as the most important thing in life.

The Catholic Church worships the one true God Who alone is worthy of worship. The Three-in-One God alone is perfect. God is He-Who-Is-to-Be-Worshipped. To worship God is not only to be true to human nature, but it is to be true to the nature of God as well. God Is He Who "never ceases to gather a people to Himself, so that from the rising of the sun to its setting a pure sacrifice may be offered to His name," to paraphrase Eucharistic Prayer III.

The Catholic Church worships God in order to respond to what Jesus reveals in the First Great Commandment, which is to love God more than anything else. The Catholic Church worships God in order to respond to what God reveals in the Third Commandment of the Ten Commandments, which is to keep holy the Lord's Day.

Those who realize God loves them—by giving them the gift of existence, by sending His Son to save them, by sending Their Spirit to guide them, and by offering them eternal happiness—want to worship God. The mature Catholic embraces the importance of worship.

Due to our fallen human nature, even the mature Catholic will not always feel like worshipping. Worshipping during those times when we feel nothing nevertheless shows God our faithfulness, which is the kind of effort needed in any good relationship. At such times, it helps to remember that there is much more to reality than what we feel.

As with prayer: if we are too busy to worship, we are too busy. Because eternity is a continuation of this life—although in a deeper/fuller/supernatural way—life without worship points to eternity without God.

WHAT IS THE ESSENCE OF CATHOLIC WORSHIP?

The way Jesus is most present on Earth between the time of His Ascension and the time of His Second Coming is the Catholic Church, which He founded. Jesus is especially present in the Catholic Church's worship.[352] All worship is an Easter in miniature because in all worship Jesus reveals his passage from death to life and celebrates it with us.[353]

The essence of every form of Catholic worship is an encounter with Jesus Christ and an opportunity to grow in relationship/friendship with Him. Because no Person of the Trinity does anything without the other Persons, an encounter with Jesus and an opportunity to grow in relationship with Him is also an encounter with and an opportunity to grow in relationship with the Father and the Holy Spirit.[354]

WHAT ARE THE SACRAMENTS?

The Catholic Church has seven Sacraments, which are sacred rituals that are more direct ways of receiving grace/sharing in the life of the Trinity than other forms of Catholic worship.[355] God's grace is both a gift

---

[352] *CCC*, 1071, 1084-1090.
[353] *CCC*, 1085.
[354] *CCC*, 1077-1112.
[355] *CCC*, 1117-1118, 1210.

and a strengthening. The Sacraments give the grace (gift) of sharing in the life of God and the grace (strength) to share in the life of God. All of the Sacraments were instituted/established by Jesus Himself.[356] The Seven Sacraments are the basis/foundation of the rest of Catholic worship. Each Sacrament gives its own particular graces.[357]

- **Baptism** joins us with Jesus for the first time in a direct way.

- **Confirmation** gives us the Holy Spirit of Jesus (and the Father) and completes Baptism.

- **The Eucharist** unites us with Jesus more closely than anything else until we enter the Kingdom.

- **Confession** reconciles us with Jesus.

- Through **Anointing of the Sick**, Jesus heals, strengthens, and consoles us.

- In **Matrimony/Marriage**, Jesus promises His love will be available in wedded love.

- Through **Holy Orders**, Jesus gives the sacred power to administer the Sacraments.

---

[356] *CCC*, 1114-116.
[357] *CCC*, 1129.

The Fullness of Life

One way to appreciate the Sacraments is to see their relationship to stages and moments in both natural life and spiritual life.[358] Baptism, Confirmation, and the Eucharist, especially First Communion, begin supernatural life and so are called the "Sacraments of Initiation."[359] Confession and Anointing of the Sick restore supernatural life lost through sin and so are called the "Sacraments of Healing."[360] Holy Orders and Matrimony/Marriage give those who receive it a mission to build up the Church and bring others to salvation through their vocations and so they are called the "Sacraments of Service," "Sacraments of Mission," or "Sacraments of Consecration."[361]

WHAT IS NECESSARY FOR THE SACRAMENTS TO BE EFFECTIVE?

The Sacraments are not magic, which supposedly is effective only when the right words are said, e.g., "Hocus pocus," and the right actions are performed, e.g., waving the magic wand. In order for a Sacrament to be effective, something is needed on the part of the person receiving the Sacrament and something is need on the part of the person administering the Sacrament.[362]

Yes, for a Sacrament to be effective, for a Sacrament to give grace, the right words and actions must be used.[363] The God-given authority to decide what words and actions are required of a minister or congregation and where the minister or congregation has freedom in the Sacraments (and all worship) belongs only to the Magisterium—not the priest, the deacon, the lay minister, the parish liturgy commission, the campus ministry department, or anyone else.[364]

The Trinity is at work in the Sacraments when they are administered by someone who is validly ordained (bishops, priests, and deacons) and

---

[358] *CCC*, 1210-1211.
[359] *CCC*, 1212.
[360] *CCC*, 1420-1421.
[361] *CCC*, 1533-1535.
[362] *CCC*, 1127-1129.
[363] *CCC*, 1153-1155.
[364] *CCC*, 1125.

when the right words and actions are used. The effectiveness of the Sacraments does NOT depend on the holiness or moral state of the Sacraments' ministers because, when they are properly administered, Jesus Himself is at work in them. A validly-administered Sacrament is still effective even when it is administered by someone who is unworthy/in a state of mortal sin.

On the part of the person receiving the Sacrament, it is only effective if it is accepted in faith. The right words and actions are not enough. The person receiving the Sacrament must be doing his best to accept God into his life.

HOW DOES THE CHURCH USE TIME TO WORSHIP GOD?

The day is one unit of time the Church uses to worship God. The day we call *Saturday* was and is the last day of the week in the Jewish calendar. In the Old Covenant, Saturday is the Lord's Day that is dedicated to worship because it is on the last day of the very first week that God rested from creating the universe (Genesis 2:2-3). The day we call *Sunday* was and is the first day of the week in the Jewish calendar. The Apostles moved the Lord's Day from Saturday to Sunday because it was on the first day of the week that Jesus rose from the dead.[365] In the New Covenant, the day dedicated to worship God is Sunday, including its vigil. TGIS—thank God it's Sunday, the most important day of the week! For a good Catholic, every week begins and ends on Sunday so that the Eucharist is the source and the summit of his life in a chronological way as well as in so many other ways.

The Church uses days as occasions to celebrate important events in the life of Christ and important aspects about Him and also to celebrate the saints. A good practice for growing in Faith is to know each day what about Jesus or what saint is being celebrated and then to learn something about that. Days in the Church year are classified as:

- Solemnities are the days of greatest importance for worship. Every Sunday and Holy Day of Obligation is a solemnity. The Solemnities that always fall on Sundays are Epiphany, Palm Sunday, Easter, Pentecost, Holy Trinity, Corpus Christi, and Christ the King. Christmas is the only Solemnity that does not always fall on

---

[365] *CCC*, 1166-1167.

The Fullness of Life

a Sunday but is always a Holy Day of Obligation. Solemnities that usually are Holy Days of Obligation (depending the decisions of bishops) are days celebrating the Holy Mother of God (January 1), Annunciation, Ascension, Assumption, All Saints, and Immaculate Conception. Solemnities that in and of themselves are not Holy Days of Obligation are the days celebrating the Baptism of the Lord, Saint Joseph, Most Sacred Heart of Jesus, Nativity of St. John the Baptist, and Sts. Peter and Paul.

- Feasts are second most important for worship. Feasts celebrate realities about Christ, e.g., the Baptism of the Lord; and they celebrate the saints, e.g., Our Lady of Guadalupe.

- Memorials rank next in importance. Memorials celebrate important saints, although some Memorials must be observed in the Masses on their days, and some Memorials are optional.

Easter is the "Feast of Feasts" and the "Solemnity of Solemnities" because it celebrates the Resurrection.[366] Every Sunday is a kind of miniature Easter. Easter falls on the first Sunday after the first full moon after the Spring Equinox in order to come as close as possible to the day of the year that Jesus rose.

Another unit of time used by the Church to worship God is the year. The Church Year, also known as the Liturgical Year, celebrates the whole truth about Jesus Christ.[367] It starts on the First Sunday of Advent, which is the fourth Sunday before Christmas. Advent is the season celebrating the First Coming of Christ at Christmas. The final Sunday of the year fittingly celebrates the Second Coming of Christ on the Solemnity of Christ the King. The Church Year ends on the Saturday after Christ the King.

There are other seasons in the Church year besides Advent. The Christmas Season begins with Christmas itself and lasts until the Solemnity of the Epiphany. The other seasons of the Church Year are the Seasons of Lent and Easter. Lent is the season before Easter and begins with Ash Wednesday. The Easter season begins with Easter itself and ends with Pentecost. The Triduum, from Holy Thursday to Easter, in a sense constitutes its own season while overlapping Lent and the Easter Season.

---

[366] *CCC*, 1169.
[367] *CCC*, 1163.

The rest of the Church Year is "Ordinary Time," which begins with the Feast of the Baptism of the Lord and during which the life of Christ is celebrated. So Ordinary Time is the time between the Christmas Season and Lent and between the Easter Season and Advent.

The days and seasons in the Church Year dictate many things about worship. One example is the prayers said at Mass, e.g., the Gloria and Creed are said on a Solemnity, the Gloria but not the Creed is said on a Feast, neither the Gloria nor the Creed is said on a Memorial. Other examples of how the day and season affect worship are the readings during the Liturgy of the Word, the color of the priest's vestments, the music selected, etc.

PERSONAL FAITH RESPONSE

Check any statements below that describe you.

In order to LIVE FULLY:

1. _____I agree with the objective truth in this chapter.

2. _____At worship, I will focus on the presence of God much more than the quality of the music, reading style, and homilizing.

3. _____I will continually learn to know what to look for at worship.

4. _____Whenever I worship, I will praise and thank God for giving me existence, sending His Son to save me and Their Spirit to guide me, and offering me eternal happiness.

5. _____I will participate in Catholic worship in order to encounter and grow in friendship with Jesus.

6. _____I will accept in faith each Sacrament I celebrate.

VOCABULARY

Worship: Public prayer done by a congregation in order to pay homage to and to get closer to God; also called **liturgy**.

Congregation: The group/assembly worshipping.

Seven Sacraments: Catholic worship that is more important than other forms of Catholic worship because (1) Sacraments were instituted by Jesus, (2) are more direct ways of encountering and growing in relationship with the Trinity than other forms of worship, and (3) are the basis of the rest of Catholic worship.

Grace: The gift of and the strength to share in the life of God.

Sacraments of Initiation: Baptism, Confirmation, and the Eucharist.

Sacraments of Healing: Penance and Anointing of the Sick.

Sacraments of Service: Holy Orders and Matrimony/Marriage. Also called the **Sacraments of Mission** or **Sacraments of Consecration**.

Solemnity: The day of greatest importance for worship, on which Mass includes the Gloria and the Creed.

Feast: The second most important day for worship, on which Mass includes the Gloria.

Memorial: The day next in rank of importance, on which Mass includes neither the Gloria nor the Creed.

Church Year: The Year that begins with the First Sunday of Advent and ends with the Saturday after the Solemnity of Christ the King. Also known as the **Liturgical Year**.

Advent: The season celebrating the First Coming of Christ.

Christmas Season: The season from Christmas itself until the Solemnity of the Epiphany.

Lent: The season before Easter beginning on Ash Wednesday.

Easter Season: The season from Easter itself until Pentecost.

The Triduum: The season from Holy Thursday to Easter.

Ordinary Time: The season between the Christmas Season and Lent and between the Easter Season and Advent.

Part 8: What Is the Fullness of Responding to Revelation?

Chapter IV:
WHAT MAKES THE EUCHARIST ESPECIALLY IMPORTANT?

WHAT IS THE HOLY EUCHARIST?

In 304 AD, the Emperor Diocletian ordered Christians not to meet on Sundays and celebrate the Eucharist. When 49 of them were caught in Abitinae, in present-day Tunisia, brought before the local authority, and asked why they had disobeyed the emperor's strict order, one of them, Emeritus, answered, "Without the Lord's Day, we are not able to live." These Abitinian Martyrs, who suffered horrible tortures and deaths, show us what all mature Catholics realize: without the Eucharist, we are not able to live.

The Eucharist is the Sacrament in which bread and wine consecrated/ made holy through the words and actions of a bishop or priest become the real Body and Blood of Jesus.[368] The Eucharist is the only Sacrament that is Jesus Himself. Jesus commanded us to celebrate the Eucharist.[369] The essence of the ritual of the Eucharist comes from Jesus Himself.[370] Over the centuries, human beings have changed inessential aspects of the ritual

---

[368] *CCC*, 1324, 1333, 1353, 1375-1377, 1381.
[369] *CCC*, 1341-1344.
[370] *CCC*, 1343, 1345-1347, 1356.

of the Eucharist e.g., the language that is used for the ritual.

Since the Eucharist is Christ Himself, it is the center of the other Sacraments.[371] The other Sacraments lead to and flow from the Eucharist.

The Eucharist is the source and summit, the cause and the goal, of the Christian life.[372] Celebrating the Eucharist is the best thing that anyone can do. To be fully alive is to have the Eucharist be the source and the summit of our lives. Sunday Mass (or its vigil) should be the starting point and the end point of our week. If it is not already, we can make it so now.

HOW IS THE LITURGY OF THE EUCHARIST A MEAL AND A SACRIFICE?

The Consecration of bread and wine into the Body and Blood of Christ takes place during the second half of the Mass: the Liturgy of the Eucharist.[373] The Liturgy of the Eucharist is a virtual/veritable time machine because it makes present two key events in Jesus' life—His Last Supper with the Twelve Apostles and His Crucifixion.[374] By going to Mass we are able to be with Christ when He ate the Last Supper and when He was crucified. So the Liturgy of the Eucharist is both a meal due to the Last Supper and a sacrifice due to the Crucifixion, and in both cases Jesus offers His Body and Blood.

How is the Liturgy of the Eucharist a meal?

At the Last Supper, when Jesus instituted the Eucharist, Jesus and the Apostles ate the Passover meal.[375] At the Consecration, the priest repeats the words Jesus said at the Last Supper, "Take this, all of you, and eat of it, for this is My Body" and "Take this, all of you, and drink from it, for this

---

[371] *CCC*, 1211, 1374.

[372] *CCC*, 1324.

[373] The Mass has two basic parts: the Liturgy of the Word, which includes readings from the Bible and ends with the Prayers of the Faithful/petitions, and the Liturgy of the Eucharist, which begins with the Preparation of the Gifts when bread, wine, and water are brought to the altar and includes the Consecration of the bread and wine and Holy Communion.

[374] *CCC*, 1363, 1366, 1383.

[375] *CCC*, 1329, 1334, 1337-1340.

The Fullness of Life

is the chalice of My Blood."

When we eat Our Lord's Body and drink His Blood, we are the most united we can be with Him (until we enter the Kingdom), and so the Eucharist inside of Mass is also called *Holy Communion* which means "union/united with."[376]

How is the Liturgy of the Eucharist a sacrifice?

There are three elements of **any ritual sacrifice** in any religion:

- The structure on which the sacrifice is conducted: an altar.
- That which is sacrificed: a victim/offering.
- The one performing the sacrifice: a priest.

There are three elements of ritual sacrifice in **the Liturgy of the Eucharist**:

- There is an altar.
- There is a victim offered for our sins: Christ Himself. The bread that is consecrated is called the "Host" because the English word *Host* comes from the Latin word *hostia*, which means "sacrificial victim."[377]

---

[376] *CCC*, 1331, 1382.

[377] Although *hosts* in "Holy, Holy, Holy, Lord God of hosts" means "armies of angels" and comes from the Latin word *hostis*.

- There is a priest: The real priest is Christ Himself who acts through the human priest.

The Liturgy of the Eucharist is an unbloody sacrifice that makes present the bloody sacrifice of Christ on the cross at Calvary to save us from our sins.[378] Thus Mass is also called the *Holy Sacrifice of the Mass*.[379]

HOW SHOULD CATHOLICS PARTICIPATE IN NON-CATHOLIC WORSHIP?

It is good for people to attend each other's worship. They can then understand better what they have in common. And they can better understand what they do not have in common.

Catholics should NOT do everything at non-Catholic worship that the non-Catholics do. At non-Catholic worship, Catholics should do nothing that contradicts Catholic Faith. They should respectfully decline if they are invited to do so. Catholics should NOT take "Communion" or the "Lord's Supper" at Protestant services. Catholics should NOT usually take the Eucharist at Eastern Orthodox liturgies.[380]

Catholics can NOT fulfill their Sunday obligation at a Protestant service. Catholics can fulfill their Sunday obligation at an Orthodox liturgy ONLY if there is not a Catholic Mass that is practical to get to.

HOW SHOULD NON-CATHOLICS PARTICIPATE AT MASS?

The Body of Christ is both the Holy Eucharist and the Church. The purpose of receiving the Eucharist/taking Communion is to be united with

---

[378] *CCC*, 1362-1372.

[379] *CCC*, 1330.

[380] A Catholic may receive the Eucharist at an Eastern Orthodox liturgy as long as it impossible to receive the Eucharist from a Catholic minister, the Catholic continues to know that the Catholic Church alone has the fullness of the means of salvation, it is better spiritually for the Catholic to receive than not to receive, and the particular Orthodox Church has no objection.

both Jesus Christ and the Catholic Church.

The Catholic Church would contradict herself if she were to invite to take Communion those who do not share her faith that the Eucharist is really the Body and Blood of Christ and who do not share the rest of her faith, life, and worship to a significant degree.

It is NOT objectively offensive not to offer Holy Communion to non-Catholics, just as it is NOT offensive not to invite everyone into your house, or not to invite every guest into every room, or not to invite every guest in a room to look in every cabinet, closet, and dresser. Being welcoming/friendly/inclusive/hospitable is NOT an all or nothing kind of thing—it is a matter of degree. Respectful guests respect their host's rules— just as respectful Catholics respect non-Catholic rules when they are the guests in non-Catholic places of worship, respectful non-Catholics respect Catholic rules when they are the guests in Catholic churches and chapels.

The above is especially true for those who are not Christian and do not recognize that Jesus is God the Son. However, Communion may be taken by Eastern Orthodox Christians who are respecting the discipline of their own churches.[381] Protestants may take Communion only in exceptional circumstances according to the directives of the local bishop and according to canon law, e.g., at the time of death with faith in the Real Presence.[382]

Catholics and all religious people still have much in common—especially in a society that is becoming more anti-religious—even if they do not share one of the most sacred parts of the Catholic Faith.

HOW IS COMMUNION RECEIVED WORTHILY?

A Catholic is obligated to attend Mass on all Sundays and holy days of obligation.[383] For a mature Catholic, especially in light of what we have already covered in this chapter, "Sunday obligation" makes as much sense as "kiss obligation" makes for someone who is truly in love, as the *Youth Catechism of the Catholic Church* puts it.

---

[381] *CCC*, 1399.
[382] *CCC*, 1400-01.
[383] *CCC*, 1389.

It is a serious/mortal sin to miss Sunday Mass (or the vigil Mass on Saturday) without a good reason.[384] It is a mortal sin to knowingly receive Communion in a state of mortal sin. Anyone aware of having committed a mortal sin must receive the Sacrament of Confession before receiving Communion. Therefore it is a mortal sin to receive Communion after having missed Sunday Mass (or the vigil Mass) without a good reason and without then going to Confession.[385]

The required fast should be kept, which in the U. S. is to abstain from food and drink (except for medicine and water) at least one hour before receiving the Eucharist, not before the beginning of Mass.[386] Those who are sick or at least sixty years old and those caring for them are exempt from this fast. All at Mass should comport themselves by wearing appropriate clothing and by having the proper conduct.

The actual act of receiving Communion needs to be done worthily. Receiving the Consecrated Wine is optional.

- Bow your head to the Host (and Chalice) either before or while the minister of Holy Communion says "The Body of Christ" (and "The Blood of Christ").
- Say "Amen" clearly AFTER the minister of Holy Communion says "The Body of Christ" (and "The Blood of Christ") but BEFORE you take the Host (and Chalice). (If the minister of Holy Communion gives you time to do so.)
- Every Catholic has the right to receive the Host either on the tongue or in the hands. Clearly give the minister of Holy Communion enough time to know which way you want to receive.
- When receiving the Host in your hands, place your hands so that it is easy for the minister of the Host to distribute It to you—not too low, not too close to the minister.
- When receiving the Host in the hands, form your hands together into a throne to receive the King of Kings by placing the hand you

---

[384] *CCC*, 1385.

[385] "Except for a grave reason where there is no opportunity for Confession. In this case, the person is to be mindful of the obligation to make an act of perfect contrition, including the intention of confessing as soon as possible (canon 916)." http://www.usccb.org/prayer-and-worship/the-mass/order-of-mass/liturgy-of-the-eucharist/guidelines-for-the-reception-of-communion.cfm

[386] *CCC*, 1387.

normally use UNDER your other hand so that you receive the Host in that other hand and put the Host in your mouth with the hand you normally use, just to minimize any awkwardness.

PERSONAL FAITH RESPONSE

Check any statements below that describe you.

In order to LIVE FULLY:

1. _____I agree with the objective truth in this chapter.

2. _____I will realize that the Eucharist really is, not symbolically is, the Body and Blood of Jesus.

3. _____I will want to be with Christ when He ate the Last Supper and when He was crucified.

4. _____I will attend Mass on all Sundays and holy days of obligation.

5. _____I will not receive Communion after having missed Sunday Mass (or the vigil Mass) without a good reason and without then going to Confession.

6. _____I will do nothing at non-Catholic worship that contradicts Catholic Faith and will respectfully decline when invited to do so.

VOCABULARY

Eucharist (or Holy Eucharist): The Sacrament in which bread and wine become the real Body and Blood of Jesus. It is called **Communion (or Holy Communion)** when it is received at Mass. It is called the **Blessed Sacrament** when it is reserved in a tabernacle.

The Consecration: The making holy of bread and wine through the words and actions of a bishop or priest so that the bread and wine become the real Body and Blood of Jesus Christ.

The Liturgy of the Eucharist: The second half of the Mass.

Part 8: What Is the Fullness of Responding to Revelation?

Chapter V:

WHAT ELSE IS IMPORTANT TO KNOW ABOUT THE SACRAMENTS?

For the sake of overview and brevity, this chapter leaves out much that is also important about the Sacraments. A good follow-up to this chapter would be reading the relevant paragraphs of the *Catechism* that are footnoted for each Sacrament.

WHAT IS IMPORTANT TO KNOW ABOUT BAPTISM?

Baptism is the Sacrament that is the foundation for the other Sacraments.[387] A person cannot receive the other six Sacraments before he receives Baptism. It is the beginning of communion with God and with the Church.

Baptism gives several graces. It connects us to Christ's redemptive death on the Cross. It frees us from the <u>ultimate</u> power of Original Sin and enables us to rise with Him to the fullness of life in the Kingdom. It does NOT free us from the <u>immediate</u> power of Original Sin. After we are baptized, we still have a fallen human nature with fallen intellects, fallen wills, fallen emotions, and fallen bodies. We still live in a fallen world. Baptism also frees us from all personal sins in the case of those who receive it after reaching the Age of Reason to know the difference between morally

---

[387] *CCC*, 1213-1284.

right action and morally wrong action/sin,[388] which is at least seven years of age. Baptism makes one a member of the Church.

Baptism is necessary for salvation. But there is Baptism of blood (dying for the Faith) and Baptism of desire (sincerely seeking God) as well as Baptism of water. We should not worry about children who died without Baptism.

The minister of Baptism is normally a bishop, priest, or deacon. However, in an emergency, Baptism can be administered by anyone, even a non-Christian (who must intend to free the baptized from Original Sin and make them a member of the Church) by following the proper ritual of pouring water over the head of the recipient and saying, "I baptize you in the name of the Father and of the Son and of the Holy Spirit."

The baptism of infants makes sense. The Church has always done it. Loving parents are committed to doing what is good for their children. Introducing their children to God and helping them grow in a relationship with Him is the best thing parents can do for their children.

Anyone interested in converting to the Catholic Church needs to ask at their local parish about the Rite of Christian Initiation for Adults (RCIA).

WHAT IS IMPORTANT TO KNOW ABOUT CONFIRMATION?

Confirmation completes Baptism.[389] It gives the grace of initiating the baptized more deeply into the life of the Holy Spirit. It especially empowers the recipient to spread and defend the Faith. And it gives the grace of initiating the baptized more deeply into the life of the Church.

Confirmation is ordinarily administered by a bishop, which expresses the recipient's greater inclusion in the life of the Church. The bishop can share the power of confirming with priests, as is necessary for all the Baptisms that take place at the many Easter Vigil Masses in a diocese.

---

[388] *CCC*, 1457.
[389] *CCC*, 1285-1321.

The Fullness of Life

WHAT IS IMPORTANT TO KNOW ABOUT CONFESSION?

Confession is the Sacrament through by which personal sins are forgiven after Baptism.[390] It is needed after Baptism because Christians continue to sin. It has other names, each of which reflects a different aspect of it: Reconciliation, Penance. Graces given are reconciliation/ reunion with God and the Church. Other graces given are consolation, re-conversion, and anticipation of meeting God face-to-face.

There is a parallel between what we need to do in order to have good relationships with other human beings and what we need to do in order to have a good relationship with God. With other people, we need to be honest with ourselves and others, admit fault when we have been wrong, and take responsibility to make things right. With God, we need to do the same.

We make a good Confession by:

- Examining our conscience which should lead to sorrow for our sins.
- Confessing/admitting our sins to the priest.
- In Confession, we are really interacting with Christ, who is represented by the priest.
- Any mortal sin should be confessed.
- Confession of venial sins is not necessary but is a great way to become better friends with God.
- Knowing whether a particular sin is mortal or venial is not necessary.
- We always have the right to anonymous confession; face-to-face confession should never be forced on someone.
- After confessing, receiving from the priest acts of satisfaction to repair the harm caused by sin which are called a *penance*.

---

[390] *CCC*, 1422-1498.

- Accepting the penance by saying An Act of Contrition to express regret for having committed sins and determination to avoid them in the future as much as possible. (We are NOT promising that we will never commit sins the rest of our lives.)
- Receiving absolution from the priest, which means he frees us of our sins by the sacred power God has given him to act for Him.
- Performing the penance, and only then are we reconciled with God and His Church.

According to the *Code of Canon Law*, the confession of mortal sin must be made at least once a year. As was pointed out in an earlier chapter, Communion must not be received while in a state of mortal sin.

The minister of Confession is a bishop or priest.

WHAT IS IMPORTANT TO KNOW ABOUT ANOINTING OF THE SICK?

The Sacrament of the Anointing of the Sick can be received by any Catholic who is seriously sick.[391] The person receiving it does NOT have to be near death. Graces given are the strength of the Holy Spirit, union with the Passion of Christ, contribution to the good of the Church, and preparation for meeting God face-to-face.

Occasionally the grace of physical healing is given. We should always remember that healing of any kind from any source only postpones the inevitable—our face-to-face meeting with God. Healing gives us more time to know, love, and serve God in this life so that we can receive the ultimate healing in the Kingdom of God.

The minister of Anointing of the Sick is a bishop or priest.

WHAT IS IMPORTANT TO KNOW ABOUT HOLY ORDERS?

The man who is ordained/receives Holy Orders receives a gift of the Holy Spirit that gives him a sacred power and mission for the Church.[392]

---

[391] *CCC*, 1499-1532.
[392] *CCC*, 1536-1600.

The Sacrament of Holy Orders has three degrees: Bishop, Priest, and Deacon. The fullness of Holy Orders is received ONLY by the bishop, which he shares to a lesser degree with priests and deacons. Only a bishop receives the fullness of Holy Orders because only a bishop is a successor of the Twelve Apostles, which is why ONLY a bishop can administer or officiate all Seven Sacraments.

WHAT IS NECESSARY FOR A SACRAMENTAL MARRIAGE?

In order for a marriage to be Sacramental, it must be between one man and one woman who freely consent to the marriage, who vow that their marriage will last as long as both of them are alive and that they will be sexually faithful to each other and so not have sex with anyone else, and who will be open to having children.[393]

Matrimony gives the couple the grace to be true to their vows. Sexual intercourse by two unmarried people is the sin of fornication. Sexual intercourse between a married person and someone to whom he or she is not married is the sin of adultery. Any genital activity between unmarried people is a sin. All Catholics who are unmarried should practice celibacy/abstention from all genital activity with another person.

The couple should know that God wants their marriage to be a living image of the love between Christ and His Church. Getting married in a Catholic wedding ceremony is a great opportunity to grow in fidelity to all Catholic doctrine. To get married in the Church without sincerely intending to grow in such fidelity disrespects God and His Church.

Marriage is the only Sacrament administered by non-ordained people—the man and the woman getting married. The bishop, priest, or deacon officiates and represents the Church.

---

[393] *CCC*, 1601-1666.

PERSONAL FAITH RESPONSE

Check any statements below that describe you.

In order to LIVE FULLY:

1. _____ I agree with the objective truth in this chapter.

2. _____ I will thank God for the Sacraments and celebrate them appropriately.

Part 8: What Is the Fullness of Responding to Revelation?

Chapter VI:

WHAT IS THE FULLNESS OF RESPONDING TO GOD IN PRAYER?

SOURCE

- Rev. Jacques Philippe, *Thirsting for Prayer* (Scepter Publishers, 2014).

WHAT IS PRAYER?

Prayer has many meanings. In this chapter *prayer* refers to the one-on-one communication between a person and God.[394]

---

[394] Prayer can also be done in groups, formally or informally. Prayer and worship can easily overlap. There are also many traditional devotions that should be prayed alone as well as by groups or families, in church or out of church, only some of which are listed here:
- Visiting the Blessed Sacrament reserved in a tabernacle
- The Stations of the Cross
- The Stations of the Resurrection
- Praying before a crucifix
- Grace before meals
- The Advent Wreath
- The Rosary

Here are excellent definitions of prayer:

- According to St. Therese of Lisieux, prayer is a simple look turned toward Heaven.

- According to St. John Damascene, prayer is the raising of one's mind and heart to God.

- According to St. Clement, prayer is conversation with God.

- According to Dr. Ralph Martin, prayer is simply paying attention to God.

- According to C. S. Lewis, prayer is getting in touch with the Father as the Son is next to us helping us while the Holy Spirit is inside us motivating us.

We need to make sure we pray to the one true God—and NOT a god we have created in our own image and likeness. We pray to the one true God by keeping all our prayer in harmony with Catholic doctrine.

WHAT DOES JESUS TEACH US ABOUT PRAYER?

Jesus often went away from others so He could pray. This teaches us the importance of finding time for prayer. A good goal is to spend at least 5 minutes in prayer every day.

Jesus explicitly teaches His disciples that prayer is necessary in order to have a relationship with God. What is necessary for any good relationship is spending time together. Prayer is spending time with God. Without a regular routine of daily prayer, our personal relationship with God will weaken and then stop (on our part—but never on God's part since God always wants to have a personal relationship with us). If we are too

---

- The Divine Mercy
- Seven Sorrows of Mary
- Novenas
- Pilgrimages
- Visiting the grave of a loved one
- Liturgy of the Hours/Divine Office
- Litanies
- Wearing a scapular or medal

busy to pray, we are too busy. Jesus teaches that perseverance will be necessary to make prayer a regular part of our day.

Jesus teaches us to approach God as our perfect Father. If we have been blessed with good fathers, we can realize how good—even better—our Heavenly Father is. If our fathers have been seriously bad as fathers, we can realize that God is even better than the fathers we wish we had.

Jesus especially teaches us a prayer that St. Thomas Aquinas calls the "most perfect of prayers": The Our Father.

WHAT ARE WAYS TO PRAY?

What follows is a very brief introduction to what Catholics have discovered about prayer from over 2,000 years of praying.

We can pray with words or without words. When we pray with words, we can use someone else's words or our own words. When we pray with someone else's words, we can use traditional prayers (e.g., the "Our Father") or devotions (e.g., the Rosary) or prayers composed by a saint or a spiritual master. A real spiritual master is someone who never contradicts Catholic doctrine.

There are two classic ways of praying without words. **Meditation** is prayer that reflects on God and His will and the mysteries of the Faith in order to understand them better. Reading can facilitate meditation. Sacred Scripture can be used, or good spiritual reading that never contradicts Catholic doctrine.

Contemplation is prayer that simply looks on or rests in or soaks up God and the mysteries of the Faith. An excellent example of contemplation comes from an old man whom St. John Vianney found in church staring at the tabernacle. When St. John asked him what he was doing, the man replied, "I look at Him, and He looks at me." Great art and architecture, pictures of families and friends, or the beauty of nature often helps contemplation.

There are classic forms of praying. **Adoration** is prayer that expresses awe and wonder and that acknowledges and praises the greatness and majesty of God. **Contrition** is prayer that expresses sorrow for sin and that asks God for His forgiveness. **Thanksgiving** is prayer that expresses gratitude to God and that thanks Him for His gifts to us. **Supplication** is prayer that expresses our neediness and that asks God for something for ourselves or others. Supplication is **petition** when it is for oneself and **intercession** when it is for others. When we pray, we can remember to include these classic forms of prayer if we memorize the acronym resulting from the first letter of each form in the order they are listed above: ACTS. Each of these classic forms of prayer can be done with words (one's own or someone else's) or without words.

WHAT ADVICE HAVE HOLY MEN AND WOMEN GIVEN?

- St. Alphonsus Liguori (1696-1787):

It often happens that we pray God to deliver us from some dangerous temptation, and yet God does not hear us but permits the temptation to continue troubling us. In such a case, let us understand that God permits even this for our greater good. When a soul in temptation recommends itself to God, and by His aid resists, O how it then advances in perfection.

- St. Antony Abbot (251-356):

[The devil] dreads fasting, prayer, humility, and good works . . . The devils tremble at the Sign of the Cross of our Lord, by which He triumphed over and disarmed them.

- St. Augustine (354-430):

Pray as though everything depended on God. Work as though everything depended on you.

- St. Benedict (480-547):

Prayer ought to be short and pure, unless it be prolonged by the inspiration of Divine grace.

- St. Bernadette Soubirous (1844-1879):

When you pass before a chapel and do not have time to stop for a while, tell your Guardian Angel to carry out your errand to Our Lord in the tabernacle. He will accomplish it and then still have time to catch up with you.

- Bl. Charles de Foucauld (1858-1916):

To receive the grace of God you must go to the desert and stay awhile.

- St. Ephraem of Syria (306-373):

Virtues are formed by prayer. Prayer preserves temperance. Prayer suppresses anger. Prayer prevents emotions of pride and envy. Prayer draws into the soul the Holy Spirit, and raises man to Heaven.

- St. Faustina Kowalska (1905-1938):

    - A soul arms itself by prayer for all kinds of combat. In whatever state the soul may be, it ought to pray. A soul which is pure and beautiful must pray, or else it will lose its beauty; a soul which is striving after this purity must pray, or else it will never attain it; a soul which is newly converted must pray, or else it will fall again; a sinful soul, plunged in sins, must pray so that it might rise again. There is no soul which is not bound to pray.

    - When I immersed myself in prayer and united myself with all the Masses that were being celebrated all over the world at that time, I implored God, for the sake of all these Holy Masses, to have mercy on the world and especially on poor sinners who were dying at that moment. At the same instant, I received an interior answer from God that a thousand souls had received grace through the prayerful mediation I had offered to God. We do not know the number of souls that is ours to save through our prayers and sacrifices; therefore, let us always pray for sinners.

- St. Gregory the Great (540-604):

Man by prayer merits to receive that which God had from all eternity determined to give him.

- St. Ignatius of Loyola (1491-1556):

We must speak to God as a friend speaks to his friend, servant to his master; now asking some favor, now acknowledging our faults, and communicating to Him all that concerns us, our thoughts, our fears, our projects, our desires, and in all things seeking His counsel.

- St. Isidore of Seville

    Prayer purifies us, reading instructs us.... If a man wants to be always in God's company, he must pray regularly and read regularly. When we pray, we talk to God; when we read, God talks to us.

- St. Jane de Chantal (1572-1641):

    When you are experiencing some physical pain or a sorrowful heart, try to endure it before God, recalling as much as you can that He is watching you at this time of affliction, especially in physical illness when very often the heart is weary and unable to pray. Don't force yourself to pray, for a simple adherence to God's will, expressed from time to time, is enough. Moreover, suffering born in the will quietly and patiently is a continual, very powerful prayer before God, regardless of the complaints and anxieties that come from the inferior part of the soul.

- St. John Chrysostom (344-407):

    - It is simply impossible to lead, without the aid of prayer, a virtuous life.

    - Prayer is the place of refuge for every worry, a foundation for cheerfulness, a source of constant happiness, a protection against sadness.

- St. John Vianney (1786-1859):

    My little children, your hearts, are small, but prayer stretches them and makes them capable of loving God.

- St. Josemaria Escriva (1902-1975):

    You don't know how to pray? Put yourself in the presence of God, and as soon as you have said, "Lord, I don't know how to pray!" you can be sure you have already begun.

- St. Julian of Norwich (1342-1416):

    For God says: Pray wholeheartedly . . . though you may feel nothing, though you may see nothing . . . For in dryness and in barrenness, in sickness and in weakness, then is your prayer most pleasing to Me.

The Fullness of Life

- Bl. Mary MacKillop (1842-1909):

  Let us all resign ourselves into His hands, and pray that in all things He may guide us to do His Holy Will . . . When thoughts of this or that come, I turn to Him and say: "Only what you will, my God. Use me as You will."

- St. Mary Magdalen de Pazzi (1566-1607):

  Prayer ought to be humble, fervent, resigned, persevering, and accompanied with great reverence. One should consider that he stands in the presence of a God, and speaks with a Lord before whom the angels tremble from awe and fear.

- St. Peter Julian Eymard (1811-1868):

  - In order to succeed in [prayer], it should be done when we first awaken, when our whole being is calm and recollected. We need to make our meditation before anything else.

  - As far as possible, you should pray in quiet and silent devotion. Try to have a favorite topic of prayer, such as a devotion to the passion of Jesus, the Blessed Sacrament, awareness of the divine presence; go directly to Jesus without too much fuss.

  - Have confidence in prayer. It is the unfailing power which God has given us. By means of it you will obtain the salvation of the dear souls whom God has given you and all your loved ones.

- St. Pio (Padre Pio) of Pietrelcina (1887-1968):

  - He who does not meditate acts as one who never looks into the mirror and so does not bother to put himself in order, since he can be dirty without knowing it. The person who meditates and turns his thoughts to God, who is the mirror of the soul, seeks to know his defects and tries to correct them, moderates himself in his impulses, and puts his conscience in order.

  - Say to God: Do you want greater love from me? I have no more. Give me more, therefore, and I will offer it to You. Don't doubt. God will accept this offer.

- When you have distractions, don't distract yourself still more by stopping to consider the why and the wherefore.

- Continue to pray that God may console you when you feel that the weight of the Cross is becoming too burdensome. Acting thus you are not doing anything against the will of God, but are with the Son of God who, in the garden, asked His Father for some relief.

- St. Teresa of Avila (1515-1582):

    - You pay God a compliment by asking great things of Him.

    - The most potent and acceptable prayer is the prayer that leaves the best effects. I don't mean it must immediately fill the soul with desire . . . The best effects [are] those that are followed up by actions—when the soul not only desires the honor of God, but really strives for it.

    - How often I failed in my duty to God, because I was not leaning on the strong pillar of prayer.

    - Don't imagine that, if you had a great deal of time, you would spend more of it in prayer. Get rid of that idea; it is no hindrance to prayer to spend your time well . . . Jacob did not cease to be a saint because he had to attend to his flocks.

    - Vocal prayer . . . must be accompanied by reflection. A prayer in which a person is not aware of Whom he is speaking to, what he is asking, who it is who is asking and of Whom, I don't call prayer—however much the lips may move.

    - One must not think that a person who is suffering is not praying. He is offering up his sufferings to God, and many a time he is praying much more truly than one who goes away by himself and meditates his head off, and, if he has squeezed out a few tears, thinks that is prayer.

    - Much more is accomplished by a single word of the Our Father said, now and then, from our heart, than by the whole prayer repeated many times in haste and without attention.

- St. Teresa of Calcutta (1910-1997):

    Everything starts with prayer. Love to pray—feel the need to pray often during the day and take the trouble to pray. If you want to pray better, you must pray more. The more you pray, the easier it becomes. Perfect prayer does not consist of many words but in the fervor of the desire which raises the heart to Jesus.

- St. Vincent de Paul (1581-1660):

    Read some chapter of a devout book . . . It is very easy and most necessary, for just as you speak to God when at prayer, God speaks to you when you read.

WHAT ARE DISCERNMENT AND SPIRITUAL DIRECTION?

When praying is an integral part of making a decision, discernment occurs. Discernment is often accompanied by spiritual direction/guidance in growing in the Faith while making a decision. The Catholic Church has developed many ways of helping its members get spiritual direction. One of these ways is a retreat, which is time away from everyday life. There are many reasons for making a retreat, from needing discernment to "catching one's breath."

There are many places retreats are made, from a retreat house to one's own house with the use of just about any form of media. Retreats take many forms, from emphasizing private time to emphasizing group prayer and discussion. Retreats take different amounts of time, from one concentrated block of time (from a couple hours to a month) to a small block of time every day for several months. Good discernment, good spiritual direction, and a good retreat NEVER contradict Catholic doctrine, but help the retreatant or directed person grow in harmony with Catholic doctrine.

Spiritual direction can also be found in membership in an organization or movement, such as Opus Dei, the Oblates of Saint Benedict, Lay Fraternities of Saint Dominic, Communion and Liberation, Courage, etc. There are many movements and organizations that call themselves Catholic, but not all are equally faithful to Catholic doctrine, which should be the litmus test for deciding whether to join.

The great temptation when getting spiritual direction is to find a "spiritual director" who will tell one what one wants to hear. We need to beware those who tell us, "God wants what you want" and "God loves you just as you are." We need to make sure that "spiritual direction" is not simply aimed at helping us feel good about ourselves, thus making God in our own image and likeness.

PERSONAL FAITH RESPONSE

Check any statements below that describe you.

In order to LIVE FULLY:

1. _____I agree with the objective truth in this chapter.

2. _____I will pray on my own at least 5 minutes every day.

3. _____I will make sure I pray to the one, true God by keeping my prayer in harmony with Catholic Doctrine.

4. _____I will pray according to everything Jesus taught about prayer.

5. _____I will try the many different ways of praying—I will pray in my own words, I will pray in someone else's words, I will meditate, I will contemplate.

6. _____Whatever method of prayer I use, my prayer will be ACTS.

7. _____I will take to heart the advice on prayer given by the holy men and women in Catholic tradition.

VOCABULARY

Prayer: Personal, one-on-one communication between a person and God.

Intercede: Pray for.

Meditation: Prayer that reflects on God and His will and the mysteries of the Faith in order to understand them better.

Contemplation: Prayer that simply looks on or rests in or soaks up God and the mysteries of the Faith, often with the help of great art and architecture, pictures of families and friends, or the beauty of nature.

Adoration: Prayer that expresses awe and wonder and that acknowledges and praises the greatness and majesty of God.

Contrition: Prayer that expresses sorrow for sin and that asks God for

His forgiveness.

Thanksgiving: Prayer that expresses gratitude to God and that thanks Him for His gifts to us.

Supplication: Prayer that expresses our neediness and that asks God for something for ourselves or others.

Petition: Supplication for oneself.

Intercession: Supplication for others.

Discernment: Making a prayerful decision.

Spiritual Direction: Guidance in growing in the Faith while growing in prayer.

Retreat: Time away from everyday life.

Part 8: What Is the Fullness of Responding to Revelation?

Chapter VII:

WHAT IS THE FULLNESS OF SHARING THE FAITH?

SOURCES

Avery Cardinal Dulles, SJ, *Evangelization for the Third Millennium* (Paulist Press, 2009).

WHY SHARE THE FAITH?

It is natural to share good news. The Catholic Faith is the best news possible: every human being can be saved from every limitation—illness and injury and disability, sadness and worry, loneliness and injustice, sin and vice, time and space! The fullness of life is possible! Christ has died and Christ is risen to begin the Kingdom of God—perfect harmony between God and humanity, between human and human, within each human, and between humanity and nature—and Christ will come again to complete the Kingdom of God! Christ has given the surest way to enter the Kingdom in the creed, morality, worship, and prayer of the Catholic Church! The Catholic Church provides the most complete knowledge about salvation and the fullness of the means of salvation! It would be unloving to not want to share this great news to those who have not heard it.

God wants to have a relationship with every human being.[395] God wants all human beings to know that He loves them, and He loves them by offering them the fullness of life. God wants all human beings to respond to His love by knowing Him, loving Him, living fully in this earthly life, and having the fullness of life in His eternal Kingdom. That is why everyone has been created. "[Your faithful] speak of the glory of Your reign and tell of Your mighty works" (Psalm 145:11).

God wants all human beings to belong to His Catholic Church.[396] It is the universal sacrament of salvation—God's primary vehicle for saving humanity from Original Sin, personal sin, and all evil. God wants all human beings to know the fullness of His Revelation, which can only be found in the Catholic Church. God wants all to respond to that Revelation with the fullness of Faith, which can only be found in the Catholic Church. God wants the Catholic Church to convert all human beings to the Catholic Faith, which is fidelity to Catholic doctrine.

As St. Paul says,

For everyone who calls upon the name of the Lord will be saved. But how can they call on Him in Whom they have not believed? And how can they believe in Him of Whom they have not heard? And how can they hear without someone to preach? And how can people preach unless they are sent? As it is written, "How beautiful are the feet of those who bring the good news!" (Romans 10:13-15)

Of course, we often hesitate to share the Good News as we often hesitate to share any good news. We doubt our know-how and ability. We know that good news is not always received as it should be. There might be a lack of interest. There might be hostility, especially on the part of those who are already looking for an excuse to verbally or physically assault us.

When we hesitate to share the Catholic Faith, we are urged by the command of Jesus Himself. "Go, therefore, and make disciples of all nations" (Matthew 28:19). "But whoever denies Me before others, I will deny before My heavenly Father" (Mt 10:33).

Anyone who has truly gotten to know the Lord and His goodness has the experience of the prophet Jeremiah: "I say I will not mention [the

---

[395] *CCC*, 850-851.
[396] *CCC*, 849.

The Fullness of Life

Lord], I will no longer speak His name. But then it is as if fire is burning in my heart, imprisoned in my bones; I grow weary holding back, I cannot!" (Jer 20:9).

In the words of the *Catechism*,

[Believers] proclaim the Good News to those who do not know it, in order to consolidate, complete, and raise up the truth and goodness that God has distributed among men and nations, and to purify them from error and evil for the glory of God, the confusion of the demon, and the happiness of man.397

WHAT ARE BASIC FORMS OF SHARING THE FAITH?

The Faith can be shared with those who do not believe it. This form of sharing is missionary work (from the Latin *missio*, which means "sending" or "mission") or evangelization (from the Greek *euangelizesthai*, which means "bringing good news"). Related is apologetics (from the Greek *apo* "from" and *logos* "word" and so "speech from"), which is defending and explaining the Faith. Apologetics is the exact opposite of apologizing, as that word has come to mean "being sorry for."

The Faith can also be shared with those who already have some degree of it. This is faith formation, which has two dimensions. One dimension is catechesis (from the Greek *katekheo*, which means "from the sound" and so "from hearing oral instruction"), which is religious instruction that deepens faith. The other dimension is pastoral ministry that helps Catholics grow in experiencing Catholic morality, Catholic worship, and Catholic prayer in fidelity to Catholic doctrine. In terms of developing a relationship with the Lord, catechesis focuses on knowing the Lord and pastoral ministry focuses on interacting with the Lord.

When the Faith is shared with those who had it but lost it—those who have fallen away from the Faith—it is new evangelization, a term coined by Pope St. John Paul II. Not only individuals, but also entire societies need the new evangelization. It of also called *re-evangelization*.

Missionary activity, evangelization, apologetics, faith formation,

---

397 *CCC*, 856.

pastoral ministry, and new evangelization are successful to the extent that they bring their audiences in greater fidelity to Catholic doctrine.

WHAT ARE KEY METHODS OF SHARING THE FAITH WITH NON-CATHOLICS?

So what are key methods of missionary work, evangelization, apologetics, and new evangelization?

As Pope St. John Paul II and Pope Benedict XVI often said, the Church proposes the Faith to non-Catholics, she does not impose it. The Magisterium considers the right to religious freedom to be a human right.[398] Just as the Church has the right to practice freedom of religion, so does the Church respect others' right to religious freedom. Each member of the Church should do the same. A Catholic should never be coercive, pushy, overbearing, disrespectful, patronizing, or impatient when trying to share the Faith. The choice to covert to the Catholic Faith is only meaningful if it is a free choice.

Trent Horn has made a good suggestion in his *Why We're Catholic* ((Catholic Answers Press, 2017): Listen to the other person before trying to get them to listen to what you want to say about the Catholic Faith. Give them the first word. Let them talk long enough to see that you are listening. Make your first response to what they say questions about what they mean, which give them more opportunity to express themselves, instead of statements agreeing or disagreeing. Make your exchange a conversation, not a debate. Make it the kind of conversation that can be continued in the future.

In our efforts to help others find the truth, we Catholics need to take into account "where" non-Catholics are in their search for meaning and to affirm whatever truth and goodness they have already discovered. We might often need to start by using Reason instead of Faith, especially when dialoguing with atheists and agnostics. In order to begin explaining why the Catholic Faith is true, we might well need to begin with secular, non-religious language—the language of common sense, Philosophy, Psychology, Biology, etc. It might be better to begin with talking about causation and the Uncaused Cause than with God's Revelation about the beginning of the universe in the Book of Genesis, or with human

---

[398] *CCC*, 2104-2109.

restlessness than with Original Sin and the Kingdom of God. With a Protestant, it might be better to start from the Biblical basis for the Eucharist and the primacy of Peter than from the infallibility of the Magisterium.

Sometimes the indirect sharing of faith by witnessing to it through actions instead of words. Catholics who make obvious the priority they have given to Mass and prayer, who clearly sacrifice for their families, who make their communities of Faith caring communities, who treat well those around them (neighbors, co-workers, customers, co-students, teammates, etc.), who visibly (yet humbly) participate in works of charity and service can give example that helps bring others to Our Lord. Sooner or later, words will be necessary. Actions alone will not bring Non-Catholics to the truth of Catholic doctrine and the understanding and wisdom it provides.

Guests entering a Catholic residence should know that the Catholic Faith is important to their host. A crucifix should be in a prominent place. Statues or pictures of Mary, the Holy Family, or a saint should be obvious. Catholic literature should be present, especially a Bible and a *Catechism of the Catholic Church*. The Christmas season is a great opportunity to witness to the Faith with an Advent wreath and a Nativity scene.

Let us remind ourselves that sharing the Faith is the loving thing to do. This is so because love is a commitment to do what is good for the loved one, and the best thing someone can do is to accept God's revelation in the Catholic Faith. Let us also remind ourselves that although Jesus was always perfectly loving to everyone, He was crucified. When we share the Faith, we will not always be received well. As Jesus says, "If the world hates you, realize it hated me first" (John 15:18). "Be sober and vigilant. Your opponent the devil is prowling around like a roaring lion looking for someone to devour" (1 Peter 5:8).[399]

WHAT ARE KEY METHODS OF SHARING THE FAITH IN THE FAMILY?

Because methods of faith formation, catechesis, and pastoral ministry are only relevant to those with responsibility for them—priests, deacons, teachers, directors of religious education, youth ministers, etc.—this

---

[399] Other passages about persecution are Matthew 10:16-39, 24:9-13; Acts 14:21-22; 2 Corinthians 4:8-11, 12:10; 2 Timothy 3:10-12.

section will deal with sharing the Faith in the place all Catholics have in common: family.

Each Catholic family is called to be a "domestic church."[400] When raising their children, Catholic parents should include reading a children's Bible and books about the saints along with the other books they read to their children. The family should go to Mass together as much as possible. The family should pray together—at least before meals and at bedtime. Parents should teach their children devotions, such as the Rosary; celebrate their feast days; take them to shrines; and visit the Blessed Sacrament. In a good Catholic family, the children will learn that nothing is more important than a relationship with God as God wants to be related to, that the best way to know God is from Catholic doctrine, and that the best way to relate to God is in Catholic morality, Catholic worship, and Catholic prayer. The Catholic family practices morality, worship, and prayer that are in harmony with Catholic doctrine. In order to share the Faith, parents must know the Faith and be able to answer their children's many questions with at least a basic answer.

Parents need help raising their children in the Faith. Identifying orthodox programs of catechesis and avoiding the many heterodox programs in the Church is crucial. Parents will also need to monitor what their children are being taught in all their classes since so many educators, including those in Catholic schools, have become Postmodernists. Parents must make sure that Postmodernist culture is not influencing their children. Gone are the days of pre-1950s societal consensus on Judeo-Christian values shared by most adults. The family should be a refuge without being a cocoon. Children need to be able to engage constructively with people who do not share Catholic values without losing their own Catholic identity.

What has been written elsewhere in this book about happiness and love especially apply to raising and being a Catholic family. Parents should want the right kind of happiness for their children. Parents should give their children the right kind of love. An important key to a good family is the key to good community and organizational life: "In essential things, unity; in non-essential things, liberty; in all things, charity." Parents need to pray for the wisdom to know when their children must obey and when their children may have liberty.

---

[400] *CCC*, 2201-2233.

The Fullness of Life

As children grow up and increasingly must make their own decisions, parents can help them get in the habit of asking, What does God want me to do? Parents must never forget that their children have free will. Ultimately, having the Faith must be the choice of each child as he becomes independent. The best way to share the Faith with children is to live and model the Faith. The best way for a couple to invite their children to the Faith is to love each other with the right kind of love and to make each other happy in the right way.

PERSONAL FAITH RESPONSE

Check any statements below that describe you.

In order to LIVE FULLY:

1. _____I agree with the objective truth in this chapter.

2. _____I will share the Faith in word by speaking the truth in love.

3. _____I will witness to the Faith in my actions.

VOCABULARY

Evangelization: Sharing the Faith with those who do not believe it. Also known as **missionary work**.

Apologetics: Defending and explaining the Faith.

Catechesis: Religious instruction that deepens knowledge of God.

Pastoral Ministry: Activities for experiencing Catholic morality, Catholic worship, and Catholic prayer.

New Evangelization: Sharing the Faith with those who had it but lost it. Also known as **Re-evangelization**.

Part 8: What Is the Fullness of Responding to Revelation?

Chapter VIII:
WHAT IS LIVING FULLY?

We end with a summary of the book in the form of a checklist. In the right-hand column, indicate if the statement in the left-hand column honestly describes you (even if you're not a baptized Catholic) by putting a **Y** for **Yes**, an **N** for **No**, or a **?** for **Not sure**.

Keep in mind that all of the statements below describe what a good Catholic <u>tries</u> his or her best to do. A good Catholic cannot be perfect, otherwise only God could be a good Catholic!

A good Catholic: **Describes Me:**

1. Seeks true happiness and living fully by getting what he should want even though it will not always feel good and will sometimes be very challenging. _____

2. Uses Right Reason (evidence, logic, and all areas of knowledge—psychology, finance, plumbing, etc.). _____

3. Recognizes and appreciates objective truth, goodness, and beauty outside the Catholic Church as Revelations/reflections of the one true God. _____

4. Lives to be in union with the most important reality—the one, true God Who is three Divine Persons of Father, Son, and Holy Spirit—and to share in their perfect love _____

5. Accepts that the one, true God has most fully revealed Himself in Jesus Christ, especially His Death and Resurrection, Who best shows the way to true happiness. _____

6. Finds that Jesus Christ is best known/revealed in the Sacred Scripture and Sacred Tradition of the Catholic Church, which Christ Himself founded. _____

The Fullness of Life

7. Knows that only the Magisterium, which is made up of the Pope and bishops, has the God-given authority to interpret Sacred Scripture and Sacred Tradition and thus define the Catholic Faith in doctrines that are always and everywhere true. _____

8. Agrees with the doctrine and discipline taught by the Magisterium while knowing that he does not have to agree with the Magisterium's social analysis and prudential judgments. _____

9. Realizes that the Catholic Faith is the best way to be a friend and follower of Jesus Christ and the best way to do the will of God until Christ's Second Coming when the Kingdom of God will come completely to earth. _____

10. Realizes that the Catholic Faith alone has the fullness of the means of salvation—the most complete creed, worship, morality, and prayer—which are also the ways to live fully and be happiest. _____

11. Tries to act according to Catholic moral doctrine, which is based on the Two Great Commandments of the New Testament/ Covenant and the Ten Commandments of the Old Testament/ Covenant. _____

12. Worships according to Catholic liturgical doctrine, especially by participating in Mass every week on the Lord's Day (or its vigil) and on Holy Days of Obligation and also by going to Confession regularly. _____

13. Prays daily and is constantly discovering the many forms of prayer in the Catholic Faith. _____

14. Develops a unique personal relationship with God that never contradicts Catholic doctrine. _____

15. Supports the Church, especially a parish, with his time, talent, and treasure. _____

16. Is Catholic 24 hours a day—his or her Catholic identity is what most defines him or her—more than race/ethnicity, economic class, gender, sexual orientation, culture, family, personality, physique, or anything else. _____

17. Tries to convert/invite non-Catholics to the Catholic Church, whose greatest saints include converts, while respecting the religious freedom of others by proposing and not imposing what can only be known by Faith. _____

18. Realizes that all of the above is objectively true. _____

www.ingramcontent.com/pod-product-compliance
Lightning Source LLC
Chambersburg PA
CBHW032146080426
42735CB00008B/602